W9-AST-073

APOCRYPHA:

Jewish Literature of the Hellenistic Age

The Jewish Heritage Classics Already Published

SERIES EDITORS: David Patterson · Lily Edelman

THE MISHNAH
Oral Teachings of Judaism
Selected and Translated by Eugene J. Lipman

RASHI
Commentaries on the Pentateuch
Selected and Translated by Chaim Pearl

A PORTION IN PARADISE
AND OTHER JEWISH FOLKTALES
Compiled by H. M. Nahmad

THE HOLY CITY
Jews on Jerusalem
Compiled and Edited by Avraham Holtz

REASON AND HOPE
Selections from the Jewish Writings of Hermann Cohen
Translated, Edited, and with an Introduction by Eva Jospe

THE SEPHARDIC TRADITION
Ladino and Spanish-Jewish Literature
Selected and Edited by Moshe Lazar

JUDAISM AND HUMAN RIGHTS
Edited by Milton R. Konvitz

HUNTER AND HUNTED
Human History of the Holocaust
Selected and Edited by Gerd Korman

FLAVIUS JOSEPHUS
Selected and Edited by Abraham Wasserstein

THE GOOD SOCIETY
Jewish Ethics in Action
Selected and Edited by Norman Lamm

MOSES MENDELSSOHN
Selections from His Writings
Edited and Translated by Eva Jospe, with
an Introduction by Alfred Jospe

RAMBAM
Readings in the Philosophy of Moses Maimonides
Selected and Translated with Introduction
and Commentary by Lenn Evan Goodman

GOLDEN DOOR TO AMERICA
The Jewish Immigrant Experience
Edited by Abraham Karp

Published in cooperation with the Commission
on Adult Jewish Education of B'nai B'rith

APOCRYPHA:
Jewish Literature of the Hellenistic Age

by NICHOLAS DE LANGE

The Viking Press · New York

First published in 1978 by The Viking Press
625 Madison Avenue, New York, N.Y. 10022
Published simultaneously in Canada by
Penguin Books Canada Limited

LIBRARY OF CONGRESS CATALOGING IN PUBLICATION DATA
De Lange, Nicholas Robert Michael, 1944–
Apocrypha.
(The Jewish heritage classics)
Bibliography: p.
Includes index.
1. Bible. O. T. Apocrypha—Criticism, interpretation, etc. 2. Apocryphal books (Old Testament)—Criticism, interpretation, etc.
I. Title. II. Series.
BS1700.D38 229'.06 77-19277
ISBN 0-670-12954-2

Printed in the United States of America
Set in VIP Times Roman

Thanks to the Morris Adler Publications Fund of B'nai B'rith's Commission on Adult Jewish Education for making the Jewish Heritage Classics Series possible as a memorial to the late Rabbi Morris Adler, former Chairman of that Commission.

TO THE REVERED MEMORY OF MY TEACHER

IGNAZ MAYBAUM

1897–1976

I shall pour out teaching like prophecy
and bequeath it to all generations forever.
Ben Sira 24:33

Preface

It has been no easy task to make this selection of translations from the apocryphal writings. It has involved wading through an enormous number of texts and learning to read several new languages. But the effort has been amply rewarded by the pleasure of discovery and by the challenge of translation. I shall be happy if some of the pleasure I have derived from this charming and fascinating literature communicates itself to the reader. A few words of caution and explanation are necessary, however, from the outset.

I originally intended to restrict myself to the Apocrypha in the narrow sense of the word, that is, the portions of the Greek Bible not found in the Hebrew. Nevertheless, it soon became apparent that this restriction was impossible to apply in practice, and, more important, that in Jewish terms it had no validity whatever. Consequently I have drawn on the whole body of anonymous Jewish literature of the Hellenistic Age. The reasons for this decision will be apparent from the Introduction. The books of the ''small Apocrypha'' are in any case readily available in English translation, whereas many of the other works are almost entirely unknown outside a narrow circle of scholars. I have tried to select excerpts that are interesting in themselves, and consequently many works are not represented. I hope that the bibliography at the end of the book will be of some help to the reader who wishes to delve deeper into the literature and its background.

In making the translations I have aimed to be as faithful as possible to the original, while at the same time making full use of the wide resources of the English language. Faithfulness must not be confused with literalism. A word-for-word translation is not necessarily faithful to the intention of the original author. Sometimes it is necessary to paraphrase or even to omit words or whole sentences. I have deemed it legitimate in an anthology of this kind to omit even long passages in the interests of continuity and freshness. In treating the texts in this way I can claim a legitimate precedent in the methods of the ancient translators in whose footsteps I am following.

Many of the texts survive only in ancient translations. In such cases I have allowed myself greater liberty still, in an effort to weed out later intrusions and distortions. It is not possible to reconstruct the original in its entirety, but I have at least tried to avoid using Greek or Latin forms of Hebrew names, except where they have been canonized by long English usage. I have preferred to use the Hebrew word "Torah" wherever appropriate, instead of the misleading translation "Law" which was first introduced by the ancient Greek translators.

I have tried to respect the variety of styles represented in the writings. This is a hard task for a single translator faced with the work of many different writers, particularly when so often we do not have the original texts. But it would be thoroughly misleading to employ the same English style throughout, as some translators have done. At all costs I have tried to avoid the un-English English which has been termed "translationese," with what success the reader must judge for himself. I have also made the effort to reproduce the alphabetical acrostics found in some Hebrew poems; this is not strictly legitimate, since no corresponding tradition exists in English, but the sacrifice would have been unfair to the Hebrew poets.

Throughout my work I have borne in mind two dicta of the great Jewish translator Franz Rosenzweig: "Only one who is profoundly convinced of the impossibility of translation can really undertake it." And "The true goal of the mind is translating; only when a thing has been translated does it become truly vocal, no longer to be done away with."

I should like to record my gratitude to the general editors of this series, Dr. David Patterson and Lily Edelman, for inviting me to contribute this anthology and for waiting so patiently for its completion.

Contents

PREFACE vii

INTRODUCTION
The Apocrypha as a Jewish Heritage 1
The Term "Apocrypha" 2
The Canonization of Scripture 3
The Problem of the Apocrypha 11
The Historical Background 14
Chronological Table 17
The Philosophical and Religious Background 19
A List of the Apocryphal Writings 24

ABOUT THE SCRIPTURES
Ezra Recovers the Scriptures 41
How the Torah Was Translated into Greek 44
Translator's Preface to Ben Sira 50

BIBLICAL STORIES

Abraham
Abram Discovers the True God 53
Abram's Ordeal 58

Abram in Egypt 61
The Death of Abraham 64

Joseph
Joseph and Asenath 68
The Last Words of Joseph 78

Deborah and Jephthah's Daughter
Deborah 87
Jephthah's Daughter 95

Daniel
Bel and the Serpent 99

MORAL TALES
The Adventures of Tobiah 103
Judith and Holofernes 114
The Story of Susanna 128

APOCALYPSE
The Visions of Shealtiel 133

PHILOSOPHY AND "WISDOM"
The Meaning of the Dietary Laws 153
The Wisdom of Ben Sira 158
The Wisdom of Solomon 173
Two Wisdom Poems 177

HISTORY
The Contest of the Three Young Men
and the Decree of Darius 181
The History of the Hasmoneans 186
The Martyrdom of Eleazar and the Seven Brothers 205
A Tourist's Description of Jerusalem 211

PRAYERS AND PSALMS 215

SUGGESTIONS FOR FURTHER READING 235

INDEX 240

APOCRYPHA:
Jewish Literature of the Hellenistic Age

Introduction

THE APOCRYPHA AS A JEWISH HERITAGE

At first sight the inclusion of the works known as "apocrypha" in a series devoted to the Jewish heritage may seem rather strange. If they are a Jewish heritage, then it is a curious kind of heritage, the very existence of which was unknown to tens of generations of Jews. Yet recent events have shown that it is possible to recover a lost heritage.

In 1947, on the eve of the restoration of Jewish rule in the ancient land of the Jews, came the first of a series of dramatic discoveries in the Judean Desert which brought to light the library of a Jewish community that perished centuries ago. Since the first discovery of the Qumrān Scrolls, which caused so much excitement, archeologists have unearthed other remains, including important written documents, which bring light and color to a period previously seen, as it were, in black and white. Another rich source of ancient documents, the Genizah (a kind of lumber room) of an old synagogue in Cairo, was discovered in the closing years of the last century; its contents are still being sorted and studied, but they have already produced some amazing finds.

All these various writings form part of the Jewish heritage; they were written by Jews to be read by Jews, and they bear witness to the life and thought of Jews in bygone times. The same is true of the apocryphal writings; only the manner of preservation is different. Whereas the Dead Sea Scrolls and the Cairo Genizah documents lay hidden and unknown for centuries, the apocryphal writings were unknown only to Jews; to Christians they were familiar, and indeed many of them were considered part of the sacred corpus of scripture. In this respect they have something in common with the writings of the New Testament, which were rejected by Jews as belonging to Christianity. But there is a fundamental difference between the Apocrypha and the New Testament: the apocryphal writings, although they were read and handed down in the Christian church, were not written by Christians and originally had nothing to do with Christianity. They were written by Jews and for Jews, and the fact that they were preserved by Christians and forgotten by Jews is due to a quirk of history. They are no more Christian documents than are the Old Testament scriptures, which were also adopted by the Church. And, like those scriptures, they have every right to be considered a part of the Jewish heritage.

THE TERM "APOCRYPHA"

The word "apocrypha" is plural (like "phenomena" or "media"; the singular is "apocryphon") and comes from a Greek word meaning "hidden away" or "secret." The term "apocrypha" was applied at first to works not considered suitable for general circulation. From the fourth century on it has been used in the Christian church as a collective name for those books which, while acknowledged to have a certain value and interest, were not recognized as part of the Bible. The actual list of books denoted by the term has, however, varied considerably in different places and at different times. The most important difference in the West is that the Protestant churches apply the term "apocrypha" to certain books which, although not found in the Hebrew Bible, were incorporated in the Greek and Latin texts of the Old Testament, whereas the Roman Catholic church, which accepted most of these as canonical at the Council of Trent in 1546, refers to these books as "deuterocanonical" (meaning canonical books of a later date than the others) and uses the term "apocryphal" for other books not even included in Greek and Latin Bibles. These other books are commonly referred to by Protestants as "pseudepigrapha," a term which implies that they were not really written by those whose names they bear—a very inappropriate term for some books, and one which would well fit some biblical books.

In the various Eastern Christian churches the situation is different again; indeed, they preserve some works which are virtually unknown in the Western Christian tradition. The status and history of the apocryphal writings in Judaism are a complicated question, which will be explored in the following pages. For the moment it must suffice to say that the Jews have never defined a separate corpus of "apocrypha," and consequently none of the Christian definitions has any validity for Jews.[1]

THE CANONIZATION OF SCRIPTURE

Before we can appreciate the nature and history of the apocryphal writings we must try to understand something of the process which is referred to as the "canonization" of scripture. The formation of the Hebrew Bible as we know it now took place over a long period of time. The first part to be codified was the Torah or Pentateuch ("Five Books"). The next section, the Prophets, must have been determined by the latter part of the second century B.C.E. The grandson of Ben Sira, who translated his grandfather's work into Greek at this time, says of him in the preface to that translation that he devoted himself to the study of "the Torah, the Prophets, and the other traditional writings" (see p. 51). Since the Book of Daniel was written during this same century, it was not included among the Prophets, which had been codified earlier, and appears in the Writings.

Up to this point there is general agreement as to what was and what was not part of the holy scriptures. Both the Pentateuch and the Prophets were used in the synagogue worship, and were considered to

[1] For the purposes of this book, the titles of the books of the "small Apocrypha," (that is, Greek Ezra, Apocalypse of Ezra, Tobit, Judith, Greek Esther, Wisdom of Solomon, Ben Sira, 1 Baruch, Letter of Jeremiah, Prayer of Azariah, Susanna, Bel and the Serpent, Prayer of Manasseh, 1 and 2 Maccabees) are set in Roman type. Titles of works outside the Greek Bible are italicized. This will make it clear to the reader whether a work is part of the traditional "Apocrypha" or an apocryphal work in the broader sense.

be divinely inspired, although for certain purposes the Pentateuch was seen as more authoritative than the Prophets. The controversy arose about, as Ben Sira's grandson put it, "the other traditional writings." By the beginning of the Christian Era there was a large number of such works in circulation. Most of them were attributed to authors named in the Pentateuch and Prophets, and were widely read and enjoyed. Some, particularly the Psalms, played an important part in Jewish worship. Some, of course, were older than others, some more interesting or inspiring than others. The problem was to decide which, if any, of these writings should be accorded the title "holy books."

It must be remembered that at that time there was no question of complete texts of the Bible in book form, such as we know today. The codex, the form of book made up of pages, belongs to a slightly later period. The Jewish scriptures, like most ancient literature, were written on scrolls. The text was written in columns on a long strip of papyrus or specially treated animal skin, and the result was extremely unwieldy and inconvenient. The scrolls were kept rolled up, holy books inside an ornamental covering, in boxes or on shelves, with a label attached to indicate the contents. Each time a book in this form was read, it had to be rolled back to the beginning again, and to look up a passage in the middle was no easy matter. It is not surprising, therefore, that ancient scholars carried most of their knowledge in their heads. Anyone who has read from a Sefer Torah or used a microfilm will be aware of the shortcomings of this form of book. And, of course, the longer a scroll the less easy it was to use. The Sefer Torah, containing only the Pentateuch, is already a very long scroll; a complete scroll of the Bible was out of the question. Instead, each long book would be copied on a single scroll, while smaller books might be collected together in one scroll or attached to a longer work with which they had some connection. For example, the twelve shortest prophetic books were commonly copied on one scroll. Since the scrolls were not numbered, it was difficult to keep them in any particular order, which is why to this day the order of the books is different in different versions of the Bible. It was not always easy to make sure that a scroll was not mislaid, or that a copy of another book did not find its way into the collection of holy writings, particularly if its subject matter was similar.

Another problem was that of translations. Not all Jews could read and understand Hebrew; many were more at home in other languages, especially Aramaic (a Semitic language related to Hebrew and spoken, at various times, in most parts of the Middle East) and Greek. These Jews naturally preferred to make use of translations of the holy writings into Greek and Aramaic, and they also sometimes read from Hebrew texts written in Greek or Aramaic letters (in fact, a form of Aramaic script has come to be adopted for the writing of all Hebrew texts, except by the Samaritans). By the beginning of the Christian Era most, if not all, of the scriptures were available in Greek and Aramaic translations. Some of these were fairly literal, but more often they diverged from the Hebrew, either to improve the style or to bring the biblical writings up-to-date for modern readers. The currency of translations meant that new "holy books" were not necessarily written in Hebrew. The Book of Daniel, for example, is partly written in Aramaic, and the Greek Bible contains several books composed in Greek. The history of the Greek Bible is similar to that of the Hebrew Bible in that the translations were written at different times, starting with the Pentateuch, and were only later collected together. The rabbis, on the whole, frowned on the use of translations and transliterated texts. The Greek translation, often called the Septuagint (from the Latin for "seventy") because of the legend that the translation of the Pentateuch was made miraculously by seventy (or seventy-two) scholars working independently, differed considerably from the official Hebrew Bible, and was closely connected with the Jews of Alexandria. When it was adopted by the Christian church it was rejected by the rabbinic authorities, who sponsored instead an extremely literal translation into Greek by a convert to Judaism named Aquila. This was in the early second century C.E.; in the same century another version was prepared by Theodotion, so that there came to exist a bewildering variety of Greek translations. The Aramaic translations, too, came into being in a rather haphazard way, arising out of the oral verse-by-verse translation of the synagogue Bible readings into Aramaic, and it was only much later that an official Aramaic translation was published. For some time, therefore, the same books circulated side by side in Hebrew, Greek, and Aramaic, sometimes with several different versions in the same language.

The result of all this is that instead of thinking of the Bible at this time as a single unit, we should envisage rather a loosely assembled library. To understand this important question better, we may look briefly at the nearest surviving example of such a library, namely that discovered in recent years in the caves of the Judean Desert, between Jerusalem and the Dead Sea. Here copies or fragments have been found of all the books of the Hebrew Bible except one, that of Esther. Most of these are in Hebrew but some are translated into Greek or Aramaic. There is often more than one copy of the same book, and there are also texts of numerous other works not included in the biblical canon. These include the books of Tobit, Ben Sira, *Enoch*, and *Jubilees*, in addition to biblical commentaries, hymns, and various other writings. No doubt these were not all considered to be equally holy and authoritative, and we do not have the means of determining precisely which books were considered "scriptural" and which were not; at least, though, we can have some idea of the breadth and variety of the Jewish religious literature which was available at the beginning of the Christian Era.

We have other information from the first century C.E. about the development of the canon of scripture. Philo, writing in the first half of the century, describes a Jewish contemplative sect in Egypt called the Therapeutae, who take with them into their cells "the laws, oracles uttered by the prophets, psalms, and other works which encourage and perfect knowledge and piety," but he also says that "they have writings of men of old, the founders of their sect, who left many records of their allegorical explanations," which they take as models in their own interpretation of the holy scriptures, and that they also compose hymns and psalms to God. The library of the Therapeutae seems to have been remarkably similar to that of the Dead Sea sect, whom they resemble in other ways too. Another instructive indication is provided by the quotations from the biblical writings in Philo's works, of which a considerable bulk survives. By far the greatest number of Philo's biblical quotations comes from the Pentateuch, but he refers to all the books of the present-day Jewish Bible with the exception of Ruth, Esther, Koheleth (Ecclesiastes), the Song of Songs, Lamentations, Ezekiel, and Daniel. He does not quote from any of the apocryphal books. Of course, the fact that Philo does not quote from a book does not necessarily mean that he did not know it or consider it as scriptural, and we must also bear in mind that Philo was living in Alexandria and knew only the Greek translation of the Bible. Still, his evidence, even though it is the evidence of silence, is significant. Some scholars have tried to show that Philo knew other books, including some apocryphal ones, but their arguments depend on similarities of expression, not on explicit quotations, and so they cannot be considered as proven.

Another interesting piece of evidence comes at the end of the Gospel of Luke, where Jesus speaks of "the law of Moses, the Prophets and the Psalms." Both here and in Philo's list of the scriptures of the Therapeutae there seems to be a clear hint of the division into Law, Prophets, and other writings. The same division is observed by Josephus, who is one of our most valuable witnesses. He writes as follows:

> Our scriptures, those which are truly accepted, number only twenty-two, and they contain the record of all history.
>
> Of these, five are the books of Moses, which include the laws and the traditional history from the beginning of mankind down to the death of Moses. This covers a period of just under three thousand years. After Moses the prophets wrote down the history of their times, from the death of Moses to Artaxerxes, who succeeded Xerxes as king of Persia, in thirteen books. The remaining four books contain psalms to God and precepts for the conduct of human life.
>
> The history from Artaxerxes to our own time has all been written, but it is not considered as equally authoritative with the earlier records because there was no exact succession of prophets.
>
> Our attitude to our own scriptures is clear in practice: although such a long period of time has elapsed, no one has dared to add, remove or change anything in them.
>
> (*Against Apion* I:38–42)

In addition to the distinction between the Pentateuch, the Prophets, and the other writings, Josephus states here for the first time that the list of holy scriptures is closed and numbers twenty-two books. He does not say which they are, but it is generally assumed that they are the books which make up our present Hebrew Bible. Since he specifically mentions Artaxerxes, whom he identifies with Ahasuerus, it is supposed that he included Esther among the prophetic books; it is also clear that Josephus reckons as prophetic books several more which now form part of the "Writings" (Job, Daniel, Chronicles, Ezra, and Nehemiah).

At the very end of the first Christian century, we have another very important reference to the canon and the position of the apocrypha in the Apocalypse of Ezra, where, after the scriptures have been destroyed, God dictates them again through Ezra to five men, who write them down. Ezra says:

> They wrote all day, and only ate some bread at night, but I did not stop speaking day and night. In the forty days, ninety-four books were written.
>
> When the forty days were up, the Almighty said to me, "Publish the first twenty-four books; they may be read by all the people, worthy and unworthy alike. But keep the other seventy books back; hand them over to your people's sages. They contain the springs of understanding, the fountains of wisdom, the streams of knowledge."
>
> (See p. 44).

The twenty-four books are evidently the books of the Bible. That Josephus speaks of twenty-two books and Ezra of twenty-four need not trouble us unduly: there were various ways of counting the books of the Bible. For example, several of the Christian church fathers, when recording the books of the Jewish Bible, give the total as twenty-two, taking Ruth together with Judges and the Lamentations together with Jeremiah as one book each, whereas the rabbis, who placed Ruth and Lamentations among the Writings as two of the "Five Scrolls," counted twenty-four books in all. What is significant is that, like Josephus, Ezra considers the list of biblical books to be closed. As for the seventy books which were handed over to the safekeeping of the sages, we are not told what they are, but it is not unlikely that they included many of the works now thought of as "apocrypha," which, as we have seen, originally meant "hidden books."

The picture so far is fairly straightforward, and we might be excused for supposing that by the end of the first century C.E., or, indeed, much earlier, the biblical canon was completed in the form in which we have it now. When we turn to the evidence of the rabbinic writings, however, a different situation emerges. There is clear evidence that both at this time and later there was disagreement about which books were part of holy scripture. The Mishnah (Yadaim 3:5) preserves a record of a discussion in the middle of the second century about whether or not the Song of Songs and Koheleth are holy books (or "defile the hands," as the rabbis put it). The issue was hotly disputed, and even later in the century there were those who held that Koheleth was not a holy book (Tosefta [Yadaim 2:14]). Two other "writings," Ruth and Esther, are also mentioned in these discussions. Esther, as we have seen, was probably accepted as a holy book by Josephus, but as late as the third century some rabbis declared that it was not holy. Against these discussions, however, we must set a statement which probably presents the official rabbinic view of the canon. Here, the twenty-four books of the Hebrew Bible are listed in order, following the customary division into Law, Prophets, and Writings (Babylonian Talmud [Baba Bathra 14–15]).

The rabbinic writings also present us with a certain amount of information concerning the apocryphal writings. The most explicit statement, made at some time in the first two centuries, declares: "The *gilyonim* and the books of the Minim [sectarians] are not holy scripture. The books of Ben Sira and all the books written since his time are not holy scripture" (Tosefta, [Yadaim 2:13]). Scholars disagree about the meaning of "the *gilyonim* and the books of the Minim"; some have tried to derive *gilyon* from the Greek for "gospel" (*evangelion*) and suppose that the word refers to Christian writings, and we might imagine that "the books of the Minim" include the sectarian writings of such groups as the Qumrān sect and the Therapeutae. The second sentence shows that the rabbis adopted a chronological criterion—that is, they accepted ancient books as sacred and rejected modern ones. We have already seen that this same principle was adopted by Josephus. The result of this process of limiting the number of sacred books was that the publication and use of the apocrypha were increasingly frowned on. The Midrash on Koheleth 12:4 states: "Whoever allows more than the twenty-four books into his house brings confusion into his house." The Midrash mentions as an example the book of Ben Sira, the one apocryphal book which is quite often referred to in the rabbinic writings and even quoted. In all there are sixteen passages where Ben Sira is quoted by name, besides several more where it is cited or alluded to without an explicit reference, and once (Baba Kamma 92^{b}) a quotation from Ben Sira is actually attributed to the Writings. It would appear, therefore, that the use of Ben Sira was not universally condemned.

Further light is shed on this question by a variant reading in some texts of the Talmud (Sanhedrin 100^{b}). The context is a discussion of a statement by Rabbi Akiba: "Whoever reads the 'excluded books' has no share in the world to come." "Excluded books" (*sefarim ḥiṣonim*) is explained as "the books of the Minim." The Babylonian teacher Rab Joseph is then quoted as saying: "It is also forbidden to read the book of Ben Sira. But," Rab Joseph adds, "we may teach the good things it contains." In place of this last statement, some texts read: "If the rabbis had not hidden this book away, we should be able to teach the good things it contains." Now, "hiding away" (*genizah*) was the process applied to sacred texts and other sacred objects which were no longer fit for use, and the same expression was applied to the suppression of texts not considered suitable for public reading. According to the Talmud (Shabbath 13^b, 30^b), for example, the sages had considered hiding away the books of Ezekiel and Koheleth on account of the misleading teachings they contain, but they were preserved from this fate. Another rabbinic text (*Aboth de Rabbi Nathan*) states that Proverbs, the Song of Songs, and Koheleth were hidden away at first because they were not thought to belong to the category of sacred writings. The statement that the rabbis hid away the book of Ben Sira suggests that it had previously been regarded as scriptural (which helps us to understand why it was quoted in the rabbinic literature), but that it came to be considered as unsuitable to be included in the Writings.

The reader will observe that the Hebrew word *genizah* is very close to the Greek word *apocrypha*, since both have to do with concealment. In fact, in later Hebrew *genuzim* or *sefarim genuzim* ("books which are hidden away") is used as a translation of "apocrypha." Rabbi Akiba's expression, *sefarim ḥiṣonim,* may mean books excluded from the Bible and so may also refer to the apocryphal writings, though this is not at all certain. (Some later commentators thought he was referring to Greek philosophical works, or perhaps to pornographic books.) In the third century, the word "apocrypha" was used by the church father Origen to refer to certain secret Jewish writings.

We can now begin to form a clearer picture of the way in which the apocryphal literature came into being. As the Bible was progressively canonized, the Jewish religious leaders, by an act of determined policy, excluded the writings which they did not consider to be authoritative, and gradually discouraged their use by Jews altogether. Before the invention of printing, books were produced in small quantities, and they depended for their survival on being continually copied and recopied. If a book was not copied it died. Many of the excluded books have in fact perished, and the majority survive only in translation. That any survive at all is due, apart from rare accidents, to the fact that the Christian churches took them up and gave them a new lease on life. The first Christians were, of course, Jews, and they had a high respect for the written word. At the time of the separation of the church and the synagogue, the process of codifying the scriptures and suppressing the excluded books was not complete. Many of the churches originated in Jewish communities outside the influence of the rabbinic authorities of Palestine; they treasured their traditional religious literature and would not lightly relinquish it. The churches gradually defined their own attitude to the sacred scriptures and developed their own canons, but this process was very slow and by no means uniform. Some churches rejected books accepted by others. In the meantime the apocryphal writings continued to be copied, and even works which had never been considered canonical (such as the writings of Philo and Josephus) were kept alive and widely read. In this way a considerable corpus of ancient Jewish literature was preserved until modern times by Christians. Occasionally, during the Middle Ages and more recently, the "lost" Jewish works were rediscovered by Jews and some of them translated back into Hebrew. For the most part, however, their survival is due to the labors of generations of Christian scribes and scholars.

THE PROBLEM OF THE APOCRYPHA

For a Jew the rediscovery of this lost literature is a fascinating process, fraught with difficulties. Fascinating because it opens the individual's eyes to a wealth of material that casts a new light on a whole era of the Jewish past. The great richness and variety of the material illuminate many aspects of Jewish life, thought, and belief during the period between the end of the biblical era and the rise of Rabbinic Judaism. Originating in different kinds of Jewish circles, the documents are of many different types. Some are polished literary creations, while others belong to the domain of folklore. They range from the most exalted metaphysical speculation and moral searching to simple prayers and legends. Some exhale a lofty detachment; others speak straight from the heart. Some breathe the quaint and curious air of a distant past; others have an overwhelming sense of immediacy and speak of problems still with us today.

At the same time, these documents raise many difficulties. The first and fundamental difficulty is that of the texts themselves. Very few of the works have come down to us in the form in which they were written. Even those which have survived in the original language often exist in two or more different recensions, and there are always textual problems, in the nature of all long textual traditions. Modern editors are working hard to establish critical texts, but for many of the works there are still no modern editions. The majority of the works survive only in translations, and the originals are lost. Here we are at the mercy of not only the scribes but also the translators. Some of the translations are extremely literal, but others, by no means the worse for it, have evidently taken great liberties with the texts, not only in adapting the language, but even omitting certain passages and inserting others. It is no easy task to decide what the original said; indeed, in many cases scholars cannot even agree on what the original language was or whether the "translation" is in fact a translation at all. The serious student of the apocryphal writings must master a bewildering variety of languages: Hebrew, Aramaic and Syriac, Greek, Latin, Coptic, Armenian, Ethiopic, the Slavonic languages—in fact, all the languages of the ancient Judeo-Christian world. He must study paleography (the science of reading ancient manuscripts) and thoroughly acquaint himself with the history and religious ideas of the people who wrote the works as well as their translators and transmittors. Even when he has done all this he will have only an incomplete understanding of the texts because so much of their background is unknown or speculative.

Other difficulties arise from the analysis of the texts as they have been transmitted. While some works have been handed down with remarkable fidelity, even in translation, others have been revised or completely rewritten. They are like ancient buildings: some—a very few—have been preserved virtually intact; others, in the course of long and varied use, have been partly demolished, added to, restored, or even entirely rebuilt; in certain cases the buildings themselves have been dismantled and the materials reused in other buildings; and, of course, many buildings have completely perished or have left nothing but fragmentary ruins. For a century or more scholars (almost exclusively Christian) have been laboring to analyze the texts and decide what is early and what is late, how much is the author's and how much the translator's, what is Jewish and what is Christian. The results are still far from satisfactory. While some progress has been made, particularly in discovering manuscripts and comparing versions, in many cases we are still as far as ever from disentangling the mesh of threads. Some of the documents have been so worked over that one has the feeling of being left with almost nothing at all—like a too well-peeled onion.

These difficulties press more heavily on the Jewish reader than on the Christian. While Christians are free to read and enjoy the works in the traditional form in which they have been handed down in the Church, Jews, who have no such tradition and who wish to rediscover the ancient Jewish originals, find the process of analysis a source of irritation and frustration. And yet, if they are to reclaim their lost heritage, they must face up squarely to the difficulties.

There may be Jews who will question the value of the whole exercise. Why meddle in things that do not concern them? Why attempt to rummage in the trash cans of time for the tattered relics of what the ancient rabbis in their wisdom discarded? Can they not be satisfied with what has been handed down: the body of sacred scripture, the traditional commentaries, the Mishnah, the Talmud, and the other rabbinic writings?

To this many answers might be given. Not all the works were discarded; they merely fell by the wayside. Nor were all the ancient rabbis hostile to the apocrypha; some of the materials they contain were actually incorporated in the rabbinic writings and in what one might call the folklore of the synagogue. Books like Judith and Tobit, for instance, were never entirely lost, and surely the Books of the Maccabees must have an honored place wherever the feast of Hanukkah is celebrated. Of those works which were consciously thrust out, some were rejected on doctrinal grounds or because they originated in sectarian groups. Others, however, suffered merely because they were popular in the wrong circles, or because the ideas they purveyed became unfashionable. They were innocent victims of circumstances. And in the vast majority of cases the only criterion seems to have been the question of date: works were set aside merely because they were thought to be late. In fact, some of the apocryphal writings are much earlier in date than some biblical ones, and we may well ask why if a work such as Daniel is included in the corpus of sacred scripture others of the same date and greater interest and appeal should be relegated to the dung heap.

The simple answer is the obvious one. Jews have always been deeply concerned with their origins and traditions. Nothing which can help to advance their knowledge and understanding of these matters should be overlooked. As we welcome the light that archeology, philology, literary and textual criticism, and other disciplines throw on the biblical writings and on the early history and thought of the Jewish people, so we must surely welcome these rich and valuable documents which have so much to tell about the origins and early development of Judaism. They have stood, in their fashion, the test of time: they can teach us some things to be learned from no other source.

THE HISTORICAL BACKGROUND

The apocryphal writings were composed, as we have seen, in different places, at different times, in various languages, and by Jews with very different outlooks. Consequently, it is not easy to give a brief account of their historical background or their ideas. The main period of their composition took place between the establishment of Seleucid rule in Judea in the early second century B.C.E., which marks the beginning of Hellenistic influence on the Jews, and the great and disastrous war of 115–117 C.E. which seems to have sealed the doom of Hellenistic Jewish culture. In other words it is what we may call the Hellenistic Age of Judaism.

The Hellenistic age of Judaism, in brief outline, is the name given to the period in which Greek rule and culture were extended over the peoples of the eastern Mediterranean region. This expansion, which began spectacularly with the conquest of the Persian Empire by Alexander of Macedon in the late fourth century B.C.E., caused a gradual but profound upheaval in the lives of all the peoples of the region. The Jews were no exception. Their cultural and geographical horizons were widened, but at the same time they experienced a difficult and painful period of acclimatization involving bitter ideological, political, and even military struggles.

The relationship of Israel and Hellas can properly be described as one of love-hate. Now love prevailed, now hate. Early in the period Judea was thrown into turmoil by a fierce conflict between the champions and antagonists of Greek culture. The antagonists emerged triumphant and established a measure of political autonomy in the country, but the advance of Hellenism continued unchecked among the Jews, especially in the communities lying outside Judea, in the Greek Diaspora.

It was here, particularly in Alexandria, that the influence of Hellenic culture was most strongly felt. The biblical writings were translated into Greek, and Greek-speaking Jews attempted to express an outlook on life that increasingly had its footing in both the Greek and Jewish camps. This process can best be seen at work in the writings of Philo, a highly educated Alexandrian Jew with a powerful admiration for the philosophy of Plato, and in those of Josephus, a Judean by birth but deeply influenced by Greece. Both writers tried to expound the traditional Jewish teachings in terms intelligible and attractive to Greek-speakers, Jew or Gentile. Philo and Josephus were only two among many Jewish writers pursuing the same aims, and the remains of this literature form an important part of what we have here called the Apocrypha.

The Hellenistic period of Jewish history is marked not only by bitter strife within the Jewish people but also by hostility between Jews and non-Jews. Unlike other neighboring peoples, the Jews clung resolutely to their own traditions even as many gladly embraced the pleasures and benefits of Greek civilization. Above all, they steadfastly maintained their old Semitic belief in a single, incorporeal God and obstinately refused to worship the gods of the Greek pantheon and their statues. This opposition to idolatry singled the Jews out from the other Hellenized peoples of the region and attracted hostile attention. It is to this period that the origins of anti-Semitism must be traced, and there were outbreaks of anti-Jewish violence throughout the region which led several times to full-scale civil war.

The pattern of Jewish history at this time is only complicated unnecessarily by exaggerating the part played by the Romans. Although in the latter part of the period most of the areas in which Jews lived were under Roman rule, the Romans interfered little with their lives. Displaying a toleration rare in the ancient world, they respected the desire of the Jews to maintain their own religious beliefs and practices, and left the administration of Jewish communal life entirely in Jewish hands. They interfered only when the Roman peace was threatened either by Jewish revolutionaries or by conflict between Jews and Greeks. Such evidence as there is suggests that, by and large, the Jews recognized and were grateful for the benefits of Roman rule. "Pray for the peace of the Empire," one statement puts it, "for without the fear of it we should have swallowed each other alive" (Aboth 3:2). Even after the calamitous war waged by Vespasian and his son Titus to put down a revolution in Judea, culminating in the sack of Jerusalem and the burning of the temple, a Jewish author could write (substituting, as was customary, the names of the Babylonian period): "Pray for the life of Nebuchadnezzar king of Babylon [i.e., Vespasian emperor of Rome] and his son Belshazzar [i.e., Titus], that their days on earth may last as long as heaven; may the Lord give us strength and illumination, and may we live in the shadow of Nebuchadnezzar king of Babylon and his son Belshazzar. May we render them long years of service, and may we win their favor" (1 Baruch 1:11–12).

Not all Jews shared this view, it must be admitted. There were zealots and revolutionaries, and the writings preserve some gruesome apocalyptic visions of the destruction of the "Roman beast." But the majority of the apocryphal writings on this subject share with the rabbinic commentators the firm conviction that the sufferings of the people were caused not by the Romans, but by God, and were a punishment for sin.

The Judean war of 66–73 C.E., which began with violent clashes between Jews and Greeks, came to a climax with the fall of Jerusalem, and ended with the crushing of the last pockets of zealot resistance, radically transformed the character of Judaism in the land of Israel. Variety gave way to uniformity, the authority of the high priests in Jerusalem was replaced by the authority of the rabbis in Yavneh and later in Galilee. As the power of the rabbis was consolidated, with Roman support, other strands of Judaism were progressively crushed.

In the Diaspora things were different. The Jews there were unaffected by the war in Judea. Both their intellectual life and their troubles continued as before. But toward the end of the reign of the Emperor Trajan a great commotion flared up almost simultaneously in Libya, Egypt, Cyprus, and even far to the east in Mesopotamia. Enormous numbers of Jews and Greeks were killed in the fighting and the life of many flourishing communities brought to an end. Many Hellenized Jews were won over to Christianity, which seemed to offer a solution to some of their problems, and they took their literature with them. The dream of a triumphant alliance of the best in Greek and Jewish thought turned to ashes, or rather it came true in an unexpected way, with the conversion of the Roman emperor to Christianity at the beginning of the fourth Christian century.

CHRONOLOGICAL TABLE

with approximate dates of the main apocryphal writings

B.C.E.		*Ahikar*
323	Death of Alexander	
312	Beginning of Seleucid era	Letter of Jeremiah
		Tobit
198	Judea comes under Seleucid rule	Judith
175–164	Antiochus IV Epiphanes, Seleucid king	Ben Sira
168	Civil war and rebellion break out in	Greek Ezra
	Judea	*Enoch* (parts)
164	Judah captures Jerusalem and	
	rededicates the temple	
161	Treaty with the Romans	
160	Death of Judah	
143	Syrians recognize Judean autonomy:	*Letter of Aristeas*
	Simon, high priest and ethnarch	*Testaments of the*
		Twelve Patriarchs
134	John Hyrcanus, high priest and	*Jubilees*
	ethnarch	
	Beginning of conflict between	1 Maccabees
	Sadducees and Pharisees	Greek Esther
104	Aristobulus I, high priest and king	*Enoch* (parts)
		2 Maccabees
		3 Maccabees
103	Alexander Yannai, high priest and king	Susanna

CHRONOLOGICAL TABLE (*Continued*)

B.C.E.		
76	Salome Alexandra, queen; Hyrcanus II, high priest	*Joseph and Asenath*
67	Civil War between Hyrcanus and Aristobulus II	Wisdom of Solomon
64	Pompey in Syria: end of Seleucid rule	Psalms of Solomon
63	Pompey conquers Judea. End of war and of Hasmonean monarchy. Limited Jewish self-government with Hyrcanus as high priest	
49	Roman Civil War (Pompey and Julius Caesar)	
48	Death of Pompey; Caesar in Egypt	
40	Parthians invade Judea. Roman Senate proclaims Herod king	
37	Herod captures Jerusalem	*4 Maccabees*
4	Death of Herod. His kingdom is divided among his sons, under Roman supervision	

C.E.		
6	Judea comes under direct Roman rule	
ca. 30	Execution of Jesus	*Biblical Antiquities*
ca. 34	Conflict between Jewish and Greek Christians in Jerusalem	*Assumption of Moses* *Apocalypse of Abraham*
38	Anti-Jewish riots in Alexandria	
ca. 45	Beginning of missionary journeys of Paul Death of Philo	
66	Widespread fighting between Jews and Greeks Revolt in Judea	
69	Vespasian emperor	

ered in many different ways by different Jewish thinkers, all ing to preserve the belief in God's perfection and at the same time onviction that he is intimately involved in human life and history. ne way in which the apparent chasm between God and man was ged was by means of mediators: personages sharing something of livine nature yet able to communicate with man. Our texts are full ngels, messengers of God's word, servants of his will. The fact we live now in an age unsympathetic to belief in angels and other pernatural" agencies is a great barrier when reading and trying to erstand the ancient writings. But even in antiquity there were Jews were skeptical about angels and who looked for other vehicles of nmunication between God and man. One might locate the initiative n God and dwell on revelation and the gift of prophecy, or concen- e on the human faculties, intuition and intellect, which make such nmunication possible. If man was created in God's image and like- s, it is evidently in the noncorporeal parts of man's constitution that is closest to God: the mind, the soul, the spirit. The body perishes the soul survives death to be reunited with God who gave it. The ellect, the faculty of reason, is also a divine gift which distinguishes n from the animals and enables him to understand his condition. e divine nature can operate on these noncorporeal elements so as to ercome the barriers and ultimately produce results in the physical rld.

These lines of reasoning make themselves felt in various ways, of ich the most influential is the formulation of the doctrines of divine isdom. Wisdom originates with God but it is also present in man. e should really say "she" rather than "it" because in the literature isdom comes to be personified, and is feminine: *ḥokmah* in Hebrew, *phia* in Greek. The man who possesses wisdom is called *sophos* or *kam*, which in Rabbinic Judaism came to be the title of the rabbi. isdom can take many forms, but her principal vehicle is Torah, the vealed word of God, with which she is sometimes identified. In reek, Torah was called *nomos*, "law," but Greek Jews also used the rm *logos* for the revealed word. The idea of the *logos* was also to lay an important role in the development of Christian theology.

Like Greek philosophy, Jewish philosophy had a practical as well as peculative side. The cultivation of wisdom led not only to commu- ion with God but also, through the study of the virtues, to the good

C.E.		
70	Jerusalem captured by Titus; temple destroyed	*Martyrdom of Isaiah*
73	Fall of last Zealot strongholds	1 Baruch
	Beginning of organized Rabbinic Judaism	*2 Baruch*
ca. 100	Death of Josephus	Apocalypse of Ezra
115–117	Widespread fighting between Jews and Greeks in Libya, Egypt, Cyprus, and Mesopotamia put down by Romans	Prayer of Manasseh
117	Death of Trajan: Hadrian becomes emperor	
132–5	Revolt in Judea (Bar Kosiba)	
		3 Baruch
324	Constantine, champion of Christianity, sole Roman emperor	

THE PHILOSOPHICAL AND RELIGIOUS BACKGROUND

It is hardly to be expected that so vast and varied a body of literature as the apocryphal writings should present a coherent, consistent point of view on such questions as the origin, meaning, and ultimate destiny of human life, or the ideal relationship between man and God or between man and man. The variety of viewpoints is indeed considerable, and by no means all of them are represented in this anthology. Yet it is possible to detect certain common threads which run through the great majority of the texts.

It must be borne in mind that the period in question, the Hellenistic Age, forms the bridge between the biblical period and the emergence of the doctrines that have come to be recognized as authoritative in Judaism and Christianity through the ages. On a superficial level the similarities between Judaism and Christianity would seem to derive, by and large, from their common origins in the Bible, and their differences from separate, parallel developments which took place after the split between the two movements. But in a more profound sense all the main areas of similarity and divergence can be traced back to the Hellenistic Jewish milieu from which both Rabbinic Judaism and primitive Christianity emerged. The common ground, generally speaking, is that of Hellenistic Judaism, and the divergences reflect the differences of opinion which developed during that period.

The differences between Judaism and Christianity are sometimes presented in cultural and linguistic terms: Rabbinic Judaism represents the continuation of the old Semitic tradition springing from the Hebrew Bible and developed in relative isolation in Hebrew- and Aramaic-speaking circles, whereas Christianity is heir to the Hellenized Judaism of the Greek Bible and the Greek-Jewish writers. This picture is oversimplified and misleading. Whatever validity it has lies in a later period, when Christianity had spread westward to take over the Greek- and Latin-speaking Roman Empire, stifling the organic development of Judaism in those lands and inevitably bringing to prominence the Jewish schools of the non-Roman, Aramaic-speaking (and later Arabic-speaking) East. But, despite this polarization, both Judaism and Christianity have remained remarkably faithful to the original fusion of Semitic and Hellenic ideas from which they emerged during that period.

This loyalty manifests itself in different ways, with each religion preserving different aspects of ancient belief. Christianity, for instance, has remained committed to the theories of sin and survival after death elaborated during that period but which have had a less permanent effect on Judaism. Judaism in turn has maintained attitudes to ritual law and the idea of the nation which have been less influential in Christianity. Yet each of the main tenets of Christian belief is echoed in the Jewish tradition, and vice-versa, and the abandoned doctrines have a habit of being revived from time to time. In this way the old debates of the Hellenistic Age remain with us, contributing to the freshness and enduring appeal of the ancient texts.

We need not dwell on the broad common features of the ancient literature which have survived equally in church and synagogue. The overpowering sense of the unity, power, and majesty of God; his justice and mercy; his loving care for his creation and in particular for his chosen people, is exuded by almost every page of the writings, and forms the common basis of Jewish and Christian faith to this day. It is the working out of the details that gives rise to debate and discussion: the nature of God's unity, the balance between his justice and mercy,

the ways in which his will is made known a
played.

In its resistance to pagan polytheism and
greatly strengthened by the prior existence of a
Greek opinion which had long proclaimed th
teachings of the Greek philosophical schools, go
Plato and Aristotle, were attractive to many Jew
of the obstacles inherent in popular and official
prized diversity above unity and blurred the dis
and gods. Josephus, describing the diversity of Je
benefit of Greeks, constantly refers to the main g
ophies,'' and goes so far as to equate the Pharisee
the Essenes with Pythagoreans. This must have s
obvious way for a Greek Jew to reconcile the var
ish and Greek thought. But the tendency to e
simplify the divisions and groups should be resist
Greeks the commitment to one particular school o
means the rule, and the Hellenized Jewish thinke
ideas eclectically rather than to ally themselves
tablished school. Philo, for instance, is often desc
yet he betrays the powerful influence of Stoicism a
Furthermore, for all his debt to Greek philosophy,
Jewish thinker, a worshipper of the God of Abraham,
devoted follower of the law given by God through
provides the best example of the fusion of Jewish a
simply because so much of his work survives. But i
of him as unique; on the contrary, there is a long
Greek thought behind him.

The central problem posed to Judaism by Greek p
relationship between God—perfect, eternal, un
poreal—and the imperfect, transient, physical wor
could the perfect God have made an imperfect worl
be said to have been created in God's image and lik
God, who knows no pain or death, sympathize with
creation? How can he communicate with beings who
tally alien to his nature? Indeed, since God is comple
tion and lacks nothing, how can one justify or unde
that he loves mankind and cares for his creation? These

life, the life lived in obedience to God's will as set out in Torah. The interpretation of the words of Torah varied considerably; some interpreters were content to take the words more or less as they found them in the scriptures, others erected vast and elaborate structures of exegesis to extract their hidden meaning. But for all alike the revealed word, as embodied in Torah, formed the basis for religious instruction and the regulation of the virtuous life.

One subject which provoked a wide variety of response was the question of God's justice and mercy. What was the relationship between these two attributes of God? What happened when they were in conflict? How were they exercised? Why did the righteous apparently suffer and the wicked prosper? This was a constant preoccupation of the ancient writers, closely allied, of course, to the subject of Torah and the virtuous life. It was widely accepted that man is endowed with free will, but that if he chooses to sin he will be punished. Yet many wicked men appear to escape punishment, and since all men alike must die, what is the reward of righteousness? While some texts still proclaim death as the end, Sheol as total destruction, a powerful and ever-growing belief develops that death and destruction are only apparent or temporary: the dead will be brought to life again, the righteous will be rewarded, and the wicked punished in a future existence, after death. The fortunes of the individual resemble those of the nation, which also seems to suffer at the hands of lawless enemies. For the nation, too, a new age will dawn: the enemies of Israel will be crushed, Jerusalem will be rebuilt, and peace and prosperity will come to Zion.

The Wisdom of Solomon provides a graphic denunciation of the foolishness and shortsightedness of those who think that evil goes unpunished. According to the author of this text, death came into the world only through man's own wickedness; it was not part of God's plan. Similarly, the author of *The Visions of Shealtiel,* the most poignant and moving text dealing with this difficult subject, broods on the "evil tendency" (in Hebrew *yeṣer hara*) to which men have surrendered themselves ever since Adam. Shealtiel realizes with growing horror the terrible meaning of the teaching of punishment after death, and refuses to be comforted even by the assurance that he himself will be among the saved. There is not even the hope that the righteous dead can intercede for the sinners (p. 145); each man must answer for his own deeds. In similar vein, Deborah insists (p. 95) that the dead cannot intercede for the living nor can dead sinners gain atonement by repentance. She even challenges the popular view that the stock of credit built up by the patriarchs counts in favor of their descendants: the only way the fathers can help is by their example, which later generations must follow. It is only in this life that men can save themselves from destruction.

This rather pessimistic view of God's justice is balanced by other texts that stress God's mercy. In these works God is sensitive to men's suffering and moved by prayer and repentance. His mercy is available to penitent sinners, and his ancient promises give an assurance to the people that, whatever calamities befall them through their sins, he will never abandon them to their fate. This message of hope, shining through one of the blackest periods in the history of the people, has brought comfort and strength to untold generations of Jews and Christians down through the ages.

A LIST OF THE APOCRYPHAL WRITINGS

The list that follows sets out the principal apocryphal works, with brief descriptions and notes on their origin and the form in which they have come down to us. The term "apocryphal," which is really totally inadequate to describe these writings, is to be understood in a wide sense as encompassing those Jewish writings of the Hellenistic Age which do not bear the genuine names of their authors. They have been arranged, for convenience, under various headings, but it should be observed that many of them could fit equally well in two or more categories. The bibliography at the end of the book provides fuller information about these writings.

BIBLICAL STORIES

It was during the Hellenistic period that the Bible was completed and edited, and first translated into another language. The Greek translations of the various books vary considerably in their faithfulness to the original: some are slavishly faithful, others take great liberties in rendering the Hebrew into polished Greek. Some (Jeremiah, Job) differ from the Hebrew in their contents or arrangement; others (Esther, Daniel) contain material not found in the original.

This was also the period when the first commentaries on the biblical books were written (fragments of such commentaries have been found at Qumrān). The Bible was always at the center of the religious life of the Jews, and the biblical stories were continually told and retold, with the constant addition of legendary material (in Hebrew, *aggadah*). Most of the works in this list contain some traces of *aggadah*, some are composed almost entirely of it. Some retell the biblical stories in contemporary idiom, reflecting the different preoccupations and interests of the age, supplying details or even whole episodes in the lives of the characters which either filled a supposed gap or provided a framework for the ideas of the author. Sometimes the purpose is moral—to illustrate a virtue; sometimes it is polemical—to attack undesirable religious or political influences, such as idolatry.

What follows is a list of works of widely disparate character which retell the biblical stories or contribute new details to the lives of the biblical characters. Further elaborations of a similar kind can be found in the works listed under the headings "Testaments" and "Apocalypse."

Jubilees

Also known as *The Lesser Genesis,* this is a free rendering of early biblical history from the Creation to the institution of the Passover (Exodus 12), which purports to have been dictated by an angel to Moses on Mount Sinai. This fascinating work was composed in Hebrew in the latter half of the second century B.C.E., in Judea. In retelling the biblical history, it does not limit itself to material contained in the Torah but includes a great deal of reinterpretation and additional material. A prominent feature of the work is the attempt to fix the chronology of the early history, which is arranged in "jubilees" (cycles of forty-nine years, each divided into "weeks" of seven years)—whence the work's title. Although referred to by several ancient writers, *Jubilees* was believed to have been lost until an Ethiopic version was discovered in the middle of the last century. Popular in the Ethiopic church, the book is now known in many manuscripts. Part of a Latin translation has also been discovered, and quotations from the Greek translation, on which these two later versions are based, appear in the works of various Greek Christian writers. The Hebrew original, still known in the fourth century, is almost entirely lost, but some fragments have been found at Qumrān and there are allusions to it and quotations from it in later Hebrew writings.

The Life of Adam and Eve

This aggadic retelling of the first four chapters of Genesis was probably compiled in the first century C.E. and is preserved in Greek and other languages.

Joseph and Asenath

Also called *The Prayer of Asenath*, this is a Greek work of the type known as ''romances.'' It describes the romance between Joseph and his Egyptian wife, Asenath (Genesis 41:45). It exists in various Greek manuscripts and in Syriac and other translations, and was probably written during the last century B.C.E.

Biblical Antiquities

Like *Jubilees,* this is an aggadic retelling of biblical history, in this case from Adam to the death of Saul (exactly the period summarized briefly in the first ten chapters of 1 Chronicles). The main emphasis is on the period of the Judges. It was probably composed in the first century C.E. in Hebrew, but all that survives is a Latin translation made from a lost Greek version in the fourth century, and some medieval Hebrew fragments, which do not represent the original text. The Latin translation was incorporated among the Latin versions of the works of Philo, whence its alternative title, *Pseudo-Philo*.

The Lives of the Prophets

A multitude of Greek manuscripts preserve details of the lives of the biblical prophets which go back to ancient Jewish *aggadah*. They were apparently translated and put together by a Greek writer in the first or second century C.E.

The Martyrdom of Isaiah

The account of the killing of Isaiah by King Manasseh was composed in Hebrew (or perhaps Aramaic) in Judea in the first century C.E. It is preserved in a composite Christian work called *The Ascension of Isaiah,* which exists in Latin, Ethiopic, and other languages, and partly also in an ancient Greek papyrus. The story is reproduced in the Babylonian Talmud (Yebamoth 49[b]), from a text "discovered in Jerusalem by Simeon ben Azzai" (second century C.E.), and also in the Palestinian Talmud and the Targum of Isaiah.

The Letter of Jeremiah

More of a sermon or a diatribe against idolatry, this purports to be a letter sent by the prophet Jeremiah to the Jewish captives in Babylon. It is thought to date from the late fourth century B.C.E., and was written in Hebrew, although it survives only in the Greek Bible and its translations into other languages.

Bel and the Serpent

This is made up of two dramatic short stories about Daniel that aim to combat idolatry. The date and place of composition are unknown. It has been argued that the original language was Hebrew, but the existing Hebrew version of the stories is probably a later retranslation. We have two Greek versions (the longer attributed to Theodotion), a Jewish Aramaic version of the Serpent story, and various Christian translations into other languages.

Lost and Fragmentary Works

There were many more legends in circulation in antiquity, and several of them are mentioned by ancient writers. We know, for instance, of a book of Adam, which is mentioned in the Talmud, and several legends about Abraham and Moses that have left their traces in the rabbinic literature and elsewhere. There was also a *Book of Jamnes and Jambres (or Mambres)*, the two Egyptian magicians whose miracles were outdone by Moses and Aaron. Of what was once a considerable literature little now survives, and the few ancient manuscripts that have been found only serve to emphasize how much has perished. A Greek papyrus fragment now in The British Museum in London preserves a few lines of a Joseph story. The most important ancient manuscript, which again is tantalizingly fragmentary, is an Aramaic scroll known as the Lamech Scroll or *The Genesis Apocryphon,* which was discovered at Qumrān. It contains part of an account of the miraculous birth of Noah and a longer passage about the life of Abraham, based on chapters 12–15 of Genesis. The lost apocrypha are discussed by M. R. James in his *The Lost Apocrypha of the Old Testament*, and many of the fragmentary legends were incorporated by Louis Ginzberg in his great work *The Legends of the Jews.* (See *Suggestions for Further Reading* for complete bibliographical data.)

MORAL TALES

Besides the biblical elaborations, which often have an underlying moral message, there are other similar stories centering around characters who are not mentioned in the Bible. Their very names seem to hint sometimes at the model virtue of their bearers: Tobit ''the good man,'' Judith ''the Jewess,'' Susanna ''rose'' of chastity.

Ahikar

This work presents the story of Ahikar, prime minister of Sennacherib, king of Assyria (c. 705–681 B.C.E.), interspersed with proverbs and parables. Versions of the story or allusions to it recur in the literature of virtually every people of the ancient Near East, including the *Arabian Nights* and ranging as far afield as Tibet. A fragmentary Aramaic text of the work was among the Jewish papyri discovered at Aswan in Upper Egypt, dating from the late fifth century B.C.E., and is thus the oldest surviving Jewish literary document. There are many parallels to the proverbs of Ahikar in the biblical and apocryphal wisdom literature.

Tobit

Set in Mesopotamia in the same period as Ahikar (in fact Ahikar is mentioned as Tobit's cousin), this ever-popular work tells the story of the pious Jewish exile Tobit (Tobi) and the adventures of his son Tobias (Tobiah). It is a charming tale of virtue rewarded and sorrow turned to joy. The date and language of the original composition are not known; it is thought to have been written in Egypt. Fragments have been found at Qumrān, and it survives in various Greek versions and translations into other languages.

Judith

Posing as history, this book is a message of encouragement in the face of adversity, and an exhortation to keep God's commandments. It tells how Judith killed Holofernes, Nebuchadnezzar's general, who was invading Israel. Jewish tradition associated Judith with the period of the Maccabean revolt, and the story was often told at Hanukkah time, but the book may well have been written at a slightly earlier date. The Hebrew original was apparently lost at an early stage, if we accept the statement of Origen (third century) that "the Jews do not use Judith or even have it in Hebrew in their apocrypha, as they themselves informed me." Jerome, however, at the end of the fourth century, says, "The Jews read Judith among the apocrypha," and he mentions an Aramaic text of the work. The surviving Greek, Latin and Syriac texts all go back to a single Greek translation, a very literal version. The story remained popular among Jews, and various Hebrew versions exist.

Susanna

A beautiful lesson in virtue and justice, Susanna is set in the Babylonian captivity, but was written in Judea in the early first century B.C.E., probably in Hebrew. Later it was associated with the name of Daniel, being actually appended to the Book of Daniel in the Greek, Latin and other Bibles. Several medieval Hebrew manuscripts exist, but they probably do not represent the original text.

Lost Stories

As with the biblical legends, by no means all such stories have come down to us. A manuscript from Qumrān preserves a fragment of a story of Nabonidus, the last king of Babylon, who is cured by a Jewish exorcist of both his ulcer and his idolatry.

TESTAMENTS

The *Testaments* represent a distinct and popular type of literature, falling midway between *aggadah* and apocalypse. They almost invariably follow the same pattern: a celebrated biblical figure, on his deathbed, gives an account of his life to his surviving family and commends them to a life of virtue. Some also contain a vision of the future fortunes of the people. The testament form of writing is a development of the patriarchal blessing such as we find in the Bible at the death of Jacob (Genesis 49) and in *Jubilees* at the death of Abraham (see p. 64).

Adam and Eve

A *Testament of Adam* is preserved in Greek and various other languages. A *Testament of Eve* forms part of *The Life of Adam and Eve* (see above).

Abraham

The Testament of Abraham survives in two Greek versions and several other translations, all of which are derived from a lost Hebrew or Greek original of the first century C.E. It contains an account of the death of Abraham, with a vision of the heavens and of divine judgment.

Isaac and Jacob

Testaments of Isaac and Jacob are preserved in Coptic, Arabic, and Ethiopic translation, along with *The Testament of Abraham*. In their present form they are Christian compositions but probably contain some authentic Jewish elements.

Sons of Jacob

The Testaments of the Twelve Patriarchs form a cycle in which each of the sons of Jacob in turn recounts his life, with many aggadic elaborations, while exhorting his children to follow a life of virtue. The work survives in its entirety in Greek and other languages. Fragments in Aramaic and Hebrew have been discovered at Qumrān and in the Cairo Genizah, and traces of the work are also to be found in medieval Hebrew writings. The date and place of composition and the original language of these testaments are much disputed (it has even been claimed that they are a Christian work of the second or third century), but it seems likely that they were written in Judea in the second century B.C.E.

Moses

In *The Testament of Moses* Moses at his death reveals the future history of the people to Joshua. The work was composed in Judea, early in the first century C.E., and contains an account of the political events of the region in the previous century and an interesting diatribe against a group of people who boast of their holiness while exploiting the people. The work survives only in a partly illegible Latin manuscript, probably deriving ultimately from a Hebrew original.

Job

The Testament of Job follows the usual pattern. This Greek work, derived perhaps from an Aramaic original, incorporates elements of Hebrew *aggadoth*. It has been dated to the late first century B.C.E., since it refers to the Parthian invasion of Judea in 40 B.C.E.

APOCALYPSE

"Apocalypse" is a Greek word meaning "revelation." Many of the ancient writings purport to present revelations granted by God to various biblical characters, usually by means of an angel. Living in times of violent political upheaval and troubled metaphysical speculation, the authors sought comfort and inspiration in the contemplation of the other world, in the mysteries of creation, the heavenly spheres, and the throne of God's glory, the involvement of God in human history, the imminent coming and final triumph of the Messiah. We have already mentioned one apocalyptic work, *Jubilees; The Life of Adam and Eve* and *The Martyrdom of Isaiah* have also been handed down in the apocalyptic tradition. Medieval Christian literature, particularly that of the various Eastern churches, is rich in apocalyptic writings, many of them going back to Jewish origins; medieval Jewish literature also contains many elements of such works. Listed below are only the most important of these writings, which include some of the most sensitive and thought-provoking documents in the whole of Jewish literature.

Enoch

The Book of Enoch, preserved in its entirety only in Ethiopic, is a composite work made up of various elements dating from the early second century B.C.E. and later. Essentially it is an account of a journey through the heavenly zones to the throne of God's glory, and a vision of the history of the Jewish people. A few sections have been preserved in Greek, and several Hebrew and Aramaic fragments have been found at Qumrān, where the work was evidently popular.

The mysterious figure of Enoch, who "walked with God and was not, because God took him" (Genesis 5:24), clearly excited the imagination of the ancient mystical writers, and there are many other works in a variety of languages which are associated with his name. The most important are *The Secrets of Enoch*, a Greek Jewish work of the first century C.E. now preserved only in Slavonic translations, and the Hebrew *Book of Enoch,* whose hero is Rabbi Ishmael ben Elisha (second century C.E.). Both these works, like the Ethiopic *Enoch,* narrate heavenly journeys.

Abraham

Among the various apocalyptic writings concerning Abraham, the work entitled *The Apocalypse of Abraham,* preserved in Slavonic and Rumanian translations, was originally written in Hebrew or Aramaic in the first century C.E. It contains the legend of Abraham and the idols (see p. 74) followed by a vision of the glory of God and of the past and future history of the world.

Baruch

Four distinct works bear the name of Baruch, secretary to the prophet Jeremiah:

1 Baruch is a composite work, partly written in Greek and partly translated from Hebrew. Produced in the aftermath to the capture of Jerusalem by the Romans in 70 C.E., it argues for submission to Roman rule and the pursuit of wisdom, and holds out a hope of a glorious future for Jerusalem. It is preserved in manuscripts of the Greek Bible and in other translations.

2 Baruch, written under similar circumstances, shares common features with the Apocalypse of Ezra (see below). It is a meditation on the nature of sin and punishment, accompanied by prophecies and visions. The original Hebrew is lost, and the work survives only in a Syriac translation made from the Greek.

3 Baruch is a vision of a journey through the heavenly spheres. Written in Greek during the second century C.E., it survives in Greek and in translations into various Slavonic languages.

4 Baruch, also called *The Paralipomena of Jeremiah,* is another work prompted by the capture of Jerusalem by the Romans. Written perhaps in Hebrew, it survives in Greek and other languages.

Ezra

Like Enoch, Ezra, the restorer of the religious life of the Jews after the Babylonian exile, attracted a great deal of interest, and many legends and writings were associated with his name. According to a persistent tradition, Ezra's contribution to Judaism was no less than Moses'. The Apocalypse of Ezra (also called 4 Ezra) is a composite work, edited by a Christian from mostly Jewish material. The central core is a series of visions about the nature of sin and punishment and the destiny of mankind, narrated in the first person by Salathiel (Shealtiel), who in the composite work is identified with Ezra. The fictional setting is the Babylonian exile, the actual setting the Roman conquest of Jerusalem. Other shorter texts have been incorporated, including the celebrated legend of how Ezra recovered the lost scriptures. The original Hebrew and the Greek version of the work are lost; it survives in Latin, Syriac, and other translations.

Various other apocalypses of Ezra have come down to us, in Latin,

Syriac, and other languages. These are mostly Christian compilations, though they contain Jewish elements. A similar work is preserved by the Falashas in Ethiopia.

The Sibylline Oracles

A large mass of anonymous prophecies and prognostications has come down to us in archaic Greek verse. They are a mixture of Jewish, pagan, and Christian elements. The Jewish sections were composed in different places and periods, ranging in date from the mid-second century B.C.E. to the late first century C.E. They present political and religious propaganda under the guise of pagan prophecy.

PHILOSOPHY AND WISDOM

When we speak of the Hellenization of the Jews, we have in mind particularly the influence of Greek philosophical thought. In their encounter with Hellas the Jews began with an inherited predisposition toward metaphysical speculation and inquiry, and many educated Jews immersed themselves wholeheartedly in the teachings of the Greek philosophical schools. At the same time they did not renounce their own heritage but devoted strenuous efforts to demonstrating the harmony of Jewish and Greek thought, and, indeed, the superior antiquity and merit of the Jewish tradition. This effort is seen at its best in the abundant writings of Philo, who strove to reconcile the teachings of Judaism and Platonism, but Philo represents the culmination of a long process. Though most of this literature is lost, we have interesting surviving specimens in *4 Maccabees* and *The Letter of Aristeas* (see below, p. 36).

Meanwhile, the Jews continued to develop their own tradition of folk wisdom expressed in the form of proverbs and wise sayings. This type of literature is represented in the Bible by the Book of Proverbs, ascribed to Solomon, the model of the "wise king." Among the apocryphal works it is well illustrated in the sayings of Ahikar (see p. 28) and Ben Sira. The inspiration of philosophical thought was personified as the divine Wisdom, a female personage sent by God to those who seek her devotedly, who is in time identified with Torah, the living word of God. Many poems were written in praise of her;

one (see p. 179) is frankly erotic in tone. It is noteworthy that the earliest Greek references to the Jews describe them as a race of philosophers.

Ben Sira

The Book of Ben Sira (in Greek, The Wisdom of [Jesus, son of] Sirach; in Latin, Ecclesiasticus) is a collection of moral maxims and poems resembling the biblical Book of Proverbs. It was written in Hebrew, probably in Jerusalem, at the beginning of the second century B.C.E. Unlike most of the other works in this list, Ben Sira is frequently mentioned by name and even quoted in the rabbinic literature. Ancient fragments in Hebrew have been discovered at Qumrān and Masada, and remains of medieval copies were found in the Cairo Genizah. The book survives complete in Greek and Syriac translations. The Greek version, dating from the late second century B.C.E., has an interesting preface by the translator.

The Wisdom of Solomon

This is a treatise on the justice of God, including a poetic praise of Wisdom, a diatribe against idolatry, and an exposition of the plagues and the exodus from Egypt. Written in Greek in the last century B.C.E., it is included in the Greek Bible.

4 Maccabees

This is a discourse about the triumph of reason over the passions, illustrated by a long account of the martyrdom of Eleazar and the mother and her seven children, which is also recounted in 2 Maccabees. The author was a Greek Jew, and the Greek text is found in most of the early manuscripts of the Greek Bible. The date of composition is probably the early first century C.E.

HISTORY

Under Greek influence, Jews turned to the writing of history, both of the ancient history of the Jewish people and of recent and contemporary events. The fullest surviving specimens of such work are Josephus' *Jewish Antiquities*, *Jewish War*, and *Autobiography*. Philo also wrote accounts, which survive, of the anti-Jewish demonstrations in Alexandria and the ensuing mission to Rome in which he was involved. We also possess the names of several historical writers whose works are lost, such as Demetrius, Eupolemus, Aristeas, and Justus of Tiberias. Evidently the surviving historical works represent only a small fraction of what was written. As Hellenistic Judaism gave way to Rabbinic Judaism, with its fundamentally nonhistorical (or even antihistorical) outlook, the writing of history by Jews gradually died out and was not revived until modern times.

The Greek Ezra

Called 1 Esdras in many manuscripts and in English Bibles, this is a history from Josiah's Passover (2 Chronicles 35) to the reading of the Torah by Ezra (Nehemiah 8), which duplicates parts of 2 Chronicles, Ezra, and Nehemiah, but is based on a somewhat different tradition. The date and place of composition are unknown, and the Hebrew or Aramaic sources on which it is based have perished. It survives in Greek and also in Latin (though not accepted as biblical by Roman Catholics) and other languages.

The Greek Esther

The version of the Book of Esther found in Greek Bibles differs considerably from the Hebrew in the order in which it presents the material, and also contains passages not in the Hebrew. In particular, it contains what purport to be copies of official decrees and letters, a common preoccupation of the Hellenistic Jewish historians, which makes itself felt in the other works in this section.

The Letter of Aristeas

Entitled in the manuscripts simply *Aristeas to Philocrates*, this purports to be an eyewitness account of events surrounding the translation of the Torah into Greek, written by a courtier of Ptolemy II (285–247 B.C.E.). It contains an interesting description of Jerusalem and a display of wisdom by the Jewish translators, whose aim, like that of the whole work, is to glorify Judaism. The work was written in Greek, in Egypt, probably during the second century B.C.E.

1 Maccabees

Perhaps originally entitled *The Book of the Hasmonean Dynasty*, this is a serious and important account of the history of the Jewish struggle for political independence and religious liberty, from the accession of Antiochus Epiphanes (175 B.C.E.) to the death of Simon (135 B.C.E.). Written in Hebrew, or perhaps Aramaic, in the late second century B.C.E., it incorporates some earlier material. Though the original is lost, a Greek translation survives, together with Latin and Syriac versions translated from the Greek. With 2 Maccabees and Josephus, who is of course much later, this is our principal source for the history of this crucial period.

The Scroll of Antiochus, which survives in the original Aramaic and in translations into Hebrew, Arabic, and other languages, is a later composition of no historical value, designed to be read publicly at the feast of Hanukkah in the same way as Esther is read at Purim.

2 Maccabees

A history of the Hasmonean rising from 175 to 161 B.C.E., independent of 1 Maccabees, this is not strictly an anonymous work: it is an abridged version of a much longer history (in five books) by a Greek Jew from Cyrene called Jason. Jason probably wrote in the third quarter of the second century B.C.E., and the abridgment was made in the late second or early first century. It survives in Greek and in various translations.

3 Maccabees

This work has nothing to do with the "Maccabees" but is an account of certain events set in the reign of Ptolemy IV (222–205 B.C.E.) and centered on Ptolemy's attempted persecution of Jews. A similar story, set in the reign of Ptolemy VII, is found in Josephus' *Against Apion* II:5. The work was written in Alexandria, around 100 B.C.E.

The original survives in the Greek Bible; but since it is not considered scriptural by the Roman Catholic church, it is not found in the Latin Bible.

The Fasting Scroll

This document, called in Hebrew *Megillath Ta'anith* (to be distinguished from the Mishnaic tractate Ta'anith) is not really a history but a list of joyful days on which fasting is forbidden. The dates commemorate historical events and are listed according to their order in the calendar. The work survives in Aramaic, which is probably the original language, and is thought to have been produced in Zealot circles in the early first century C.E. It is preserved in the Jewish tradition, not the Christian, and is often quoted in the Talmud.

PRAYERS AND PSALMS

The Jewish love of poetry and song is evident from the Bible. The encounter with Greece, which had its own highly developed poetic tradition, resulted in some Jews writing Greek poetry on the classical model but with Jewish themes. Our concern here, however, is with the more genuinely Jewish tradition of religious poetry, which includes psalms, hymns, and other poetic compositions. Sometimes these are independent creations, and sometimes they are found interspersed in prose works (as is also the case in the Hebrew Bible).

The tradition of writing psalms continued well into the Hellenistic period; indeed, some scholars have dated certain of the biblical psalms to this period. Other psalms have been preserved in other ways. A large scroll of psalms found at Qumrān, for example, contains, in addition to biblical psalms, several other pieces, some of which were previously known and some which were new. It seems to have been customary in antiquity for books of psalms for liturgical use to contain additional material. Thus Greek Christian psalters contain a Psalm 151, and some of them also add a collection of psalms and prayers taken from various biblical books and elsewhere. These include The Prayer of Manasseh, two psalms preserved in the Greek Daniel, and a Morning Hymn. Syriac psalters have five psalms which are not in the

Hebrew Bible. Various other prayers and psalms have come down to us, some put into the mouths of biblical characters.

At Qumrān, in addition to remains of several apocryphal psalms, a long manuscript has been found containing several hymns which were previously unknown. While they perhaps originated in sectarian circles, they have many features in common with the biblical psalms.

The Greek Book of Daniel incorporates in the story of the furnace (Daniel 3:23) two psalms not found in the original Aramaic of Daniel. The first, entitled the Prayer of Azariah, is a prayer for help for the nation after the destruction of Jerusalem, the language of which is reminiscent of the Apocalypse of Ezra and other works written in the late first century C.E. The second is a psalm in praise of God with a recurring refrain; its language, suggestive of the Jewish liturgy, has long had a place in Christian worship.

The Greek Esther, besides its other additions, records the prayers of Mordecai and of Esther just before the queen interceded with the king on behalf of her people.

The Psalms of Solomon are a collection of eighteen psalms composed in Judea in the middle of the last century B.C.E. Some of them describe the capture of Jerusalem by Pompey in 63 B.C.E. The attribution of the psalms to King Solomon reflects that of the biblical psalms to David; several other works, both biblical and apocryphal, were ascribed to Solomon. The original Hebrew is lost, and we have only Greek and Syriac translations. A collection of forty-two more poems attributed to Solomon survives in Syriac; they derive from sectarian Christian circles in the early second century C.E., but probably contain some Jewish elements.

The Prayer of Manasseh, a kind of penitential psalm, purports to be the prayer of the king of Judah when he was a prisoner in Babylon. Such a prayer is mentioned in 2 Chronicles 33:19. Our prayer, however, was written in Greek, possibly in the aftermath of the destruction of the temple.

About the Scriptures

It seems appropriate to open this anthology with three passages in which the ancient writers tell in their own words how they conceived of their literature, its history, and its contemporary relevance. The three passages are of very different character: the first takes us into the realm of the supernatural and of divine revelation; the second is cast in an historical mold; the third is a translator's preface to his own work. Despite their different character and background, however, they all have certain features in common. They are all written in the first person, although in two out of the three this is merely a literary device. More important are the honor and respect the writers all pay to the ancient writings and the urgency they express for their preservation, translation, and study. Their interest in the writings is far more than antiquarianism. The Torah is for them the guide to the right life, and it is essential to make it available to everyone, in every generation, in the form in which it can be understood and put into practice.

EZRA RECOVERS THE SCRIPTURES

Ezra is described, in the biblical book of the Old Testament bearing his name, as "a scribe learned in the Torah of Moses, which the Lord their God had given to Israel. . . . He had devoted himself to the study and observance of the Torah of the Lord and to teaching statute and ordinance in Israel'' (Ezra 7:6, 10). Jewish tradition, as exemplified in *The Apocalypse of Ezra,* ascribes to him a most important role in the history of the transmission and preservation of the Torah. According to this tradition, the Torah had been lost during the Babylonian exile, and after the return of the Jews to Jerusalem he miraculously recovered it and made it available to the people once more.

The classical rabbinic account of the history of the Torah, which opens the tractate Aboth, does not even mention Ezra:

> Moses received the Torah at Sinai and handed it on to Joshua; Joshua handed it on to the Elders, the Elders to the Prophets, and the Prophets to the men of the Great Assembly.

The emphasis is on continuity of tradition; there is no hint of an interruption in the chain. Yet there is evidence that the rabbis were aware of the traditional role of Ezra:

> Resh Lakish said: In ancient times, when the Torah was forgotten in Israel, Ezra came up from Babylon and restored it.
>
> (Babylonian Talmud [Sukkah 20[a]])

Resh Lakish was a Palestinian teacher of the late third century C.E., but an earlier authority, the mid-second-century Tanna Yose, mentions two striking features of the tradition—the comparison between Ezra and Moses, and the new alphabet:

> Rabbi Yose said: Ezra was worthy to have the Torah given through him to Israel, if Moses had not got there first. But even though it was not given through him, it was through him that the script was changed.
>
> (Babylonian Talmud [Sanhedrin 21[b]]; Tosefta [Sanhedrin 4:7])

The rabbis were aware that the square script, which is in use to this day, and which they called ''Assyrian writing,'' had not always been used for writing Hebrew. The old Hebrew script, which they called ''jagged writing'' and which is still used by the Samaritans, continued for a while to be used for writing the sacred four-letter name of God and is found on coins of the rabbinic period. Opinions were divided about which was the original script in which the Torah had been given, but even those who claimed that the square script was the original still agreed that Ezra had restored it after an interval:

Rabbi [Judah] said: The Torah was originally given to Israel in the Assyrian script. When they sinned it was changed to "jagged" script, but when they returned in the time of Ezra the old Assyrian writing was restored.

(Tosefta [Sanhedrin 4:7]; Babylonian Talmud [Sanhedrin 22[a]]; Palestinian Talmud [Sanhedrin 1:9, 10[a]])

A curious feature of the text that follows is that in addition to the twenty-four books which must be presumed to be the twenty-four books of the Hebrew Bible (see above, p. 8), Ezra received a further seventy books which are to be handed over to the secret keeping of the "sages." In rabbinic Hebrew and Greek, the term "sages" is normally reserved for the rabbis, and it would be reasonable to suppose that these seventy books are the books of the Mishnah. As we have it, however, the Mishnah consists of sixty-three books, and there is no evidence that it ever contained seventy. It is likely that "seventy" is not meant to be a precise figure but merely a large number. In view of the fact that the seventy books are to be kept hidden, many scholars have assumed they are the apocrypha.

The Apocalypse of Ezra (4 *Ezra*) 14

One day, as I was sitting under an oak tree, I suddenly heard a voice calling me from a bush opposite: "Ezra! Ezra!"

"Yes?" I said, and I got to my feet.

"I revealed myself from a bush," the voice said, "and spoke to Moses when my people were slaves in Egypt. On my orders he brought my people out of Egypt and led them through the desert. I made him climb Mount Sinai and I kept him with me for many days. I told him many wonderful things, I showed him the secrets of history, and I taught him about the end of time. I ordered him to publish part of what I had said, but to hold the rest back.

"Now I say to you, store up the signs I have shown you in your mind. You are going to be taken away from the world of men; you will wait with other like-minded souls until the end of time. The world is no longer young; time is growing old. Put your affairs in order; address your people for the last time, comforting the pious and teaching the wise; and prepare to take your leave of mortal life."

"Lord," I said, "grant me one favor. I will go as you command, and instruct the people for the last time. But who will instruct those still unborn? The world has sunk into darkness, its inhabitants live without light, because your Torah has been burnt. Nobody will know what you have done, or what you are going to do in the future. Grant me the gift of your spirit, Lord, and let me write down everything that has happened in the world since the beginning, and everything that was written in your Torah, so that people will be able to find the right path, and so that those who desire the life of the new age will learn the way."

"Very well," he answered. "Go and summon your people. Tell them not to look for you for forty days. Prepare a large number of writing tablets and come back here, bringing with you five scribes who can write quickly. I shall light a lamp of understanding in your mind which will not go out until you have finished writing everything you are to write. When you have finished, you are to publish part of it, and the rest hand over to the sages to be kept hidden. You will start writing at this time tomorrow."

I went and summoned the people and addressed them as he had told me. Then I collected the five men, and together we went back to the place and waited. Next day I suddenly heard a voice calling me, "Ezra! Ezra! Open your mouth and drink what I shall give you."

I opened my mouth and saw a cup full of what looked like liquid fire. I took it and drank, and as I drank my mind filled with understanding and my heart with wisdom; I retained my consciousness and my memory. My mouth was opened, and the Almighty inspired the five men to write down what was said continuously, in a previously unknown script. I stayed there for forty days; they wrote all day, and only ate some bread at night, but I did not stop speaking day and night. In the forty days, ninety-four books were written.

When the forty days were up, the Almighty said to me, "Publish the first twenty-four books; they may be read by all the people, worthy and unworthy alike. But keep the other seventy books back; hand them over to your people's sages. They contain the springs of understanding, the fountains of wisdom, the streams of knowledge."

HOW THE TORAH WAS TRANSLATED INTO GREEK

The passage which follows has been excerpted from *The Letter of Aristeas*, in which the author, who pretends to be a non-Jewish courtier of Ptolemy II (285–247 B.C.E.) in Alexandria, describes the circumstances of the translation of the Torah into Greek. The first translation of a Jewish scripture into any other language, it hence became the foundation not only for subsequent translations but for the whole Greek literature of the Jews. The story of the seventy-two translators was naturally familiar to Greek Jews and is preserved in several sources, of which this is probably the oldest. Josephus refers to it in the introduction to his *Jewish Antiquities,* explaining that Ptolemy only had the five books of the Torah translated whereas it is his own intention to expound the whole five-thousand-year-old history of the Jewish people. He comments:

> The main lesson to be learnt from this history is that men who follow the will of God, and do not contravene the excellent provisions of the law, prosper beyond belief and are rewarded by God with happiness, whereas the further men depart from the strict observance of the laws, the more they find that things become impossible and all their good intentions end in irremediable disaster.

Later, when he comes to the reign of Ptolemy II, he describes the translation at great length, reproducing the account given in *The Letter of Aristeas* (*Jewish Antiquities* XII:12–118).

The story is also told by Philo, in his *Life of Moses*, in a section devoted to the excellence of the law. Philo does not cling to the account of our text, as Josephus does, but describes the events in his own words. Like the author of the passage from *The Letter of Aristeas*, he emphasizes the wisdom and universal appeal of the Mosaic legislation; it is evident that both share the aim of impressing Jews and Gentiles alike with the superiority of the Jewish laws. Unlike our author, however, Philo imports a distinctly supernatural element into the story, and he also adds an interesting postscript:

> The island of Pharos lies in front of Alexandria, connected to the city by a narrow strip of land, and enclosed by shallow water, so that the distant boom and roar of the sea are muffled. They selected this as the most suitable place where they could find the peace and quiet necessary for the soul to commune in solitude with the laws. They took the holy books and held them up to heaven and asked for God to grant success to their efforts. He answered their prayers, so that most if not all of the human race might benefit by being led to found their lives on those philosophical and thoroughly excellent ordinances.

> Hidden away here with no other company but the natural elements, earth, water, air and heaven, which were to be the first subject of their sacred task since the laws begin with the creation of the world, they were seemingly inspired: instead of producing several different versions of the prophecies, they all wrote the same words, as though taking dictation from an invisible source. . . . A comparison of the translation with the original shows, if one knows both languages, that they are as like as two sisters. Indeed, they are identical in substance and language, and one can only revere these men, not as translators, but as priests and prophets, whose purity of mind led them to an encounter with the pure spirit of Moses himself.
>
> To this day a festive public gathering is held every year on the island of Pharos. Not only Jews but throngs of non-Jews cross to the island to show their veneration for the place where the light of the translation first flashed out and their gratitude to God for this ancient gift which enjoys eternal youth. After the prayers and thanksgivings they feast with their family and friends, some building shelters on the seashore and others lying in the open air on the sandy beaches, which they consider more luxurious than dwelling in a royal palace.
>
> In this way the leaders and laymen alike show how worthwhile and desirable they find the laws, even though for some years now our nation has been dogged by misfortune. When one is not prospering one is bound to be under a certain cloud, but if our prospects were suddenly to take a brighter turn, what a change we might see! I believe that then the other nations would abandon their own institutions and wave goodbye to their ancestral ways, and all turn to honoring our laws alone. Coupled to national prosperity, our laws would outshine the rest as the rising sun outshines the stars.

It is sad to reflect how hollow the test of time had made Philo's resolute optimism seem. The clouds of which he speaks were not dispelled but became thicker still, and darkness descended on his world. All the more interesting to observe that even in his own day there were those who saw the translation of the Torah into Greek as the beginning of a dark age for the Jewish people. This idea is expanded with many elaborations in the Midrash; it is expressed with epigrammatic brevity in *The Fasting Scroll*:

> On the eighth of Tebeth the Torah was translated into Greek in the reign of King Ptolemy, and darkness descended on the world for three days.

The Letter of Aristeas 9–11, 121–123, 172–186, 301–318

When Demetrios of Phaleron was put in charge of the king's library he was assigned generous funds with instructions to assemble, if possible, a complete collection of the literature of the world, a project that he carried out to the best of his ability by means of purchase and copying.

I was present once when he was asked by the king how many books had already been collected. "More than two hundred thousand, Your Majesty," he replied, "and I shall make every effort to bring the total up to half a million as soon as possible. I am told," he added, "that the legal literature of the Jews is also worth having copied and deposited in your library."

"What is stopping you, then?" answered the king. "All the necessary means have been put at your disposal."

"It will have to be translated first," Demetrios said, "because the Jews use a language and script of their own, like the Egyptians. It is commonly supposed that they use Syriac, but that is not the case."

The king ascertained the details and gave instructions for a letter to be written to the high priest of the Jews so that the project could be put into effect.

The high priest, Eleazar, selected the best men available to act as translators. They were men of noble birth and great learning who were equally proficient in the literature of the Jews and the Greeks. They were experienced spokesmen, well equipped to expound the law and answer questions about it. They were also men of moderation and outstanding modesty who had earned Eleazar's high esteem and affection.

Having selected the translators, Eleazor offered sacrifices and prepared many gifts for the king. Then he sent us on our way with a heavily armed escort.

As soon as we arrived in Alexandria the king was informed. He was so keen to meet the delegates that he summoned them to court and ordered all the other officials to withdraw. This struck everyone as very strange since the usual procedure was that even those who arrived on official business had to wait five days before being admitted to the king's presence, while envoys from other kings or eminent cities were rarely admitted within thirty days. But so high was his opinion of these visitors and the man who had sent them that he immediately dismissed those he considered superfluous and paced impatiently up and down waiting to greet them.

They soon arrived, bearing the gifts and several leather scrolls. As soon as the king caught sight of them he asked to see the books. They took the scrolls out of their wrappings and unrolled them. The law was written in gold in Jewish writing; the parchment was wonderfully worked and the joins between the sheets were invisible.

The king stood looking for a long time. Then he bowed respectfully seven times and said, "Gentlemen, I am grateful to you and even more to him who sent you, but most of all to God, whose holy words these are."

Everyone present, newcomers and courtiers alike, gave their unanimous approval to these words. Nervous strain and excitement crowned success with tears: the king wept for joy. He had the scrolls put away, and then at last he greeted the men: "You are God-fearing men: you will agree that it was only right that I should first pay my respects to the objects that are the reason for your being here before holding out my hand to you. I declare this day on which you have arrived a great day. It will be celebrated annually as long as I live. It happens also to be the anniversary of my naval victory over Antigonos, and I wish to dine with you today. Everything," he added, "will be prepared according to your customs, for me as well as for you."

They expressed their gratification, and he gave instructions for them to be given the best accommodation, near the citadel, and for preparations for the banquet to be put in hand.

Under the arrangements instituted by the king, which are still followed to this day, each nation that had its own special customs regarding eating, drinking, and service at table was allotted to a particular official, so that whenever they came to court their own customs could be followed and they could enjoy themselves without any awkwardness. So it was on this occasion. The arrangements were entrusted to Dorotheos, who was a most painstaking man. He saw to it that special food was served and that they were seated on either side of the king. Every possible honor was shown them.

When they were seated, the king gave orders for the usual procedure when there were guests from Judea to be followed. The sacred heralds, sacrificers, and others who usually offered the prayers were dispensed with, and instead he asked the senior priest in the party, Eleazar, to offer a prayer. He stood up and spoke these memorable words: "Your Majesty, may Almighty God give you your fill of all the good things that he has created. May he grant you, your wife, your children, and all your well-wishers uninterrupted enjoyment of them all the days of their lives."

His words were received with a burst of applause, and it was some time before the shouts of joy died away. Only then did they turn their attention to the delights which had been prepared for them. . . .

The banquet was repeated every day for seven days. Three days later the librarian, Demetrios, led the visitors along the causeway, which is nearly a mile long, to the island of Pharos and then over the bridge to the northern part of the island. Here, in a magnificently appointed building situated in a quiet location by the seashore, he held a meeting and invited them to set to work on the translation. Everything they might need had been provided.

So they set to work. They consulted together and agreed on each point, and the approved version was written down by Demetrios. The sessions lasted until the middle of the afternoon. Then they would break off and turn to recreation. Everything they wanted was lavishly provided, and every day they were served with royal feasts by Dorotheos, on the king's instructions.

They appeared at court every day at dawn to greet the king before going off to work. And before they began the work of reading and interpreting they washed their hands in the sea, as is the custom of all Jews,[1] and prayed to God. So they gathered each day as I have described in this charming spot, with its peace and quiet and its clear light, and in due course they completed the project. As if by coincidence, the translation was finished in exactly seventy-two days.

When the work was finished, Demetrios held a public meeting of the Jews at the place where the translation had been made and read it

[1] I asked them why they washed their hands before praying, and they explained that it was a sign they had done no wrong because all actions are done with the hands. Their way of making everything a symbol of righteousness and truth is beautiful and shows great piety. [Author's note]

out in the presence of the translators, who received a great ovation from the crowd in recognition of the great service they had rendered. They showed their approval of Demetrios in the same way, and requested him to have a copy made of the whole law and present it to their leading men.

After the reading of the scrolls, the priests, the senior translators, and the leaders of the community stood forward and said, "This translation is so beautiful and faithful and so accurate in every respect that it ought to remain just as it is, and there should never be a new edition."

The suggestion was received with universal acclaim, and it was agreed that the customary curse should be pronounced on anyone who should revise what had been written by addition, alteration, or deletion. They were right to do this so that it would be kept forever as a permanent and enduring monument.

When the king heard the news he was delighted at the safe completion of his project. The whole work was read out to him as well and he was most impressed by the lawgiver's mind. He bowed respectfully and gave orders that the books should be carefully looked after and preserved with due reverence. He told the translators that they were free to return to Judea but invited them to visit him often. He would regard them as his friends, he said, and treat them with the consideration they so richly deserved.

TRANSLATOR'S PREFACE TO BEN SIRA

In this short preface the translator explains how he came to translate his grandfather's work into Greek. Visiting Egypt in the reign of Ptolemy IX Euergetes (145–117 B.C.E.), he was struck by the urgent need for Jewish books in Greek. He has something to say of his grandfather's aims and of the difficulty of translations (he does not seem to share Philo's opinion of the miraculous success of the Greek translation of the Torah), but above all he stresses the benefits to be derived from the Torah and the other writings and the need to give the Torah practical application in one's life.

* * *

Many great benefits have accrued to us through the Torah and the Prophets and the other works which follow them, and for this credit is due to the Jewish tradition of education and scholarship. It is essential that this tradition be not only exploited by students but that it be made available to the world at large by scholars through both their oral teaching and their writings. It was in accordance with this tenet that my grandfather, Joshua, having devoted himself over a long period to the study of the Torah, the Prophets, and the other traditional writings, decided to write his own book on the subject of education and scholarship, with the aim of encouraging future scholars to familiarize themselves with the subject and so to make their own contribution to the practical application of Torah.

I must crave the reader's sympathetic attention and beg him to excuse any apparent inadequacies in the translation. Hebrew is not an easy language to translate; even the Torah, the Prophets, and the other writings seem quite different when read in the original.

When I was thirty-eight I went to Egypt, in the reign of King Euergetes. After spending some time there I realized what a great demand there was for education. I decided that it was essential for me to apply my efforts to translating this book. I devoted all my skill and spare time, burning the candle at both ends, to completing the work. I am publishing it for the benefit of those in the Diaspora who have a desire for scholarship and who wish to make the Torah a reality in their lives.

In these few tersely-worded sentences the Book of Genesis tells us all that we know from the Bible about the birth and early life of Abraham. There was ample scope for legend to embroider the details: the relationship between Abram and his family, the mysterious early death of Haran, above all the childhood of Abram and the paths by which he came to a knowledge of the true God.

The Book of Jubilees is the earliest surviving source for such legends, although Josephus (*Jewish Antiquities* I:158–160) refers to other ancient writings which mention Abraham. *Jubilees* places the marriage of Terah in the eighth year of the thirty-ninth jubilee—that is, in the year 1870 of the world—and the birth of Abraham six years later, in 1876.

Even as a child, Abram began to draw apart from the idolatry of his family, who actually owned and ran an idol factory. The first episode of the story combines the miraculous and the scientific: Abram solves the problem of the crows which, we have been told earlier, were sent by the devil to make life hard for men. It is a common feature of the Hellenistic Jewish writings that they make the biblical patriarchs responsible for the important inventions which make civilized life possible. This was a response to the Greek accusations that the Jews were a recent people who had contributed nothing to civilization. In addition to Abraham, Noah and Jacob are also credited with agricultural improvements.

The story of the destruction of the idols is one of the most celebrated legends about Abraham. Different versions of it occur in many sources, notably in *The Apocalypse of Abraham* and in several Hebrew Midrashim.

Jubilees 11:14–12:29

[*An angel is speaking.*]

In the thirty-ninth jubilee, in the first year of the second week, Terah married his father's sister's daughter. Her name was Edna, daughter of Abram. In the seventh year of the same week she bore him a son, and he named him Abram, after his mother's father, who had died before his grandson was conceived.

Biblical Stor

Abraham

This brief selection of biblical legends begins with stories abo Abraham, the father of the Jewish people. Innumerable such stori circulated in antiquity, filling in the background to the biblical narr tive and elaborating on the piety and steadfastness of the patriarc Only a few can be included here; a fuller selection, together wit many other stories covering the whole of biblical history, can be foun in Louis Ginzberg's *The Legends of the Jews*. (See *Suggestions fo Further Reading* for full bibliographical data.)

ABRAM DISCOVERS THE TRUE GOD

Terah had three sons, Abram, Nahor and Haran, and Haran had a son called Lot. Haran died before his father Terah in his birthplace, Ur of the Chaldeans. Abram and Nahor both married: Abram's wife was called Sarai and Nahor's was called Milcah daughter of Haran. . . . Terah took his son Abram, his grandson Lot son of Haran, and his daughter-in-law Sarai, Abram's wife, and they left Ur of the Chaldeans together to go to the Land of Canaan; but when they reached Haran they settled there.

(Genesis 11:26–32)

Gradually the child began to understand the errors of mankind, who were worshipping idols and indulging in immorality. His father taught him to read and write, but when he was fourteen he moved apart from his father because he did not want to worship idols. He began to pray to the Creator of all things to save him from the errors of mankind and not to let him fall victim to lust and immorality.

When sowing time came round and they all went out to scare the crows off the seed, Abram, who was still a child of fourteen, went with them. A flock of crows came to eat the seed, but before they could settle on the ground Abram ran up to them and said, "Shoo! Go back to the place you came from."

The crows all turned tail and fled. That day he turned away seventy flocks of crows, and not a single crow landed in all the fields where Abram was. The people who were with him saw him call out and make the crows go away, and he became famous all over Chaldea. Whenever anyone wanted to sow that year, they took Abram with them, and for once they harvested enough grain to feed them in plenty.

In the first year of the fifth week Abram taught the craftsmen who made the farming equipment to make a container and fix it to the plough. The seed was put in the container, and it fell onto the ploughshare and was buried so that they no longer had to fear the crows. They made these containers and fitted them to all the ploughs and sowed as Abram had shown them, and after that they no longer feared the birds.

In the seventh year of the sixth week Abram said to his father, Terah, "Father?"

"Yes, son?"

"These idols you worship and bow down to—what good are they to us? They are dumb and deceptive: Do not worship them. Worship the God of heaven who sends the dew and rain to the earth and does everything in the world. He has created everything by his word and all life comes from him. Why do you worship things that have no spirit? They are made by men, you carry them about, they cannot help you. They bring shame on those who make them and delude those who worship them. Do not worship them."

His father replied, "I know, son, but what can I do about the people who make me work for them? If I tell the truth they will kill me because they are bent on honoring and worshipping them. So keep quiet, son, or they may kill you."

Abram said the same thing to his two brothers, and they were angry with him. So he kept silent.

In the fortieth jubilee, in the seventh year of the second week, Abram married Sarai, his father's daughter.[1] His brother Haran married in the third year of the third week, and in the seventh year his wife had a son, whom he named Lot. His other brother, Nahor, also married.

In the fourth year of the fourth week, when Abram was in his sixtieth year, he got up one night and secretly set fire to the idol factory and all its contents. The others got out of bed and tried to save their gods from the flames, and Haran was burned to death in the attempt. So he died in Ur of the Chaldeans before his father, Terah, and he was buried in Ur of the Chaldeans.

Then Terah left Ur of the Chaldeans together with his sons to go to Lebanon and Canaan. On the way he stopped in Haran, and Abram stayed in Haran with his father, Terah, for two weeks of years.

In the fifth year of the sixth week, on the new moon of the seventh month, Abram sat up all night to watch the stars, to forecast the rainfall for the coming year. While he was sitting alone and watching, a word came into his heart and he said, "All the signs of the stars, the moon, and the sun are in the power of the Lord. Why am I studying them? If he wishes, he makes it rain morning and evening. If he wishes, he holds back the rain. Everything is in his power."

That night he prayed:

"My God, Most High God, you are my only God,
  and I have chosen you and your rule.
You are the Creator of all things;
  everything that exists is the work of your hands.
Rescue me from the power of evil spirits who have power over men's minds,
  and do not let them lead me away from you, my God.
Strengthen me and my descendants forever,
  do not let us go astray from now and forever more."

[1] According to Genesis 20:12 she was his half-sister.

And he added, "Should I go back to Ur of the Chaldeans, who are clamoring for me to return, or should I stay here? Guide me in the right path and do not let me take a false turn, my God."

When he had finished speaking and praying, the word of the Lord was sent to him through me:[2]

"Leave your country, your family, and your father's house, and go to a land which I shall show you, and I shall make you a great and mighty nation.

"I shall bless you.
I shall make you famous.
You will be blessed throughout the world,
and all the families of the earth will be blessed by you.
I shall bless those who bless you,
and those who curse you I shall curse.[3]

"I shall be your God, and your son's and grandson's, and all your descendants'. Do not be afraid: from now to the last generation on earth I am your God."

Then the Lord God said, "Open his mouth and his ears, and let him speak and understand the language of revelation."[4]

So I opened his mouth and his ears, and I began to speak to him in Hebrew, in the language of the Creation. He took the books of his forefathers, which were in Hebrew, and transcribed them and began to study them. He studied them during the six rainy months, and I explained whatever he could not understand.

In the seventh year of the sixth week he spoke to his father, and announced that he was leaving Haran to go and see the land of Canaan, and that he would return. Then his father, Terah, said to him:

"May the eternal God make your path straight.
May the Lord protect you from all harm.
May He grant you grace, mercy and favor from those you meet,
and may no man have power to harm you.
Go in peace."

[2] An angel is speaking.
[3] See Genesis 12:1–3.
[4] Which men had stopped speaking ever since the destruction. [Author's note]

ABRAM'S ORDEAL

In *The Apocalypse of Abraham* the episode of the destruction of the idols ends with a great fire which destroys the factory, similar to the fire which kills Haran in the version of *Jubilees*. There are several legends which associate Abraham with a fire, and their source is probably to be found in an interpretation of the name "Ur," which can mean "fire." In Genesis 15:7 God says to Abram: "I am the Lord who brought you out of *Ur of the Chaldeans*" [italics mine], and in most of these legends Abram is saved from a fire. One such legend follows. It occurs in several versions, including some in Hebrew; the one given here is translated from the Latin of *The Book of Biblical Antiquities*.

It is thought that the author of *Biblical Antiquities* had read *Jubilees* since he seems to take care not to repeat the stories about Abraham appearing there. The story of Abram's ordeal does not appear in *Jubilees*. If it did, the logical place for it would be that occupied by the fire which killed Haran and which immediately preceded the departure from Ur of the Chaldeans. *Biblical Antiquities,* however, has combined it with another famous biblical story, the building of the tower of Babel. (In *Jubilees* the tower was built some two hundred years before Abraham was born.) It begins with a paraphrase of Genesis 11:1–4, and continues to tell how Abram, with a handful of companions, refused to participate in this challenge to God's sovereignty.

The principal instigators of the challenge, according to *Biblical Antiquities,* are the leaders of the three main divisions of mankind: Penech for the sons of Japheth, Nimrod for the descendants of his grandfather, Ham, and Joktan for the Semites. In our version Joktan plays the leading part, but in other versions it is Nimrod, described as "a mighty hunter before the Lord" (Genesis 10:8–9), who is responsible for persecuting Abram.

Biblical Antiquities 6

The inhabitants of the world, who had been divided, reunited and lived together. Traveling from the east, they came on a plain in the land of Babylon and settled there. They said to one another, "We may become dispersed, and in time to come we may end up fighting among ourselves. Let us build a tower that will scrape the sky, and make a name for ourselves in the world. Let us take bricks and each write our name on them, and then we shall bake them. Those that are well baked will serve as bricks, and the rest will make mortar."

So they all took bricks, except for twelve men who refused. The people arrested them and took them to their leaders. They said, "These are the men who have disobeyed us and refused to take part in our plan."

The leaders said to them, "Why would you not bake your bricks with the other people?"

They replied, "We bake no bricks with you. We do not share your desire. We acknowledge one Lord, and we worship him. Even if you throw us in the fire with your bricks we will not obey you."

The leaders were furious and said, "Do exactly as they have said. If they do not agree to bake bricks with you, burn them in the fire with your bricks."

But Joktan, who was the chief of the leaders, said, "No. Let them have seven days' grace. If they abandon their wicked ideas and agree to bake bricks with you, let them live. If not, then let them be burnt as you have decided." He was trying to find a way to save them from the people because he was from the same tribe as they and worshipped God.

So he took them and locked them up in the palace. That evening he had fifty warriors summoned to him, and he said to them, "Go tonight and take the men who are locked up in my house and load ten mules with provisions for them. Bring the men to me and take the mules with the provisions into the mountains and keep them there. I warn you: if anyone gets to hear of what I have told you, I shall burn you in the fire."

So the men went and did everything that their chief had told them. They fetched the men from his house by night, and they loaded the provisions onto mules and led them into the mountains as he had said.

The chief called the twelve men and said to them, "Cheer up, do not be afraid: you are not going to die. The God you trust in is strong. Be firm in your faith: he will rescue you and free you. Listen: I have sent fifty men with provisions from my house to go ahead of you into the mountains and to look after you in a valley there. I shall give you another fifty men to take you there. Go and hide in the valley. You will have water to drink; it flows out of the rocks. Stay there for thirty days, until the anger of the people has died down and God has vented his rage on them and smashed them. I know that their evil plans will come to nothing; they are idle fancies. When the seven days are up and they come to find you, I shall say, 'They broke down the prison door and escaped into the night. I have sent one hundred men out to search for them.' That way I shall foil their fury."

Eleven of the men replied, "You are very kind to rescue us from the hands of these ruffians."

Abram alone said nothing.

The chief said, "Abram, servant of God, why don't you answer me?"

Abram replied, "Suppose I run away and hide in the mountains today; I may escape being burnt, but the wild beasts in the mountains may eat us, or we may run out of food and starve to death, and we will die as sinners for running away from the people of the land. By the life of him in whom I trust, I will not leave the place where I have been put. If I am a sinner and the fire burns me, God's will be done."

Then the chief said, "If you refuse to leave with these men, be it on your own head. If you choose, you will be set free. If you prefer to stay behind, by all means do so."

"I am not going," Abram said. "I will stay here."

The chief sent fifty more men with the eleven, with these orders, "Wait in the mountains with the first fifty men I sent. At the end of a fortnight come back and say that you have not found them. I have said the same to the first detachment. I warn you: anyone who fails to carry out all my instructions to the letter will be burnt to death."

So the men left, and he took Abram and locked him up again in the same place as before. After seven days the people gathered and said to the chief, "Hand over the men who refused to obey us so that we can burn them to death."

When the officers were sent to fetch them, they found Abram all alone. The people assembled and said to their leaders, "The men you imprisoned have escaped. They have eluded us."

Penech and Nimrod said to Joktan, "Where are the men you imprisoned?"

"They broke out at night," he replied. "I have sent out one hundred men to search for them with orders, if they find them, not only to burn them to death but to leave their bodies for the birds of the air to destroy.''

''Well,'' the people said, ''let's fetch the one who is left.''

So they seized Abram and took him to their leaders, and they said to him, ''Where are the others who were with you?''

''I was asleep,'' he replied. ''When I woke up in the morning, they were gone.''

So the people seized Abram and they built a furnace. They lit a fire in it and put baked bricks inside it. Then Joktan's mind was deranged; he took hold of Abram and put him in the furnace with the bricks. But God made a great earthquake, and the fire burst out of the furnace in flames and sparks and burnt all the people who were standing round watching. 83,500 people were burned to death, but on Abram there was not the slightest trace of a burn. He stepped out of the furnace and the furnace collapsed. So Abram was saved. He went to the eleven men who were hiding in the mountains and told them what had happened to him. They came down from the mountains with him joyfully calling God's name, and no one came to meet them to frighten them. They named the place after Abram's God, calling it Deli, which is the Chaldean word for God.

ABRAM IN EGYPT

In the biblical narrative, Abram leaves Haran at God's bidding and goes to the land of Canaan. Here there is a famine which forces him to spend some time in Egypt. The next story is based on the episode which follows (Genesis 12:9–20), although it is influenced by a similar story in Genesis 20. It is preserved only in one ancient manuscript, found at Qumrān, and unfortunately this manuscript is damaged so that parts of the story are missing or mutilated. In this translation these have been summarized for the sake of continuity.

Genesis Apocryphon cols. 19–20

[*Abraham is the narrator.*]

Our land was totally famine-stricken. Hearing that there was corn in Egypt, we left it and went to the land of the Hamites, the land of Egypt.

The first night after we had arrived in Egypt, I, Abram, had a dream of a cedar and a palm tree. Some men came and tried to cut down and uproot the cedar, leaving the palm tree on its own. But the palm tree cried out, "Do not cut down the cedar. Whoever fells it will be cursed." So the cedar was spared because of the palm tree.

I woke up in the middle of the night and said to my wife, Sarai, "I've had a frightening dream."

"Tell me about it," she said.

So I told her about the dream, and I explained that it meant that someone would try to kill me but to spare her. "Tell them," I said, "that I am your brother, and they will spare me for your sake because otherwise they will certainly kill me."

Sarai cried at what I told her that night, and as we traveled on together to Zoan I made her swear not to let any man see her.

But when we had been there five years, three Egyptian princes came on orders from the Pharaoh of Zoan to inquire about my business and about my wife. . . .

[*Abram apparently entertains them to a feast in the course of which they see Sarai. Later they give the king a detailed report about her beauty.*]

"She has a beautiful face and lovely hair. She has beautiful eyes and a charming nose, and her whole face glows. She has lovely breasts and her skin is beautifully white. Her arms are shapely and her hands are perfect, with lovely palms and long, slender fingers. She has beautiful legs and faultless thighs. She is the most beautiful woman who exists; there is not a virgin or a bride to touch her. And not only is she beautiful, she is also clever, and does everything well."

When the king heard the unanimous report of Harkenosh and his two companions, he felt a strong longing for her. He ordered her to be brought to him at once, and as soon as he saw her, he was overwhelmed by her beauty. He took her as his wife and was going to kill me. But Sarai pleaded for me and said I was her brother, and so, thanks to her, I was spared.

Nevertheless, I cried. I, Abram, was reduced to tears. My nephew Lot and I both wept that night when Sarai was taken away from me by force. As I wept that night, I prayed and implored and supplicated: "Blessed are you, Almighty God, Lord to all eternity. You are Lord and ruler of all things, and you rule over all earthly kings and punish their wrongdoings. Lord, I invoke your aid against Pharaoh of Zoan, king of Egypt. My wife has been taken away from me by force. Punish him for me. Show me your mighty hand raised against him and all his household. Do not let him defile my wife tonight. Show them, Lord, that you are the lord of all earthly kings!''

That night, while I was weeping, the Almighty sent an evil spirit to afflict him and all his household. He could not go near her, and for the two years she was with him he did not sleep with her.

The plagues and afflictions on him and his household grew worse and worse, till at the end of two years he summoned all the wise men and magicians and doctors in Egypt to see if they could cure them. But the spirit attacked them all, and they left.

Finally Harkenosh came to see me and begged me to go to the king and pray for him and lay my hands on him to heal him, because he had dreamed of me. But Lot said to him, ''My uncle Abram cannot pray for the king while Sarai, his wife, is with him. Go and tell the king to send the wife back to her husband. Then he will pray for him and save him.''

When Harkenosh heard what Lot said he went back to the king and told him, ''Sarai, Abram's wife, is the cause of all these plagues and afflictions you are suffering. Send Sarai back to her husband, Abram, and the plague and the evil spirit will leave you.''

So the king summoned me and said, ''What have you done to me? You told me Sarai was your sister, and I married her. I didn't know she was your wife. Here, take your wife and get out of Egypt. But first pray for me and my household, and rid us of this evil spirit.''

Then I prayed for him and laid my hand on his head, and the evil spirit left him; the plague went away and he was healed. He thanked me and swore not to harm me. He gave rich gifts of silver and gold and fine linen and purple to Sarai and also to Hagar, and he sent men to escort me out of Egypt.

So I left Egypt a rich man, with huge flocks and silver and gold. My nephew, Lot, came with me, and he too had huge flocks, and also a wife he had married in Egypt.

THE DEATH OF ABRAHAM

We return to *The Book of Jubilees* for our final episode from the life of Abraham, namely his last words and death. In the Bible this is described very briefly:

> Abraham had lived for a hundred and seventy-five years when he breathed his last. He died at a ripe old age, after a very long life, and rejoined his forefathers. He was buried by his sons Isaac and Ishmael in the cave of Machpelah. . . . There Abraham was buried beside his wife Sarah.
>
> (Genesis 25:7–10)

Jubilees, in its usual manner, expands the story and gives us a full account of the circumstantial details and of Abraham's last advice to his grandson Jacob and his blessing. The story resembles the account of the death of Jacob in Genesis 49:1–50:4, both in its general plan and also in some detail of its phraseology.

Jubilees 22–23

In the forty-fourth jubilee, in the second year of the first week, that is the year of Abraham's death, Isaac and Ishmael came from Beersheba to Abraham, their father, to celebrate the Feast of Weeks, the feast of first-fruits of the harvest. Abraham was delighted that both his sons had come. Isaac, who had property in Beersheba, was in the habit of going to see it and visiting his father, but this time Ishmael also came to see his father, so they both came together. Isaac sacrificed a burnt offering on the altar which his father had set up in Hebron, and he also made a thank-offering and threw a party for his brother Ishmael. Rebecca baked cakes from the new flour and gave them to her son Jacob to take to his father so that he could eat the first-fruits of his land and bless the Creator of all things before he died, and Isaac gave him the best parts of the thank-offering to take to Abraham so that he should eat and drink. So Abraham ate and drank, and blessed Almighty God, "who has created heaven and earth, and made the rich produce of the land, and given it to mankind for them to eat and drink and bless their Creator."

"And now," he said, "I thank you, my God, for permitting me to see this day. I am one hundred and seventy-five years old, I am an old man, yet all my days have been peaceful. The enemy's sword has not vanquished me for everything you have given me and my children all my life to this day. My God, may your mercy and peace be upon your servant and upon his sons' descendants. May they be your chosen people and your inheritance out of all the peoples of the world, from now to the last generation on earth, and for all time."

Then he called Jacob and he said, "Jacob, my child, may the God of all bless you and strengthen you to do right and to perform his will. May he choose you and your descendants to be the people of his inheritance according to his will forever. Now, Jacob, my child, come here and kiss me."

Jacob came close and kissed him, and Abraham said:

"May Almighty God bless Jacob, my child
and all his sons to the end of time.
May God give you righteous descendants
and may he make some of your sons holy in the world.
May peoples serve you,
and all nations bow down to your descendants.
Be strong among men
and rule over all the sons of Seth.
Then you and your sons will live justly
and become a holy nation.
May Almighty God bless you
just as he blessed me and Noah and Adam;
may blessings rest on your children's holy heads
from generation to generation forever.
May he keep you pure of all wickedness and injustice
and forgive all your wrongdoings and omissions.
May he strengthen and bless you,
and may you inherit the whole world.
May he renew his covenant with you,
may you be the nation of his inheritance forever;
may he be your God and your children's God
in truth and justice for all time.
Jacob, my child, remember my words
and hold fast[1] to the precepts of Abraham, your father.

[1] There is a pun in Ethiopic on the name of Jacob.

Cut yourself off from the nations and do not eat with them;
do not behave like them and do not mix with them:
they are unclean, and all their ways are impurity, foulness, and filth.
They sacrifice to the dead and worship demons,
they eat over graves, and all they do is vain and worthless.
They have no mind to understand or eyes to see
what they are doing or how they go wrong
when they say to wood 'You are my God'
and to stone 'You are my Lord and Redeemer.'
Jacob, my child:
May Almighty God help you
and the God of heaven bless you
and keep you from their impurity and all their mistakes.
Jacob, my child, beware of marrying a daughter of Canaan:
all his descendants will be destroyed from the world.
Because of the sin of Ham,[2] Canaan became a wrongdoer;
all his descendants will be destroyed from the world,
and none of them will be saved on judgment day.
As for all worshippers of idols,
they have no hope in the land of the living;
they will go down to Sheol
and to the place of condemnation
they will not be remembered on earth.
As the children of Sodom were removed from the world
so will all those who worship idols be removed.
Jacob, my child, do not be frightened,
do not be afraid, child of Abraham:
God Almighty will save you from destruction
and preserve you from the paths of error.

"I have founded this house to put my name on it in the world: it will be called the House of Abraham. It is yours and your descendants' forever because you will build my house and preserve my name before God forever. Your descendants and your name will continue till the last generation on earth."

[2] See Genesis 9:22.

When he had finished instructing him and blessing him, they lay on the bed together, and Jacob slept in his grandfather Abraham's arms. Abraham kissed him seven times and was full of love for him. He blessed God in these words:

> "God Almighty, God of all, Creator of all, who brought me out of Ur of the Chaldeans to give me this land as a perpetual inheritance and to found a holy family, blessed be the Almighty forever."

And he also blessed Jacob:

> "May your grace and mercy rest on my child, whom I love with all my heart, and on his descendants forever. Do not abandon or forsake him for all time but keep a watchful eye on him and his descendants. Look after him, bless him, and make him the holy nation of your inheritance. Bless him with all your blessings from now to the end of time, and renew your covenant and your love with him and all his descendants according to your will to the last generation on earth."

Then he placed two of Jacob's fingers on his eyes, blessed the God of gods, covered his face and stretched out his legs, and he slept the eternal sleep and rejoined his forefathers.

Jacob, meanwhile, was lying in his arms, and did not know that his grandfather, Abraham, was dead. When Jacob woke up, Abraham was as cold as ice. He said, "Father, father," but there was no reply, and he realized that he was dead. He got up and ran to tell Rebecca, his mother, and Rebecca went out in the dark to tell Isaac. They went in together, with Jacob holding a lamp, and found Abraham lying dead. Isaac threw himself on his father and wept and kissed him. The noise woke Ishmael, who went to his father, Abraham, and wept over him, and all Abraham's household wept loudly.

Abraham was buried by his sons Isaac and Ishmael in the cave of Machpelah, beside Sarah, his wife, and he was mourned for forty days by all his household, Isaac and Ishmael and all their sons, and all the children of Keturah. He had lived for three jubilees and four weeks of years, one hundred and seventy-five years in all, and ended his days in great old age.

Joseph

JOSEPH AND ASENATH

The Book of Genesis tells how, after prophesying a serious famine and outlining a program of grain reserves to mitigate it, Joseph is elevated by Pharaoh to a position of authority over the whole land of Egypt. The text continues:

> Pharaoh named him Zaphenath-paneah, and he gave him as wife Asenath, the daughter of Potiphera, priest of On. And Joseph's authority extended over the whole of Egypt.
>
> Genesis 41:45

On the basis of this brief allusion, the romance *Joseph and Asenath* sets out in great detail the love story of the young couple. Asenath, when we first meet her, is eighteen years old, beautiful and chaste but haughty and disdainful of men. The story continues with Joseph's arrival at Heliopolis (On) in connection with his preparations for the years of famine. Asenath falls violently in love with him and, in the best romantic tradition, they marry and live happily ever after.

The central portion of the story, slightly abridged in the present version, concerns the repentance of Asenath, her abandonment of idolatry, and her conversion to the worship of God. The language of this passage provides a fascinating insight into the attitude to conversion at that time and even the ceremonies followed. The expression "renewed, remade, given new life" is probably a survival from an ancient conversion ritual.

We leave Joseph and Asenath at the birth of their sons Manasseh and Ephraim (Genesis 41:50–52). The rest of the romance is taken up with the jealousy of Pharaoh's eldest son, who is in love with Asenath. He tries to seize her by force but is foiled by Joseph's brothers. He is killed as a result of a wound inflicted by Benjamin, and Pharaoh dies of grief, leaving his throne to Joseph, who rules Egypt as regent for forty-eight years.

Joseph and Asenath 3–21

On the eighteenth day of the fourth month Joseph arrived at Heliopolis. As he approached the city, he sent twelve men on ahead to Potiphera, the priest of Heliopolis, with this message:

> I shall visit you today because it is midday and lunchtime; the sun is very hot and I should like to rest under your roof.

When Potiphera heard this, he was delighted, and he said, "Blessed be the Lord God of Joseph." He summoned his majordomo and said to him, "Quickly; get the house ready and prepare a great feast because today Joseph, the mighty one of God, is coming."

When Asenath heard that her mother and father had come back from visiting their estates she was happy and decided to see them. She hurriedly dressed in a violet linen tunic woven with gold thread and fastened with a gold belt, and golden trousers. She put bracelets on her wrists and ankles and a necklace round her neck. She was dripping with precious stones; the bracelets and stones were engraved all over with the names of the gods of Egypt, and the images of the gods were carved on the stones. She placed a tiara on her head, fixed a diadem round her temples, and covered her head with a veil.

Then she hurried downstairs to greet her father and mother. Potiphera and his wife were delighted to see their daughter dressed up like a bride of God. They unpacked all the good things they had brought back from their estates and gave them to Asenath, who was thrilled with all the wonderful fruits, the grapes and dates, the doves, the pomegranates and the figs.

"My dear," Potiphera said to his daughter, "come and sit down between us and let me tell you my news."

Asenath sat down between her father and her mother, and Potiphera took her hand and said, "My child, Joseph, the mighty one of God, is coming today. He is the governor of the whole of Egypt. Pharaoh has made him governor of all the land, and he is distributing corn to the whole country. He is going to save us from that famine that is coming. He is a pious and modest man, as virginal as you are. He is also a man of great wisdom and knowledge; the spirit of God rests on him and the grace of God goes with him. Let me give you to him as his wife, my child. You will be his bride and he will be your bridegroom forever."

Asenath, on hearing this, flushed deeply, and gave her father a furious sideways look. "Father, what are you saying?" she exclaimed. "Why do you want to hand me over as a prisoner to this foreigner, this refugee, this slave? Isn't he the son of a Canaanite shepherd whose father disowned him? Isn't he the man who slept with his master's wife, and then his master threw him in the dungeon, but Pharaoh released him because he interpreted a dream for him? No, I want to marry the king's eldest son: he is the real king of the whole land."

Hearing this furious and haughty reply, Potiphera was cowed and said nothing more to his daughter on the subject of Joseph.

Then a servant stepped forward and announced: "Joseph is outside the gate."

At this Asenath left her parents and ran upstairs to her bedroom. But she stood at the great east-facing window to get a view of the visitor.

Meanwhile Potiphera went out with his wife and all his family to greet Joseph. The east gates were thrown open, and Joseph entered the courtyard in Pharaoh's viceregal carriage. The carriage was overlaid with gold leaf and was drawn by four snow-white horses with golden bridles. Joseph was wearing a splendid white robe and a cloak of purple linen woven with gold thread. On his head he wore a gold crown set with twelve peerless jewels and surmounted by twelve golden rays, and in his right hand he held a royal sceptre. He also held an outstretched olive branch heavy with olives.

When he had entered the courtyard the sentries closed the gates, shutting out the crowds. Potiphera and his wife and all his family apart from Asenath came forward and fell on their faces in homage to Joseph, who descended from the carriage and raised his right hand in greeting.

As soon as Asenath set eyes on Joseph she was stunned. Her stomach turned over and she went weak at the knees. Trembling all over with fear she said with a groan, "Where can I go to hide from him? What will Joseph, the son of God, think of me for the wicked things I've said about him? Where can I hide? Surely he sees everything—he is so full of light! O God of Joseph, be gracious to me, because in my ignorance I said terrible things. Poor wretch, what will happen to me? I said 'Joseph, the son of a Canaanite shepherd, is coming,' and now the sun has come down from heaven in his chariot and entered our house. I was stupid and arrogant. I scorned him and said terrible things about him. I didn't realize that Joseph was the son of God. What human womb could have produced such beauty, such light? Stupid wretch, how could I have said such terrible things to my father? If only my father would give me to Joseph as his servant, I'd gladly slave for him forever and ever."

Joseph, meanwhile, had entered the house. Potiphera seated him on a throne, washed his feet, and laid a table for him by himself because Joseph did not eat with Egyptians since it was an abomination for him. Joseph said to Potiphera: "Who was that woman I saw standing at a window on the terrace? Get rid of her!"

The reason for this was that Joseph was afraid that she would pester him. He was forever being pestered by women; all the daughters of the great men and local governors of Egypt wanted to sleep with him. As soon as they saw him they were stirred by his beauty, and they kept sending him gold and silver and expensive presents. Joseph always sent them back with threatening messages. "I shall not sin before the God of Israel," he would say. He always treasured a vivid mental image of his father, Jacob, and he remembered what Jacob had said to Joseph and his brothers: "My sons, keep away from foreign women. Have nothing to do with them. They spell death and destruction." That was why he said "Get rid of that woman."

"My lord," Potiphera replied, "that woman you saw upstairs is no stranger. She is our daughter. She is a virgin, she hates men, and you are the first man ever to set eyes on her. If you wish, though, she can come and speak to you, because our daughter is your sister.''

Joseph was overjoyed to hear Potiphera say, ''She is a virgin, she hates men.'' He said to Potiphera and his wife, ''If she is your daughter, let her come. She is my sister and from this day on I shall love her as my sister.''

So Asenath's mother went upstairs and fetched her, and Potiphera said, ''Asenath, say hello to your brother. He is a virgin like you, and he hates strange women just as you hate strange men.''

Asenath said, ''Greetings, lord, blessed by Almighty God.''

And Joseph answered, ''May God who gives life to all things bless you.''

Potiphera said, ''Now step forward and kiss your brother.''

But as she came forward to kiss him, Joseph put out his right hand and laid it on her chest. ''It is not right,'' he said, ''for a god-fearing man, who blesses the living God with his mouth and eats the blessed bread of life, to kiss a strange woman who blesses dead dumb idols with her mouth and eats the bread of death from their altars. A god-fearing man only kisses his mother and his sister of his own tribe and family, and his wife who shares his bed, because they bless the living God with their mouths. And similarly it is not right for a god-fearing woman to kiss a strange man. It is an abomination before God.''

Asenath, hearing these words, was smitten with grief and started sobbing. She stared at Joseph with tear-filled eyes. When Joseph saw her he felt very sorry for her because he was a gentle and sympathetic man who feared the Lord. He placed his right hand above her head and said:

''Lord God of my father Israel,
Almighty, All-powerful,
who gives life to all things,
who summons forth from darkness to light,
from falsehood to truth,
from death to life,
Lord, grant life
and blessing to this virgin.

"Renew her by your spirit,
remake her by your hand,
breathe new life into her,
let her eat your bread of life
and drink your cup of blessing.
You chose her before her birth,
let her enter into the rest
you have prepared for your chosen ones."

Asenath was overjoyed at Joseph's blessing. She hurried up to her room and fell limply on her bed. She felt happy and sad and frightened all at once, and she flushed at the thought of the words that Joseph had spoken to her in the name of Almighty God. She wept long and bitterly and forsook the gods she worshipped. And she waited for the evening.

Meanwhile, when Joseph had finished eating and drinking, he said to his servants, "Harness the horses to my carriage. I must continue my tour of the city and the countryside."

"Stay the night, my lord," Potiphera said. "Tomorrow you can be on your way."

"No," Joseph replied, "I must go today. This is the day on which God began the work of creation. But in eight days' time I shall come back and spend the night."

Potiphera and his family went off to their estate, leaving Asenath alone with her maids. She lay and wept until the sun went down. She ate no bread and drank no water, and when the others were asleep she alone was still awake. Then she went downstairs and unfastened the curtain which hung over the door. This she filled with ashes and carried it up to her room and laid it on the floor. Next she carefully locked and bolted her door and began sobbing and groaning. Her favorite maid, hearing her sobs, came and stood outside the locked door and asked her what was the matter. "I've got a terrible headache," Asenath answered from inside; "I'm in bed. I can't get up to open the door, I feel exhausted. Go back to bed."

Then she got up, quietly opened the door, and went into the next room where she kept her clothes. From a chest she took out a dark, mournful-colored dress that she had worn when her eldest brother died. She took off her regal tunic and put on the black dress. Instead of the golden belt she fastened it with a length of cord. She also took off the tiara, the diadem, and the bracelets. Then she threw all her best clothes out of the window for the paupers and, shattering her countless gold and silver gods to smithereens, she threw them out for the poor and needy. She picked up her dinner and the sacrificial meat and libation wine and threw it all to the dogs. After that she scattered the ashes on the floor, wrapped herself in sackcloth, untied her hair, and lay down in the ashes. She lay there beating her breast and wailing all night long. When morning came she got up and saw that the ashes had turned to mud with her tears. She lay face down in the ashes again until the sun set, and she did the same for the next seven days, without eating anything.

On the eighth day she raised her head from the floor; the rest of her body was paralyzed from her self-abasement.

She stretched her arms out toward the east, raised her eyes to heaven, and said:

"Lord, eternal God,
who gave the breath of life to all,
who brought unseen things to light,
who created all and made the invisible visible,
who stretched out the heavens on high
and laid the foundations of the earth on the waters,
who set the great rocks in the watery depths
so that they will never be submerged,
but will obey your will to the last,
O Lord my God, when I call on you
hearken to my plea.
I shall confess my sins to you,
and display my wrongs before you.
I have sinned, Lord, I have sinned,
I have done wrong, I have acted impiously, I have spoken wickedly
before you.
My mouth has been soiled by sacrifices to idols,
and from the tables of the gods of Egypt.
Lord, I have sinned before you and wronged you

in worshipping dead dumb idols,
and I am not worthy to open my mouth to you.
Lord, I have sinned before you,
I, the daughter of Potiphera, the priest,
the haughty and arrogant,
I lay my plea before you, Lord,
and call out to you
as a child calls to its father and mother:
save me from my pursuers.
Spread out your hands over me, Lord,
like a loving, tender father,
and snatch me from the hand of the foe.
The ancient raging lion pursues me
and his cubs, the gods of Egypt,
whom I threw away and shattered,
their father, the Devil, wants to devour me.
Lord, save me from his hands,
snatch me from his jaws,
do not let him seize me and tear me like a wolf,
and hurl me into the fiery depths
and the tempestuous sea
to be devoured by the great crocodile.
Save me, Lord, I am an orphan,
my father and mother have disowned me
because I shattered their gods.
I have no hope but you, Lord,
you are the father of the fatherless,
protector of the persecuted,
helper of the afflicted.

"All the wealth of my father, Potiphera, is transient and uncertain, but the habitations of your heritage, Lord, are imperishable and eternal.

"Lord, consider my orphaned state; I have made you my refuge. I have cast off the trappings of my splendor and put on sackcloth and ashes. I have neither eaten nor drunk for seven days, and I am worn out with weeping. Pardon me, Lord, because I sinned from ignorance when I slandered my lord Joseph. I did not know he was your son; people said he was the son of a shepherd from Canaan and I believed them. So I was misled and despised him, not realizing that he was your son. What mortal has fathered such beauty, what man is as powerful and wise as Joseph? I commend him to you, Lord, because I love him more than myself. Protect him in your gracious wisdom and give me to him as a servant, to wash his feet and serve him and slave for him to my last day.''

Just as Asenath concluded this confession to the Lord, the morning star rose in the eastern sky. When she saw it she was glad, and said, ''God has heard me. This star is a herald of the light of the great day.''

Soon afterward the sky was rent apart and an indescribable light dawned. Asenath fell on her face in the ashes. Suddenly a man came toward her out of the sky. He stood over her and called her name.

''Who is that calling me?'' she said. ''The door is locked and my tower is too high to climb. How can he have got into my room?''

Then the man called her a second time and Asenath replied, ''Here I am, my lord. Tell me who you are.'' ''I am the commander of the Lord's household and commander-in-chief of the army of the Almighty. Stand up and let me speak to you.''

Asenath looked up and saw a man who looked just like Joseph, with the same cloak and crown and scepter, except that his face was like lightning, his eyes like the sun, his hair like fire, and his hands and feet like red-hot iron. Asenath was terrified at the sight of him and fell at his feet.

''Be brave, Asenath,'' he said. ''Do not be afraid. Stand up and let me speak to you.''

Asenath stood up and the man continued, ''Take off that black dress and the sackcloth, shake the ashes out of your hair, and go and wash your face in cold water. Then put on a clean dress and your double sash of virginity, and come back and hear the message I have been sent to bring you.''

Asenath did as he had said, covered her head with a fine veil, and returned.

''Take off that veil,'' the man said. ''Today you are a pure virgin and your head is like a young man's.''

So she took off the veil and the man said, ''Be brave, Asenath. The

Lord has heard your confession. Your name has been inscribed in the book of life and will never be erased. From this day you have been renewed and remade and given new life; you will eat the bread of life and drink the cup of immortality. Be brave, Asenath. The Lord has given you to Joseph as his bride, and he will be your bridegroom. You shall no longer be called Asenath, but your name will be 'City of Refuge,' because many nations will take refuge in you and many peoples will shelter under your wings, and those who turn to God in repentance will find protection within your walls. Now I am going to Joseph, and I shall tell him about you. He will come to you today, he will be glad to see you, and he will be your bridegroom. Now put on your wedding robe, dress up as a bride, and prepare yourself to meet him."

When he had finished speaking Asenath fell at his feet, full of joy, and said, "Blessed be the Lord God who has sent you to rescue me from darkness and to lead me to the light. Blessed be his name forever."

Then the man blessed her and vanished. . . .

Just then a servant arrived from Joseph's entourage and announced, "Joseph, the mighty one of God, is coming to you today."

Asenath summoned her majordomo and said, "Prepare a fine feast because Joseph, the mighty one of God, is coming."

Then she went to her chest and took out her radiant wedding dress and put it on. She fastened on a regal sash studded with precious stones. She put on golden bracelets and golden trousers, a precious necklace, and a gold crown set with precious stones, and she covered her head with a veil. Her face shone like the sun and her eyes gleamed like the morning star.

Then a little slave-boy came in and announced, "Joseph is outside the gate."

Asenath went down to greet him with her seven maidens. When Joseph saw her he said, "Come here, my pure virgin. I have heard all your good news from a messenger from heaven." He held out his arms and embraced her and she embraced him, and they kissed for a long time.

Eventually Asenath said, "Come, my lord, enter my house." She took him by the hand and led him into the house. Seating him on the throne of her father, Potiphera, she fetched water to wash his feet.

Joseph remonstrated with her: "Let one of your maidens wash my feet."

But Asenath replied, "No, my lord, my hands are your hands and your feet are my feet. No one but I shall wash your feet." So she forced him to let her wash his feet. Then Joseph took her right hand and kissed it, and Asenath kissed Joseph's head.

When her parents came home from the country and saw Asenath sitting with Joseph and dressed up as a bride, they were delighted. They praised God, and ate and drank.

Potiphera said to Joseph, "Tomorrow I shall send invitations to all the great men and governors of Egypt. I shall arrange the marriage and you will take Asenath as your wife."

Joseph said, "First I must tell Pharaoh about her. He is my father, and he will give Asenath away to me."

Joseph spent the rest of the day with Potiphera and did not go to Asenath's room because he did not think it right for a god-fearing man to sleep with his wife before they were married.

Joseph got up early the next morning and went to tell Pharaoh about Asenath. Pharaoh was much impressed by her beauty. He married them and blessed them, and ordered that anyone who worked during the seven days of the marriage feast would die a terrible death. When the feasting was over Joseph went into Asenath, and she conceived and bore him Manasseh and his brother, Ephraim.

THE LAST WORDS OF JOSEPH

The biblical Book of Genesis ends with the death of Joseph:

Joseph remained in Egypt together with his father's family. He lived there to be a hundred and ten years old; he saw Ephraim's children to the third generation, and he also recognized the children of Manasseh's son Machir. He said to his brothers: 'I am going to die, but God will not fail to come to your aid and take you away from here to the land which he promised to Abraham, Isaac and Jacob.' And he made the sons of Israel swear that when

this happened they would take his bones with them. Joseph died at the age of one hundred and ten, and he was embalmed and put in a coffin in Egypt.
(Genesis 50:22–26)

The text which follows comes from a series of similar writings known as *The Testaments of the Twelve Patriarchs*, in which each of the sons of Jacob, on his deathbed, gives an account of his life and commands his children to live a virtuous life.

Joseph begins his address with the praise of God. As in some rabbinic homilies, he shows from his own life how God himself exemplifies the social virtues, such as visiting the sick and feeding the hungry.

The rest of his speech falls into three parts. The first, in which he gives his own version of his adventure with Potiphar's wife, illustrates the virtues of chastity and steadfastness in the face of adversity.

The next section praises brotherly love. Joseph claims that he never admitted to anyone that his brothers had sold him into slavery so as not to shame them, and he urges his children to love one another and be loyal to the family.

The last section is an eschatological vision, in which he foretells the dispersion of the Israelites and the coming of the Messiah.

The Testament of Joseph

When Joseph was about to die he summoned his children and his brothers and addressed them as follows:

"My brothers, my children, listen to Joseph, the beloved of Israel. My sons, pay attention to your father. In my life I have experienced envy and death but I never went astray, I always clung to the truth of the Lord. My brothers here hated me but the Lord loved me. They tried to kill me but the God of my fathers protected me. They threw me into a pit but the Almighty took me out of it. I was sold into slavery but the Lord of All liberated me. I was taken captive but his strong hand supported me. When I was starving the Lord himself fed me. When I was lonely God comforted me. When I was sick the Lord visited me. When I was in prison my God was kind to me. He released me when I was in chains. He spoke up for me when I was maligned.

He saved me when I was being attacked by the Egyptians. He promoted me when the other slaves were jealous of me.''

CHASTITY AND STEADFASTNESS

''When Pharaoh's prime minister took me into his household I had to struggle against a shameless woman who was urging me to sin with her, but the God of my father Israel saved me from her fire. I was imprisoned and beaten but the Lord made my jailer take pity on me.

''The Lord does not abandon those who fear him, even in dark times, in chains, in troubles and torments. God is never frightened like a man; he is always nearby to offer comfort even if he occasionally withdraws to test your mettle.

''He tested me ten times, and each time I passed the test. Steadfastness is a great healer, and endurance brings many benefits.

''How often that Egyptian woman threatened me with death. How often she had me punished. Then she would send for me again and threaten me, and when I still refused to sleep with her, she tried coaxing me: 'You will be my husband, the lord of all my household, if only you give yourself to me.' But I remembered my father's words and went to my room to pray to the Lord.

''Throughout those seven years I fasted. The Egyptians thought I looked effeminate because those who fast for God's sake develop delicate faces. Whenever my master was away I drank no wine. I refused my food for three days and gave it to the poor and sick. I prayed to the Lord from early morning and I wept because of the Egyptian woman.

''She never stopped pestering me. She made excuses to visit me at night. Because she had no male child she pretended to regard me as her son. She kissed me like a son—I didn't realize what she was doing. Gradually she tried to draw me into making love with her. Then I understood her trickery. I suddenly came to my senses. I was miserable for days. I spoke to her about the teachings of the Almighty and tried to deflect her from her shameful desire. At this she began praising me as a holy man. She was cunning. She would praise my chastity when she was talking to her husband, but when we were alone together she tried to trap me. 'Don't be afraid of my husband,' she would say. 'He is convinced of your chastity. Even if someone tells him about us, he won't believe them.' I threw myself on the ground and implored God to save me from her tricks.

"When she saw that she was getting nowhere, she came to me pretending to want instruction. She said she wanted to learn the word of God. 'If you want me to abandon my idols,' she said, 'then sleep with me. I'll persuade my husband to give up idolatry too, and we'll follow the way of the Lord.' 'God doesn't want unclean worshippers,' I replied. 'He has no time for adulterers.' She said nothing but went on planning to have her evil way. And I redoubled my fasts and my prayers to the Lord to save me from her.

"Another time she said to me, 'If you object to committing adultery, I'll poison my husband and marry you.' At this, I tore my clothes and said, 'In the name of God, woman, don't do such a terrible thing. If you do, I'll tell the world about it.' She was frightened then and begged me not to tell a soul. She went away and sent me every imaginable sort of present.

"Next she tried sending me drugged food. When the eunuch brought it, I had a vision of a terrifying man holding out a sword with the dish, and I realized that this was another of her tricks. I was reduced to tears. I didn't touch that or any other food she sent. Next day she came and saw the food and asked me why I hadn't eaten it. 'Because you've filled it full of drugs,' I answered. 'And you said you would give up idols and follow the Lord. The God of my fathers sent an angel to betray your trickery. I've kept the food so that I could confront you with it and make you regret it. But just to show you that the evil schemes of the godless have no power over those who worship God in chastity, I shall eat it now.' So saying, I prayed, 'The God of my fathers and the angel of Abraham be with me,' and I ate it. Then she fell weeping at my feet. I helped her up and spoke severely to her, and she promised not to do it again.

"But still she did not abandon her evil schemes to seduce me. She started sighing and groaning. When her husband asked her the reason, she said, 'I have a pain in my heart; I'm groaning in agony.' So he pampered her even though she was not sick. Then, taking advantage of an occasion when her husband was away, she came rushing in and said to me, 'If you won't come to bed with me, I'll hang myself or throw myself over a cliff.' I realized that she was possessed by a demon. I prayed to the Lord and I said to her, 'You're distracted; your sinfulness has blinded you. Have you forgotten that if you kill yourself, your husband's concubine, Asetho, your rival, will beat your children? She will destroy all memory of you.' 'So you do love me after all,' she said. 'I'm glad. So long as you want me to live I have hopes of achieving my desire.' She did not understand that I was speaking out of loyalty to my master, not out of love for her. People who become obsessed with evil desires, like her, interpret everything they hear as having a bearing on their passion.

"I tell you, children, it was about midday when she left me, and I spent the rest of the day and the whole night kneeling before the Lord, weeping, and praying to be left alone by her. When at last, toward dawn, I got to my feet, she came and seized hold of my clothes, and tried to force me physically to mate with her. When I found that she was clinging to my robe like a mad thing, I slipped out of it and ran away with nothing on. But she took the robe and told lies about me to her husband, and he had me locked up. Next day he had me beaten and sent to Pharaoh's prison.

"When I was in prison, the Egyptian woman was sick with grief and she used to come and listen to me gladly singing God's praise in the dungeon and thanking him for saving me from her lust. She sent messages to me, offering to have me released if I would gratify her desire, but I didn't give them a moment's thought. God prefers a man to be chaste and to fast in a den of iniquity rather than to live richly but licentiously in a royal palace. Even though she was sick she used to come at odd times and listen to me praying. But I was unmoved by her groans. When I was living in her house she often uncovered her arms and legs and breasts to make me sleep with her; she was very beautiful and had made herself up specially to attract me but the Lord protected me against her tricks.

"So you see, children, how much steadfastness, fasting, and prayer can achieve. If you pursue purity and chastity steadfastly, with prayer and fasting and humility, the Lord will dwell among you too because he loves chastity. And then, whatever happens to you—envy, slavery, false accusations—the Lord will not only protect and save you but he will reward you richly, just as he did me."

BROTHERLY LOVE

"My children, in everything you do be conscious of the fear of God and also honor your brothers. The Lord loves everyone who obeys his Torah. Even when I was a child I feared God. I never boasted to my brothers how much my father loved me; I honored them. So much so that even when I was being sold I did not tell the Ishmaelites that I was the son of Jacob, a powerful and influential man.

"When we reached the Red Sea I was asked if I was a slave, and I said I was so as not to dishonor my brothers. 'You're no slave,' said the chief. 'That's clear from your appearance.' But I insisted that I was a slave.

"When we arrived in Egypt they could not decide who should buy me so they agreed to leave me with their agent there until they returned with their next consignment. The Lord made the agent kind to me, and he put me in charge of his household. I was with him for three months and five days, and during that time God blessed him with silver and gold.

"Meanwhile Potiphar's wife got to hear of me, and she told her husband about how the agent had become wealthy because of a young Hebrew. 'They say he was stolen from Canaan,' she said. 'Why don't you bring the man to justice and take the boy into your own house? Then the God of the Hebrews will bless you because the youth possesses grace from heaven.'

"Potiphar agreed and had the agent brought before him. 'What's this I hear,' he said, 'that you kidnap people in Canaan and sell them as slaves?' The agent groveled at his feet and swore that he didn't know what he was talking about. 'Where does the Hebrew slave come from, then?' Potiphar asked. 'The Ishmaelites left him with me till they return,' he answered. Potiphar did not believe him and had him stripped and flogged. When he persistently repeated the same story, he sent for me. I saluted him respectfully because he was the third in rank of all Pharaoh's ministers, and he took me to one side and said, 'Are you a slave or a freeman?' 'I am a slave,' I replied. 'Whose?' he asked. 'The Ishmaelites',' I said. 'How did you come to be their slave?' 'They bought me in Canaan.' 'You're lying,' he said and he had me stripped and flogged too.

"His wife, who was watching from a window of her house, sent him a message, accusing him of injustice because he was punishing a free man who had been kidnapped as though he had committed some crime. When I did not change my story he had me imprisoned 'until the slave's owners arrive,' as he put it.

" 'How can you keep such a nobly-born lad in prison?' his wife asked. 'He ought to be set free and treated with respect.' (It was her lust which made her want to see me but I knew nothing of such things.) 'Egyptians don't take other people's property away without proof,' he said (referring to the agent); 'the boy must be detained in custody.'

"After twenty-four days the Ishmaelites came back. They had heard that my father, Jacob, was in deep mourning over me. They came to see me and said, 'Why did you tell us you were a slave? We have heard that you are the son of a powerful man in Canaan who is in deep mourning for you.' When I heard this I felt a faintness in my stomach and I thought my heart would break. I wanted to cry but I stopped myself so as not to dishonor my brothers. 'I know nothing about that,' I said. 'I'm a slave.'

"Then they decided to sell me in case they were caught in possession of me. They were frightened that my father would punish them because they had heard that he was influential with God and with men. And their agent was begging them to release him from Potiphar's judgment against him. So they came and asked me to say that they had bought me for money so that we would be released.

"Potiphar's wife heard that I was for sale and asked her husband to buy me. She sent a eunuch to the Ishmaelites to make an offer for me but they would not accept it, and so he went back to his mistress and told her that they were asking a high price. So she sent another eunuch and told him that money was no object, she must have me whatever the price. The eunuch paid them eighty pieces of gold for me but he told his mistress that I had cost a hundred. I knew the truth but said nothing, to save the eunuch's honor.

"So you see, children, the sufferings I put up with so as not to dishonor my brothers. I want you also to love each other and to cover up for each other's faults even if you suffer for it. God is pleased with brothers who stick together and love one another.

"When my brothers came to Egypt they found that I returned their money and I wasn't angry with them, and I was kind to them. After our father died I loved them even more, and I did everything he had told me for them. I made sure they didn't suffer in any way, and I gave them everything that was in my power to give them. Their children were my children, and my children were their servants. Their life was my life, their suffering was my suffering, their sickness was my sickness. My land was their land, and whatever they wanted, I did. I never treated them arrogantly, though I was in a position of great honor, but I was always humble with them.

"Children, follow the commandments of the Lord, and he will raise you high and bless you with good things forever and ever. If ever anyone tries to harm you, be kind to him and pray for him, and the Lord will protect you. Look at my reward for my modesty and steadfastness: I married the daughter of the priest of Heliopolis, and she brought me one hundred talents of gold. And he made me as beautiful as a flower, more beautiful than any other Israelite, and he made my beauty last into old age, because I was just like Jacob in everything I did."

A VISION

"Listen, my children, to a vision I saw. There were twelve deer feeding. Nine of them were scattered, and three were left. The next day the three were also scattered. Then I saw them become three lambs. They cried out to the Lord, and he led them into a green, well-watered place. He led them from darkness into light. They cried to the Lord again and the nine deer were also brought back, and they became twelve sheep, and after a while they bred and became many flocks.

"Then I saw twelve calves being suckled by one cow. She produced such a quantity of milk that it fed countless herds. The horns of the fourth bull rose up to heaven like a wall, and a third horn grew between them. And I saw a calf which protected the bulls.

"Then a lamb was born that was attacked by all the wild beasts but conquered them and trampled them underfoot. This victory caused great rejoicing among angels and men. The whole land rejoiced.

"All this will come to pass in due course, in the last days. So keep the Lord's commandments, children, and honor Levi and Judah because from them will come the one who will rescue Israel, whose kingdom will last forever.

"But my kingdom will come to an end, like a harvest watchman's hammock which vanishes at the end of the summer. I know that after my death the Egyptians will make your life a misery. But God will not fail to come to your aid and take you to the land which he promised to your fathers. Take my bones with you when you go. Take your mother, Asenath, too, and bury her near my mother, Rachel."

When Joseph had finished speaking he stretched out his legs and died. All Israel mourned him, and so did the Egyptians because he had always ruled them with kindness and sympathy.

And when the Israelites left Egypt they took Joseph's bones with them, and they buried them in Hebron with his forefathers. He had lived for one hundred and ten years.

Deborah and Jephthah's Daughter

A peculiar feature of *The Book of Biblical Antiquities* is the large amount of space devoted to the history of the Judges, equalling that devoted to the first six books of the Bible. The judges, in order, are: Kenaz, Zebul, Deborah, Gideon, Abimelech, Jephthah, Abdon, Elon, Samson. The account of this period fills in many "gaps" in the biblical narrative. We have selected here two passages: the story of Deborah and that of Jephthah's daughter. Both these stories of noble women begin from the biblical text but supply elaborations and expansions of great interest.

The story of Deborah, found in the Bible in Judges 4 and 5, tells how Deborah and Barak defeat Sisera and how he is killed by Jael, wife of Heber the Kenite. Chapter 5 contains the song that Deborah and Barak sang after their great victory. *Biblical Antiquities* contains less circumstantial detail about Deborah and Barak and their relationship but compensates with a much longer account of the death of Sisera and with the speeches delivered by Deborah on the eve of the battle and before her death. It also records the brief but moving lament sung by the Israelites after her death. The long song of Deborah and Barak is quite different from that found in the Bible. It emphasizes the history of Israel and God's covenant with his people. An extraordinary aspect of the story is the supernatural intervention of the stars, based on a brief phrase in the biblical song (Judges 5:20):

> The stars fought from heaven,
> the stars in their courses fought against Sisera.

According to *Biblical Antiquities* the Israelites did not actually engage the enemy forces because they were burnt up by the stars; perhaps a shower of meteorites is meant. One other aspect is striking: the stress on the part played by women. One woman (Deborah) attacks Sisera, and another (Jael) kills him, and at the end of the story Deborah is addressed by the Israelites as their mother.

Biblical Antiquities 30–33; 39–40

The Israelites had no one they could make their judge. They fell away and forgot the promises, and they disobeyed the commandments that Moses and Joshua, God's spokesmen, had given them. They wooed the Amorite women and worshipped their gods.

The Lord was angry with them and sent his angel to say, "One people have I chosen out of all the nations on earth in which to establish my glory in this world. I sent Moses, my servant, to them to tell them of my greatness and my justice, but they have disobeyed my commandments. I shall stir up their enemies against them and let them rule over them until they admit that the reason for their misfortune is that they disobeyed the commandments of God and their fathers. Then I shall send a woman to rule them and be a beacon to them for forty years."

So the Lord stirred up Jabin, the king of Assyria, to make war on them. His general, who was called Sisera, attacked the Israelites in Mount Ephraim with nine thousand iron-clad chariots. The terrified Israelites lacked the will to resist him. When they had reached the depths of gloom, they assembled in the Judean Hills and made this unanimous acknowledgment: "We, who once called ourselves the happiest people on earth, have become the lowest of the low. We cannot live freely in our own land; our enemies are dominating us. Who is responsible for this? We are. We have deserted the Lord our fathers worshipped, and we have steered a disastrous course. Let us fast for seven days and hope that God will be reconciled to his chosen vineyard."

So they wore sackcloth and fasted for seven days, and on the seventh day God sent them Deborah.

She made this speech: "You are going to the slaughter like sheep who have nothing to say for themselves. But you were born to be God's own flock. He led you into the cloudy heights, trampling angels underfoot. He gave you the Torah. He sent prophets to guide you and generals to punish you. He worked miracles for you: the sun and moon stood still for you and hailstones rained down on your enemies and killed them.[1] But you disobeyed the commandments he gave you through Moses, Joshua, Kenaz, and Zebul. You were loyal to God so long as they lived, but when they died your heart died too. You are like iron which melts when it is put in the furnace but hardens again when it is removed. If the Lord takes pity on you today it will not be for your own sakes but because of the covenant he made with your fathers, when he swore never to desert you. When I am gone you will start sinning again, but even then he will work wonders for you and give you victory over your enemies. Your fathers are dead but the God who made the covenant with them is life itself."

Then she sent for Barak and said to him, "Pull yourself together like a man. Go and fight against Sisera. I can see the stars and the lightning preparing to fight on your side. Sisera boasts of his strength, he claims he will share our plunder among his slaves and take our beautiful women into his bed. Hear God's reply: A weak woman will fight against him, our maidservants will take his plunder, and he himself will fall into the hands of a woman."

As soon as Deborah and Barak and the people went out to meet the enemy, the Lord set the stars in motion. "Hurry," he said. "The enemy is upon you. Smash their power, shatter their strength, because I want my people to win. Even if my people sin, I still have pity on them."

At this the stars did as they were told and burnt up the enemy. Ninety times ninety-seven thousand men were burnt in a single hour. But they left Sisera alone, as they had been commanded.

[1] See Joshua 10:11–13.

Sisera was riding for his life when he came face to face with Jael, the wife of Heber the Kenite. She was a beautiful woman, and she had put on all her jewelery. "Come inside," she said. "You can sleep here and this evening when you are fresh I shall send you on with my servants. I know that you will remember my good turn."

Sisera went in, and found the bed strewn with rose petals. "Jael," he said, "if I am spared I shall take you home to my mother and make you my wife." Then, feeling thirsty, he said, "Give me some water. I feel faint. I'm on fire with the flames that came from the stars."

"First rest and then drink," Jael replied.

When Sisera was asleep, she went and milked her sheep, and as she milked she said, "Lord, when you divided the tribes of mankind you chose Israel to be your own people, and you compared him to a ram who walks at the head of the flock and leads it. Sisera said to himself, 'I shall go and punish the flock of the Almighty.' Now I am going to take the milk of the animal to which you likened your people, and give it to him to drink. When he has drunk he will feel faint, and then I shall kill him. Give me a sign, Lord: if when I go in Sisera wakes up and immediately asks me for water, I shall know that my prayer has been heard."

As soon as she went back in, Sisera woke up and said, "Give me a drink. I am on fire. I feel as if I'm burning."

Jael poured some wine into the milk and gave it to him to drink, and as soon as he had drunk it he fell asleep again. Then Jael took a wooden stake in her left hand, and as she approached him she said to herself, "If the Lord makes me a sign, I shall know that Sisera was meant to fall into my hands; if I can push him off the bed without his feeling anything I shall know that he's mine." She pushed him off the bed and he felt nothing because he had passed out completely.

Jael prayed, "Strengthen my arm this day, for your sake, for your people's sake, and for the sake of those who hope in you."

Then she placed the stake against his temple and hit it with a mallet. As he was dying, Sisera said to her, "Jael, I'm in pain. I'm dying like a woman."

"Go and boast to your father in hell," Jael replied. "Tell him you have been killed by a woman." She finished killing him and laid his corpse out ready for Barak.

While all this was happening, Sisera's mother, whose name was

Temech, was inviting her lady friends to go out with her to greet her son and to see the Hebrew girls he was bringing back to share his bed.

Meanwhile Barak had given up pursuing Sisera. He was very upset because he had not found him. Jael came out to meet him and said, "Welcome and God bless you. Come inside. I shall give you the enemy you have been chasing so hard." Barak went in and found Sisera lying there, dead. "Blessed be the Lord," he exclaimed. "He said that Sisera would fall into the hands of a woman." So saying, he cut off his head and sent it to Sisera's mother with the message: "Here is your son that you were expecting to return with plunder."

This is the hymn that Deborah and Barak, son of Abinoam, and all the people sang together on that day:

"The Lord has shown forth his glory on high,
just as he did in the past.
He spoke and confused men's speech.
He chose our nation.
He chose Abraham out of all his brothers,
and saved him from the fire, from the furnace of bricks.
He gave him a son in his old age,
the fruit of a barren womb.
But the angels were jealous, and God said,
'Kill the son I have given you, sacrifice him to me.'
Abraham did not protest,
he set out right away.
He said to his son, 'I am offering you to God,
I am returning you to him who gave you to me.'
'Father,' said his son,
'a lamb is acceptable as a sweet-smelling offering to the Lord,
and sheep may be killed for the sins of men.
If man is destined to inherit eternity
then you are offering me the heritage of a life of safety
and time beyond all measure.
If I had not been born,
I could not be offered as a sacrifice to him who made me.
I shall be the most blessed of men;

it will not happen again.
Through me the nations shall learn
that man is a worthy sacrifice to the Lord.'
When his father had bound his feet and placed him on the altar,
when he was about to kill him,
then the Almighty spoke from on high, saying,
'Do not kill your son.
Now I have sealed the mouths of your enemies.
Your memory will be before me forever.
Your name and his will live through every generation.'
He gave Isaac two sons, also from a closed womb;
after three years of marriage
Esau and Jacob were born.
God loved Jacob,
but Esau he hated for his deeds.
When Isaac was old he blessed Jacob,
he sent him to Mesopotamia, where he had twelve sons.
They went down to Egypt, and lived there.
When their enemies oppressed them
the people cried out to the Lord.
He heard their prayer and led them out.
He took them to Mount Sinai
and gave them the foundation of understanding prepared since the birth of the world.
There was earthquake, lightning, and storm,
the earth shook to its foundations,
mountains and peaks trembled,
and the clouds surged up against the flame, to save the world from burning.
The deep was stirred
and the ocean floods converged.
Then, as the fruits of his inspiration were given,
Paradise shuddered, and the cedars of Lebanon,
the wild beasts trembled in the forests
and all his works assembled to see
the Lord making his covenant with the children of Israel.
Everything the Almighty said, he kept;
his witness was Moses, his beloved.

When Moses was dying he showed him the heavens,
saying, 'The sky you entered and the earth you walked
shall witness between me and you and my people.
The sun and moon and stars shall be our ministers.'
So when Joshua was fighting the enemy,
and evening drew on as the battle still raged,
he spoke to the sun and the moon:
'You are ministers between the Almighty and his sons:
The battle continues, and you neglect your duty.
Stand still; give light to his sons and darkness to their foes.'
And they did so.
Then Sisera came to make us slaves;
we called on the Lord and he commanded the stars:
'Come down from your places and burn my enemies,
let them learn my power.'
So the stars came down and stormed their camp,
effortlessly they guarded us.
For this we shall never cease praising him,
our mouths shall always tell of his wonders;
he remembered his promise, new and old,
and he showed us his deliverance.
Jael, too, shall be famous among women;
she led the way and killed Sisera with her own hands.
Go, earth,
go, heavens and lightnings,
go, angels of the heavenly army,
go and say to our fathers in the treasuries of souls:
'The Almighty has not forgotten the promises he made you;
he told you little but for your sons he has done much.'
From now on let it be known that what God says he will do, he will do.
Sing praises, Deborah, sing praises,
may the holy spirit move in you,
recount the works of the Almighty.
Such a day shall not be seen again,
when the stars fought against the enemies of Israel.
From now on if Israel is in difficulties
they can call on these witnesses and ministers

to appear before the Almighty and remind him of this day,
and he will call to mind his covenant and send help.
Deborah, tell what you saw on the battlefield,
how the people strolled in safety
while the stars fought for them.
Earth, rejoice for your inhabitants,
because the army of the Lord is near to guard them.
Rightly did God take Adam's rib,
knowing that from it Israel would be born.
Let this bear witness
to what the Lord does for his people.
Linger, hours of daylight, do not hurry away,
let us expound what our minds can utter.
Night will soon be upon us,
like the night when God smote the firstborn of Egypt for his firstborn.
I shall not cease my song
until the time prepared for his righteous ones comes.
I shall sing his praises till creation is renewed;
the people will remember how he saved them.
This shall be their witness.
And let the sea which God dried up before our fathers witness
that the stars came down from their places and fought against our enemies."

When Deborah had finished, she went up with all the people to Shiloh, and they offered sacrifices and sounded the broad trumpets. She said, "The trumpets are a witness between the stars and their Lord."

After that Deborah judged Israel for forty years.

When she was about to die, she assembled the people and made this speech: "My people, listen to what I say. Let me advise you as a woman of God and enlighten you as a woman. Listen to me as you would listen to your mother; listen to what I say because you too will die, like me.

"Direct your hearts to the Lord your God while you are alive, because you will not be able to repent once you are dead. By then your time is up and your doom is sealed. Even if you try to sin in Sheol you will not be able to because the desire to sin will cease and the evil inclination will have lost its power. Once you have been sent to Sheol you cannot be released except by order of him who sent you there. So pay heed to my advice, my children, while you still have time: guide your lives by the light of the Torah."

When the people heard these words, they cried and said, "Mother, you are abandoning your children. Pray for us when you are dead; remember us forever."

Deborah replied, "A man can pray for himself and for his children while he is alive but once dead he cannot pray, nor can he remember anyone. So do not put your hope in your fathers. The only way they can help you is if you show yourselves to be like them. Then you will be like the stars of heaven, whom you have seen with your own eyes."

Deborah died and slept with her fathers, and was buried in her ancestral city. The people mourned her for seventy days and sang this lament for her:

"A mother has died from Israel,
a saint who ruled the house of Jacob.
She built a fence around her people;
we shall miss her."

JEPHTHAH'S DAUGHTER

[The moving story of Jephthah's sacrifice of his daughter is told in the Bible in Judges 11:29–40. Biblical Antiquities, in its usual manner, expands the story and inserts the lament sung by the daughter over her untimely death.]

The king of the Ammonites would not listen to Jephthah so he armed the people for war, and he made this vow: "When I have conquered the Ammonites, the first thing I see on my return shall be a burnt offering to the Lord."

The Lord was furious at this. He said, "Jephthah has vowed that he will offer me whatever he sees first. Suppose the first thing he meets is a dog, will he offer me a dog? I shall make his vow fall on his first and only child, his daughter. I will indeed save the people: not for his sake but because of the prayers of the Israelites.''

So when Jephthah fought the Ammonites he defeated them and sacked sixty of their cities. When he returned from the battle the women danced out to meet him, and they were led by his only daughter, Sheila. When Jephthah saw her he nearly fainted.

''Sheila,'' he said, ''you are appropriately named: you are required for a sacrifice. All my joy is canceled out by this sorrow. I have made a vow to the Lord, and I cannot take it back.''

''Who can die sad when they see the people saved?'' Sheila replied. ''Don't you remember what happened to our forefathers? The father offered his son as a burnt offering. He did not begrudge him but was happy to comply. They were both glad, the father and the son. So do not cancel your vow. Just grant me this one favor before I die: let me go up into the mountains with my girl friends, to pour out my tears and feel the sympathetic sorrow of the beasts and the trees. I am not sad to die but I want to offer myself willingly so that my sacrifice will be acceptable. Let me go and tell the mountains, and I shall come straight back.''

''Go,'' said her father.

Before she went she consulted the wise men, but they could not contradict her. So she went to the mountains with her girl friends.

That night the Lord thought about Sheila: I silenced the wise men so that they could not answer Jephthah's daughter, to prevent them interfering with my plan; but even so I see that she is cleverer than her father and wiser than all the wise men here. Let her give her life as she has asked; her death will always be dear to me.

When she reached the mountain, she uttered this lament:

''Mountains, hear my lament;
hills, see my tears;
rocks, witness my sorrow.
Let my death not be in vain.
May my words reach the sky.
may be tears be inscribed in heaven.
May my father not hinder the fulfilment of his vow;
may our ruler agree to the sacrifice of his daughter.

I have never known the satisfaction of the marriage bed,
never put on my bridal wreath, my perfumes, my splendor.
Mother, you have borne your only child for nothing;
death has become my bridal chamber.
Pour away the precious perfumes,
let the moth eat my wedding dress,
my wreath of flowers must wither,
my violet and purple counterpane is food for worms,
my bridesmaids shall weep for me.
Trees, droop your boughs and weep for my youth;
beasts of the forest, come and trample on my virginity.
I am cut off before my time.
the rest of my life is darkness."

When she had finished she went down to her father, who did as she had asked and offered her as a burnt offering. All the unmarried girls of Israel gathered and buried her. The daughters of Israel mourned her and decided to assemble every year on the fourteenth day of that month to weep for four days in memory of Jephthah's daughter.

Daniel

The two stories of the idol Bel and the serpent share a common destiny with the story of Susanna (see p. 128), although there is no intrinsic connection between them. Like Susanna, they were associated with the names of both Habakkuk and Daniel. The earlier Greek translation bears the heading "From the prophecy of Habakkuk, the son of Jesus of the tribe of Levi," and in both versions it is Habakkuk who feeds Daniel in the lion pit, though no doubt this is a later addition to the story. (There is a spirited attack on idolatry in Habakkuk 2:18–19). The later version adds a further historical reference at the beginning: "After the death of King Astyages, Cyrus the Persian received his kingdom. Daniel was a confidant of the king and the most honored of the King's Friends."

As with other similar stories, the historical setting cannot be taken seriously. The actual circumstances of composition are extremely uncertain, but it is not unlikely that these two interconnected stories, like parts of the Book of Daniel and the story of Susanna, were composed in Judea during the Hasmonean period. The message of the stories is the futility of idol worship, but it is not clear whether they are intended as propaganda in favor of Judaism aimed at non-Jews or whether they are attacking the supposedly idolatrous practices of Hellenized Jews.

In both stories Daniel is told to worship a cult object, in each case by means of food offerings. In the first story, involving the Babylonian god Bel (Baal, i.e. Marduk), Daniel shows that it is ridiculous to think that an idol can eat food. In the second story the object of worship is a huge snake (called a dragon in the older English translations). The snake, of course, *can* eat food but Daniel demonstrated how easily it can be destroyed. There is a different account of Daniel's adventure in the lion's pit in Daniel 6.

There are medieval Hebrew and Aramaic texts of our stories, including an account of the destruction of the serpent in some texts of *Genesis Rabba* 68:13, beginning with a very apposite quotation from Jeremiah (51:44): "I will punish Bel in Babylon and make him bring up what he has swallowed."

Bel and the Serpent

There was a priest called Daniel, son of Abal, who was a confidant of the king of Babylon. The Babylonians worshipped an idol called Bel, and every day they offered him eighteen bushels of fine wheat flour, forty sheep, and fifty gallons of wine. The king revered him and went every day to worship, but Daniel worshipped the Lord.

One day the king asked Daniel why he did not worship Bel.

"Because I do not believe in man-made gods," Daniel replied. "I worship the Lord God who created heaven and earth and is king of all men."

"Isn't Bel a god?" said the king. "Haven't you seen how much he eats and drinks every day?"

Daniel laughed and said, "Don't you believe it. Your idol is made of clay on the inside and bronze on the outside. It has never eaten anything."

At this the king was angry, and he summoned the priests. "If you do not tell me who eats all this food I'll have you put to death," he said. "But if you can prove to me that Bel eats it then Daniel will be killed because he has blasphemed against Bel."

Daniel agreed to a test, and the priests[1] accompanied Daniel and the king to the temple. There the food and mixed wine were set out for Bel in their presence.

Daniel said, "Now that everything has been properly laid out, Your Majesty, have the temple closed and seal the locks."

The king agreed. Daniel then told his servants to see all the others out of the temple and then to sprinkle the floor with ashes without their knowledge. After that he closed the door of the temple and had it sealed with the king's signet ring.

Next morning they all assembled again, but in the meantime the priests had come in through a secret entrance and eaten all the food and drunk the wine.

Daniel said, "Is everything in order? Are the seals intact?"

They found that the seals were intact, and broke them and opened the door. When they saw that the food which had been laid out for Bel had been eaten and the table was bare, the king was delighted and said to Daniel, "Great is Bel. There is no deception in him."

Daniel burst out laughing and said to the king, "No, but come and see the priests' deception! Whose footprints are these?"

"Men, women and children," said the king.

Then he went to the priests' house and found the remains of Bel's food and wine. Daniel also showed him the secret entrance through which the priests used to go into the temple to take the food. So the king killed the priests, destroyed the idol, and gave Daniel the rest of the food and drink which he had provided for Bel.

There was also a great serpent which the Babylonians worshipped. The king said to Daniel, "You wouldn't say that this was made of bronze, would you? He is alive, and eats and drinks. You ought to worship him."

"With Your Majesty's permission," Daniel said, "I shall destroy the snake without using a sword or a stick."

The king gave his consent, and Daniel took some pitch and fat and hair, boiled them up together and threw lumps of the mixture into the

[1] There were seventy priests of Bel, in addition to their wives and children. [Author's note]

snake's mouth. The snake swallowed them and burst. Daniel showed the pieces to the king and said, "Are these the gods you worship?"

The Babylonians, when they heard about all this, said, "The king has become a Jew. He has killed the priests and destroyed Bel and killed the serpent." So they planned a revolution against him.

When the king saw the mob rebelling, he summoned his Friends and announced that Daniel was to be handed over to be killed.

Now there was a pit of lions where they used to throw anyone who plotted against the king. There were seven lions in it, and every day two condemned prisoners were thrown in. The mob threw Daniel into the pit to be eaten by the lions, and he stayed there unharmed for six days.

Meanwhile in Judea, the prophet Habakkuk had prepared a meal and was taking it with a plate of bread and a jug of wine to the harvesters in the field. But an angel of God came to him and said, "Take the food you are carrying and give it to Daniel, in the lion pit in Babylon."

"Lord God," Habakkuk said, "I have never been to Babylon and I don't know where the lion pit is."

So the angel of God picked Habakkuk up by his hair, carried him to Babylon, and held him up over the lion pit. "Daniel," he called out, "take the food which God has sent you."

Then Daniel said, "God has remembered me. He does not abandon those who love him."

Daniel ate the food, and the angel immediately put Habakkuk back in his place.

Next day the king went to mourn for Daniel, but when he looked into the pit he saw him sitting there. "Great is the Lord God," the king shouted aloud. "There is no other god but him!"

He had Daniel lifted out of the pit and threw the men who had tried to kill him down instead, and they were eaten in a moment while Daniel looked on.

Moral Tales

THE ADVENTURES OF TOBIAH

Tobit is an attractive story, a moral lesson of virtue and piety rewarded. The date, place, and language of the original composition are a matter for scholarly controversy, but it was most probably written in Egypt at the beginning of the second century B.C.E. At the earliest it dates from the mid-fourth century, and the historical setting is no more than a literary device.

The Book of Tobit was highly respected in Jewish circles from an early date. References to it have been detected in the Book of Daniel, in the Psalms, and in other works of the Hasmonean period; copies of the work in Hebrew and Aramaic have been discovered at Qumrān. There are also allusions to it in the New Testament, which show that it was still popular in the first Christian century. Its continuing popularity is witnessed by surviving Aramaic, Hebrew, and even Jewish Persian manuscripts which show that the story of Tobit was told and retold as a living tradition up to the Middle Ages and even later. It has also served as the subject for numerous paintings, dramas, and musical compositions.

Tobit begins with an introduction telling of the piety and righteousness of Tobit (Tobi), an Israelite who is taken captive by the Assyrians in the reign of Shalmaneser (721 B.C.E.) and carried off to Nineveh.

Tobit has a wife, Anna (Hannah), and a son, Tobias (Tobiah). In prosperous times he had left a sum of money on deposit in Media with a certain Gabael. (This was a common practice in the ancient world in the absence of banks.) Later, in times of hardship and persecution, impoverished and blinded, he is driven so far as to pray to God to kill him and release him from his troubles.

We take up the story at the point where Tobit decides to send his son on the hazardous journey to Media in search of the money. The adventures of Tobiah are told with vividness, sympathy, and great charm.

In the sequel, not reproduced here, Raphael reveals himself as one of the seven angels who minister to the Lord. Tobit utters a long prayer of thanksgiving and eventually dies at the age of one hundred and twelve, after prophesying the destruction of Assyria and the eventual return of the people to their land. When Anna dies, Tobias buries her by Tobit's side and then leaves Nineveh and settles at Ecbatana with his father-in-law. Before he himself dies, wealthy and greatly respected, at the age of one hundred and seventeen, he hears that his father's prophecy has come true and that Nineveh has been destroyed by Ahasuerus, king of Media.

The work survives in various Greek, Aramaic, Hebrew, and Latin texts, which differ considerably in length and detail. These texts fall into two main groups; the shorter, and less attractive, form of the story is translated in the English Revised Version. The translation here is based on the Greek text in the Codex Sinaiticus (one of the earliest manuscripts of the Greek Bible, copied in the first half of the fourth century C.E. and now in the British Museum in London), but some readings from the Aramaic and the better Hebrew texts have been included and the Hebrew forms of the names restored.

Tobit 4–11

Tobi suddenly remembered the money which he had left on deposit with Gabael in Rages, in Media, and he said to himself, "I have prayed for death. Before I die, why not call Tobiah in and tell him about the money?"

So he called Tobiah and said to him, "Give me a decent burial, son, and take care of your mother. Look after her for the rest of her life, do whatever she tells you, and don't give her cause to worry. Remember what she went through for you when she brought you into the world. When she dies, bury her next to me.

"Follow this advice, son, and you won't go far wrong. Always remember the Lord, and don't sin or break his commandments. Do what's right all your life. Give generously to charity. If you don't neglect the poor, God won't neglect you. Give as much as you can afford. If you've got a lot, give a lot; if you've only got a little don't be afraid to give what you can. Charity is a good investment. It wards off death, and it's an offering which is pleasing to the Almighty.

"Keep away from loose women, son. Marry one of our girls, don't marry out of the clan. We're descended from the prophets. Remember Noah, the first prophet, and our ancestors, Abraham, Isaac, and Jacob. They all married in the clan, and their children were a blessing to them. Their descendants will inherit the land some day. Love your people; don't look down on them and marry out. Scorn brings trouble. And idleness brings poverty. Don't put off paying your employees their wages. Settle with them on the spot. If you do what God says, you'll be rewarded. Always be careful what you do, son, and try to live decently. Don't do to anyone else what you're not fond of yourself. Don't drink too much and walk around drunk. Feed the hungry and clothe the naked. Be charitable, and give generously. Honor the memory of the just, and don't give anything to sinners. Always ask wise men for their advice, and never refuse good advice when it's offered you. Always bless the Lord your God; pray to him to give you a good and successful life. God rules everything we do: he decides whom to reward and whom to punish. Remember this advice, son. Don't forget it.

"Now something else, son. I want to tell you that I left ten talents of silver on deposit with Gabael, the brother of Gabri, at Rages in Media. But don't worry because we're not well off any more. If you fear God and keep clear of sin and live the kind of life that God approves of, you'll be very rich."

"Father, I'll do everything you say," Tobiah replied. "But how will I be able to get the money from him? He doesn't know me, and I don't know him. What proof can I give him so that he'll know who I am and trust me and give me the money? And how will I find my way to Media?''

''We wrote out a document and cut it in half,'' Tobi answered. ''Here's one half, and the other half is with the money. Now, son, go and find a trustworthy man to go with you. We'll pay him his wages until you get back. Then go and fetch the money.''

So Tobiah went out to look for a man who knew the way to Media and would go with him. When he got outside he met the angel Raphael, but he did not realize that he was an angel of God.

''Where are you from?'' Tobiah said.

''I'm an Israelite like you,'' Raphael replied. ''I've come here to look for work.''

''Do you know the way to Media?''

''Yes, I've been there often. I know it well and I know all the roads. I often used to go to Media and stay with our cousin Gabael, who lives in Rages, which is in Media. It's two normal days' travel to Rages from Ecbatana. Ecbatana is in the plain, but Rages is in the hills.''

''Wait here while I go and tell my father,'' Tobiah said. ''I need you to go with me. I'll pay you good wages.''

''I'll wait,'' said Raphael, ''but don't be too long.''

Tobiah went inside and told Tobi that he had found an Israelite to go with him.

''Bring him in,'' said Tobi. ''Let me see which family he comes from and which tribe he belongs to, and whether he's a responsible person to go with you, son.''

So Tobiah went out and told Raphael that his father wanted to see him. When he went in Tobi greeted him, and Raphael answered, ''How do you do?''

''What do you mean 'How do I do'?'' Tobi said. ''I'm a blind man. I can't see the light of day. I sit in darkness like a dead man. I'm dead while I'm still alive. I can hear men's voices but I can't see them.''

''Cheer up,'' Raphael said. ''God can heal you.''

''My son Tobiah wants to go to Media,'' said Tobi. ''Can you go with him and show him the way? I'll pay you a fair wage.''

''I can go with him,'' he said. ''I know all the roads. I've often been to Media. I've been all over the plains and all over the mountains. I know all the roads.''

"Tell me, friend," Tobi said, "what's your family, and which is your tribe?"

"Why do you want to know my tribe? If you don't like the look of me, find someone else to go with your son."

"Don't get angry, friend. It's just that I'd very much like to know what your name is, and which tribe you belong to."

"Very well. I am Azariah, son of Hananel, a great man and a relative of yours."

"Welcome, cousin. Don't be angry with me because I wanted to know your family. Yes, we're related. You come of good stock. I used to know Hananel and Nathan, the two sons of Shelomiah, who was also a great man. We used to go to Jerusalem together to worship. They didn't abandon the faith. You come from a good family, and I'm glad to welcome you. I'll give you a drachma a day for your wages, and all found. Go with my son, and if you bring him back safely I'll give you a bonus."

"I'll go with him," Raphael replied, "and don't worry. We'll get there and back all right. It's a safe journey."

"God bless you, cousin," Tobi said.

Then he said to Tobiah, "Get everything you need ready for the journey and go with your cousin. May God in heaven protect you and bring you safely back to me, and may his angel go with you and look after you, my son."

When Tobiah was ready to leave, he kissed his father and mother. Tobi said goodbye. Hannah, in tears, said to him, "Why have you sent my boy away like this? He's our only child, the comfort of our old age. Forget about the money; it's a small price to pay for our son's life. God has given us enough to live on."

"Don't worry," Tobi said. "Our boy will come back safely. You'll see. Don't worry about them, dear. A good angel will look after him, and he'll come back to us safely."

At this, Hannah stopped crying.

So Tobiah set out with the angel, and the dog ran after them. On they went together, and when night fell they camped by the river Tigris. Tobiah went down to the river to wash his feet, and a huge fish leaped out of the water and nearly bit his foot off. Tobiah screamed, and the angel called out, "Catch hold of the fish!"

So he caught hold of the fish, and dragged it up out of the water.

"Cut it open," the angel said, "and take out the gall and the heart and the liver, and keep them. You can throw away the rest of the guts, but the gall and heart and liver are useful for medicine."

Tobiah opened up the fish and took out the gall and the heart and the liver. He grilled and ate part of the fish, and the rest he salted.

As they were traveling on toward Media, Tobiah said to the angel, "Cousin Azariah, what is the medical use of the heart and the liver and the gall of the fish?"

"If a man or woman is attacked by a demon or an evil spirit," he replied, "you burn the heart and liver of the fish, and the smoke drives him out forever. As for the gall, if a man has a white film over his eyes, you rub it on the eyes or blow into them with it and it will cure him."

When they were already in Media and were nearing Ecbatana, Raphael said, "Cousin Tobiah."

"Yes?"

"We're going to stay the night with Reuel, who is a relative of yours. He has a daughter called Sarah. Sarah is his only child. You are her nearest relative who is eligible to marry her, and it's right that you should inherit her father's property. She's a good girl, and she's also intelligent and has a lot of character. You ought to marry her. Listen: I'll talk to her father tonight and arrange for you to marry her. We can celebrate the wedding when we come back from Rages. I know that Reuel won't refuse to marry her to you or give her to anyone else because he knows that by rights you have first claim on her and that to refuse is forbidden on pain of death in the law of Moses. So listen, cousin: Tonight we'll talk to him about the girl and make the engagement, and on our way back from Rages we'll collect her and take her to your home."

"Cousin Azariah," Tobiah replied, "I've heard that this girl has already been given to seven men, and each of them died in the bedroom on the wedding night. People say they were killed by a demon. He doesn't harm her, but he kills any man who tries to go near her. I'm afraid. I'm an only child; if I die the shock will kill my poor parents, and then who'll bury them? They haven't got any other children, only me."

"Don't you remember what your father said? He told you to find a wife in our family. Now listen, cousin. Forget about the demon. Marry her—I know that you'll be engaged to her tonight. When you go into the bedroom, take the liver and the heart of the fish and put them on the cinders in the incense burner. When the smell spreads, the demon will smell it and vanish, and he won't come back again. And before you get into bed with her, you must both stand up and pray to God in heaven to have mercy and save you. Don't be afraid. She was meant for you before ever the world began. You'll save her, and she'll go with you, and you'll have a fine family. Don't worry."

When Tobiah heard everything that Raphael had to say, he felt very excited and very much in love with the girl.

When they reached Ecbatana, Tobiah said, "Cousin Azariah, take me straight to our cousin Reuel."

They found him sitting by the courtyard door. They greeted him, and he welcomed them and led them inside.

"This young man looks just like my cousin Tobi," he said to his wife Edna.

"Where do you come from?" Edna asked them.

"We're from the tribe of Naphtali, who are captives in Nineveh."

"Do you know our cousin Tobi?" she said.

"Yes, we do."

"How is he?"

"He is alive and well," they said, and Tobiah added, "He is my father."

Then Reuel leaped up and kissed him, and cried.

"Bless you, child," he said. "You're the son of a good and noble man. Oh, what a tragedy, for such a good and charitable man to go blind!" Then he put his arm around Tobiah and cried, and Edna and Sarah also cried, and Reuel went out and killed a sheep in their honor.

After they had bathed and washed their hands and sat down to dinner, Tobiah said to Raphael, "Cousin Azariah, talk to Reuel about giving me Sarah."

Reuel overheard him and said, "Eat and drink and enjoy yourself. No one has more of a right to marry my daughter than you, and I couldn't even offer her to anyone else because you're my nearest relation. I'll tell you the truth, my boy. I've given her to seven different men, and they all died on the wedding night. But now eat and drink, my boy. God will have mercy on you."

But Tobiah said, "I won't touch food or drink until you settle this affair."

"Very well," said Reuel. "She is yours according to the law of Moses and the decree of heaven. Take her; from now on you are her brother and she is your sister. She is yours forever. May the Lord of heaven have mercy on you, my boy, and grant you success tonight."

Then Reuel called Sarah, took her by the hand, and gave her to him.

"Take her according to the law of Moses," he said. "Have her and take her safely to your father's house, and may God in heaven grant you prosperity and peace."

He called to her mother to fetch a notebook, and he wrote out a marriage document to say that he gave her to him as his wife according to the law of Moses. Then they ate and drank.

Meanwhile Reuel said to his wife, "Edna, dearest, get the spare bedroom ready and take her in."

She went and made the bed up and took the girl in. Wiping away her tears, she said, "Be happy, darling: the Lord of heaven has turned your sorrow to joy. Be happy." Then she left the room.

When they had finished eating and drinking and it was time for bed, they escorted the young man to the bedroom. Tobiah remembered what Raphael had said; he took the liver and heart of the fish out of his bag and put them on the cinders in the censer. The smell of the fish banished the demon, who fled to the farthest corner of Egypt, where Raphael caught him and put him in chains. Then, when they were locked in the bedroom, Tobiah told Sarah to get up and pray to God to have mercy on them and save them. She stood up and prayed, and Tobiah prayed this prayer:

"Blessed are you, God of our fathers, blessed is your name forever and ever. May the heavens bless you and all your creation forevermore. You made Adam, and you made Eve, his wife, to help him and sustain him. All mankind come from them. You said: It is not good for the man to be alone; let us make a helper for him. And now, Lord, you know that I am not taking this sister of mine out of lust but with a pure heart and according to your law. Have pity on us both, and let us grow old together.''

They both said Amen, and then they went to sleep.

Meanwhile, Reuel got out of bed and called the servants and they went outside to dig a grave. ''Otherwise,'' he said, ''if he dies, people will accuse us and make fun of us.''

When they had dug the grave he went indoors and said to his wife, ''Send one of the servant girls to the bedroom to see if he is alive. If he's dead we can bury him and no one will be the wiser.''

The servant girl lit a lamp and went into the bedroom, where she found them fast asleep in each other's arms. She came back and told Reuel that he was alive and well, and he blessed God in heaven and said, ''Blessed are you, God, with purest blessing. May you be blessed forever. Blessed are you because you have made me happy; you had great pity on us, and it did not turn out as I feared it would. Blessed are you because you have spared a pair of only children. Have pity on them and save them, Lord, and fill their lives with gladness and peace.''

He told the servants to fill in the grave before morning, and he asked his wife to bake plenty of bread. He himself went out and fetched two cows and four sheep and told them to prepare them. Then he called Tobiah and said, ''You must not leave this house for fourteen days. You will stay here and eat and drink and celebrate and make my poor daughter happy. Afterward you may take half of everything I possess and go home safely to your father. When my wife and I die, the other half is yours too. Be happy, my son: from now on I am your father and Edna is your mother. Be happy.''

Tobiah said to Raphael, ''Cousin Azariah, take four servants and two camels and go to Rages. Give Gabael the document, get the money, and bring him back with you to the wedding feast. You know how my father will be counting the days till I get back; each extra day will be agony for him. But you heard what Reuel said—I can't disappoint him.''

So Raphael went to Rages with four servants and two camels, and called on Gabael. Raphael gave him the document and announced to him that Tobiah, Tobi's son, was getting married and invited him to the wedding feast. Gabael counted out the bags with their seals intact and loaded them on the camels, and early next morning they set out for the wedding feast. When they arrived at Reuel's house they found Tobiah sitting at table. He leaped up to greet them, and Gabael cried as he said, "You are a good, honest son of a good, honest father. The blessings of heaven on you and your wife, and on your parents and hers. God be praised that I have seen my cousin Tobiah!"

Tobi, meanwhile, was counting the days that it would take Tobiah to go to Rages and return home. When the days were up and his son had not returned, he began to worry. Perhaps he had been detained in Rages; perhaps Gabael was dead and there was no one to give him the money?

Hannah was convinced her son had been killed. She cried and mourned for him and rued the day she had let him go. Tobi tried to cheer her up.

"Don't worry, dear," he would say. "He's all right. Don't be so upset. No doubt he's caught up in business of some sort. The man who went with him is reliable—he's one of us. Don't cry over him, dearest, he'll soon be here."

But she replied, "Don't try to deceive me. My child is dead."

Every morning she went out early and spent the whole day watching the road along which her son had left; she would not listen to anyone. When the sun set she went indoors and lay awake all night crying.

When the fourteen days which Reuel had set for the celebration of his daughter's wedding were over, Tobiah went up to him and said, "Let me go now. I know that my father and mother have given up hope of ever seeing me again. Please, father, let me go home to my father. I have already told you about how I left him."

"Stay here, my boy, with me," Reuel said. "I'll send messengers to your father to tell him what has happened to you."

But Tobiah said, "No, please. Let me go to see my father."

So Reuel handed over to Tobiah his daughter Sarah and half of all he possessed: servants and serving girls, sheep and cattle, donkeys and camels, clothes, money and goods. He kissed him and said, "Good-bye, my boy. Have a safe journey. God bless you and Sarah, your wife. I hope I'll see my grandchildren before I die.''

And to his daughter he said, ''Off you go now to your father-in-law. From now on they are your parents. Good-bye, dearest. I hope I'll always hear good news of you.''

When he had kissed them and said good-bye, Edna said to Tobiah, ''God bless you, my son, and give you a safe journey. I hope to see your children and Sarah's before I die. I'm trusting my daughter to you, before God; be good to her always. Good-bye, my dear. From now on I am your mother and Sarah is your sister. May we all live happily all our lives.'' And she kissed them both good-bye.

Tobiah took his leave of Reuel and gave thanks to God for crowning his journey with success.

When they were not far from Nineveh, Raphael said, ''You know how we left your father. Let's go ahead of your wife, and get everything ready for her.''

So the two of them went on ahead. Hannah was sitting watching the road and when she saw them coming, with the dog running along behind them, she called out to Tobi. Meanwhile, Raphael said to Tobiah, ''Have the fish gall ready, and rub it into your father's eyes. The medicine will draw the white films off his eyes and he will be able to see again.''

Sarah came running and threw her arms round her son. ''Now that I've seen you, my son,'' she said, ''I can die happy.'' She burst into tears, and Tobi rose and stumbled over to the front door. Tobiah ran up to him with the gall in his hand and blew into his father's eyes with it, and rubbed it into his eyes, and the white films came away. Tobi put his arms round him and cried and said, ''I can see you, son. Blessed is God, blessed is his great name, blessed are all his holy angels. May his great name be blessed for ever and ever. He has healed me and let me see my son, Tobiah.''

Tobiah was overjoyed and thanked God and told his father how successful his journey had been. He had brought the money and married Reuel's daughter, and she was nearing the gate of Nineveh at that moment. Tobi, too, was glad, and thanked God, and he went to the gate of Nineveh to meet his daughter-in-law. When the people of Nineveh saw him striding boldly past, instead of being led by the arm, they were amazed. Tobi thanked God publicly for being merciful to him and opening his eyes. When he came up to his daughter-in-law he blessed her and said, "Welcome, my daughter. Blessed is God who has brought you to us. Blessed is your father, blessed is Tobiah my son, and blessed are you, my daughter. Welcome to your new home."

JUDITH AND HOLOFERNES

The story of Judith and Holofernes is a famous story of virtue and heroism, dressed up as history. It is set in the reign of Nebuchadnezzar, whose commander-in-chief, Holofernes, has invaded Judea with a powerful army. An Ammonite leader, Achior, speaks up and advises Holofernes that he will never conquer the people of Israel as long as they are faithful to their God and he protects them. Holofernes has him bound and handed over to the Israelites in their fortified city of Bethuliah, and proceeds to besiege the city. It is at this point, with the Israelites inside the city in deep despair, that we first encounter the virtuous widow Judith, and the rest of the book is taken up with her bold and brilliant plan to kill Holofernes and save her people.

The story of Judith has obvious similarities to the story of that other valiant heroine, Deborah, notably the repetition of the theme that a mighty warrior is defeated by a woman. Most of the places mentioned in the story, including Bethuliah itself, are otherwise unknown, and this accords with the legendary nature of this romantic story. The historical details of the reign of Nebuchadnezzar (d. 562 B.C.E.) are likewise fictitious. The story is thought to have been written in Hebrew in the second century B.C.E., although it is not impossible that it embodies a traditional recollection of actual events about which nothing more is known.

A striking feature of the story is the emphasis on the attachment of the heroine to the religious law; she even goes so far as to take her own pots and pans with her to the Assyrian camp. It has been claimed that this shows that the author was a Pharisee. At any rate it has always been popular in Jewish circles. It is alluded to in the Hanukkah liturgy, and various versions of the story are told in the Hebrew Midrashim.

The story has also won great popularity in the Christian church, and, like the other stories in this section, has been a favorite subject for Christian artists.

Judith 8–16

News of all this reached Judith, the daughter of Merari, son of Uz, son of Joseph, son of Uzziel, son of Helkiah, son of Hananiah, son of Gideon, son of Raphael, son of Ahitub, son of Elihu, son of Eliab, son of Nathanael, son of Shelomiel, son of Sarishaddai, son of Israel. Her husband, Manasseh, a member of her own tribe and family, had died during a barley harvest. He had suffered sunstroke while supervising the binding of the sheaves, been put to bed, and died in his home town of Bethuliah. He was buried in the graveyard between Dothaim and Balamon. Judith had been a widow for three years and four months, and all that time she had lived in a hut on the roof of her house, wearing widow's weeds and fasting every single day except for Sabbath eves, Sabbaths, eves of New Moon, New Moon, and the feasts and festivals of the house of Israel. Judith was an outstandingly beautiful woman, and her husband, Manasseh, had left her gold and silver, servants, livestock, and property on which she herself lived. No one spoke ill of her because she was a very God-fearing woman.

Now, when Judith heard that the people had spoken up against the Governor because of the desperate shortage of water, and that Uzziah had sworn to surrender the city to the Assyrians after five days, she sent her maid, who had charge of all her affairs, to summon Uzziah and Kabri and Karmi, the city elders. When they arrived, she addressed them as follows:

"Rulers of the people of Bethuliah, listen to what I have to say. You did wrong today in swearing to surrender the city to our enemy if the Lord does not help you within the next five days. Who are you to test God in this way and to put yourselves in God's place? If you try to test God, then you know nothing. You do not even understand the minds of men, or understand what they are thinking; how then can you fathom the mind of God, who has brought all this about? How can you know his thoughts or comprehend his purpose? No, my brothers, do not provoke the Lord our God to anger. If he is not inclined to help us within the next five days, he has the power to deliver us whenever he wishes, or else to destroy us before our enemies. Do not commit the

Lord our God to your plans: God is not like man, who can be threatened or persuaded by pleas. Let us wait for the salvation which is his to send, and call on him to help us, and if he so wishes, he will hear our cry. No one nowadays, no individual or family or tribe or city, worships gods made by men's hands, as happened in the past, and for which our forefathers were butchered and captured and massacred by our enemies. But we have never recognized any other God except him, and so we may hope that he will not reject us or any of our race. If we are captured, the whole of Judea will fall and our sanctuary will be ravaged, and he will hold us responsible. The slaughter of our brethren, the occupation of our land, and the destruction of our heritage will all be punished on us, wherever we are scattered as slaves to the Gentiles, and we shall be detested and despised by our captors. Our captivity will not even be honorable captivity but will be shameful. And so, my brothers, let us set an example to our brethren because their lives depend on us, and the sanctuary and the Temple and the altar also depend on us. Furthermore, let us give thanks to the Lord our God, who tests us, just as he tested our forefathers. Remember all the things he did to Abraham, all the ways he tested Isaac, and all the things which happened to Jacob in Mesopotamia, when he served as shepherd to his uncle Laban. He has not tried us in the fire, as he did to them, to search out their hearts, nor has he taken vengeance on us. The Lord afflicts those who are near to him, to admonish them."

Then Uzziah said to her, "Everything you have said you have said with the best of intentions, and no one will contradict you. This is not the first occasion that you have displayed your wisdom; everyone has always been conscious of your understanding because your heart is in the right place. But the people were so very thirsty that they compelled us to do what we did, and we cannot go back on our word. But now, because you are a godly woman, pray for us and the Lord will send us rain to fill our cisterns, and we shall no longer be faint with thirst."

Judith said to them, "Listen. I shall do something which will go down in the annals of our people. Be at the gate tonight and let me go out with my maid. Within the time limit which you have set for the surrender of the city, the Lord will rescue Israel through me. But do not ask what it is I am planning. I shall not reveal it until my purpose has been completed."

Then Uzziah and the other rulers said to her, "Go in peace, and may the Lord God go with you, to take vengeance on our enemies."

They left her hut and went to their respective places.

Then Judith lay flat on her face, covered her head with ashes, and uncovered the sackcloth she wore, and at the time the evening incense was being offered in the house of the Lord in Jerusalem she cried out aloud to the Lord, "O Lord God of my forefather, Simeon, you placed a sword in his hand to exact vengeance from the foreigners who had ravished a virgin and defiled her. You had said 'It shall not be,' and yet they did it,

so you caused their rulers to be slain, and their couch to be dyed with blood,
you struck down the servants with the princes, and the princes on their thrones,
you let their wives be taken as plunder and their daughters as captives,
and all their spoils be divided among your beloved children
who, inspired by zeal for you and appalled by the pollution of their blood,
called upon you to help them.[1]

"O God, my God, hear a widow's prayer. You brought about both what happened before those things and also what has happened since. You have planned both what is happening now and what is still to come, and what you plan comes to be. The things you choose to do stand before you and say, 'Here we are.' All your ways are prepared beforehand, and your judgments are grounded in foreknowledge.

"You see now how mighty and powerful the Assyrians have become. They boast of their horses and their horsemen, and revel in the strength of their infantry. They trust in their shields and spears and bows and slings, and they know not that 'The Lord is a man of war, the Lord is his name.'[2] Shatter their strength with your might and humble their force with your wrath, for they intend to profane your sanctuary, defile the tabernacle where your glorious name rests, and cut down with the sword the horns of your altar. Look on their arro-

[1] See Genesis 34.
[2] Exodus 15:3.

gance and punish it with your wrath. Give me, a widow, the strength to carry out my plan. By means of my trickery strike down 'the servant with the prince, and the prince with his servant.' Smash their splendor by means of a mere woman. Your strength does not lie in numbers or your might in strong men; you are the God of the afflicted, the helper of the oppressed, the upholder of the weak, the protector of the defenceless and the savior of the hopeless. O God of my father, God of the inheritance of Israel, Lord of heaven and earth, Creator of the waters, King of all creation, hear my prayer. Make my trickery bring destruction on those who have plotted violence against your covenant, your hallowed house, Mount Zion's summit, the house of your children's possession. And make every nation and every tribe which is yours know that you are God, the God of all power and might, and that Israel has no other protector but you."

When she has finished crying aloud to the God of Israel in these words, she stood up, called her maid and went down into the house where she lived only on Sabbaths and feast days. She pulled off her sackcloth, and took off her widow's weeds, washed her body all over with water, rubbed expensive oils into her skin, dressed her hair and fastened it with a tiara, and then put on her most festive clothes, which she had not worn since her husband, Manasseh, had died. She chose a pair of sandals, put on her necklaces, bracelets, rings, earrings, and all her other jewelry, and made herself beautiful to attract the attention of any man who saw her. Then she handed her maid a leather flask of wine, a bottle of oil, and a hamper packed with parched corn, pressed figs, fine bread and cheese; she also packed her own plates and handed them to her.

When they reached the city gates of Bethuliah, they found Uzziah standing there with the other city elders, Kabri and Karmi. When they saw her finely dressed and made up they were deeply struck with her beauty. They said to her, "May the God of our fathers favor you and fulfil your plan, for the glory of the children of Israel and the exaltation of Jerusalem."

Then she uttered a prayer, and said to them, "Tell them to open the city gates for me, and I shall go out to do what we have spoken of."

They ordered the guards to open up for her, as she had asked. When they had done so, Judith went out with her maid and the people in the city watched her go down the mountainside until she reached the end of the valley and passed out of sight. And as they went on down the valley the Assyrian guards intercepted her and asked her, "What is your nationality? Where have you come from? Where are you going?"

"I am a Hebrew woman," she said, "but I am running away from these people because they are about to be given over to you to be destroyed, and I am on my way to your general, Holofernes, to tell him the truth. I am going to show him a way to conquer all the hill country without the loss of a single man."

Hearing what she had to say, and observing the extreme beauty of her face, the men said to her, "You have saved your life by coming down to see our general. Come along to his tent now—some of us will escort you to him. And when you are standing in front of him do not be afraid, but tell him what you have just told us and he will treat you well."

They detailed one hundred of their number to escort Judith and her maid, and they took them to Holofernes' tent.

Meanwhile, word of her coming had passed round the camp, and a great throng collected and surrounded her as she stood outside Holofernes' tent waiting to be announced. They admired her beauty and because of her they also admired the children of Israel, and they said to one another, "Who can despise a people which produce women like this? It would be a mistake to leave one of them alive; if they are spared they could seduce the whole world."

Then Holofernes' attendants and servants came out and took her into the tent. Holofernes was lying on his couch under a canopy woven with purple and gold and emeralds and other precious stones. When Judith was announced he came out into the antechamber, preceded by silver lamps. When he and his servants caught sight of Judith they were all impressed by her beauty. She fell on her face as a mark of respect, but his servants raised her up and Holofernes said to her, "Take heart, dear lady, and do not be afraid: I never harm anyone who has chosen to serve Nebuchadnezzar, king of all the earth. If your people who live in the hill country had not shown contempt towards me I should not have lifted up spear against them. They have brought all this on their own heads. Now tell me, why have you deserted them and come to us? You have come to save your life—well, rest assured, you shall live, both tonight and in future. No one shall harm you; everyone will treat you well, like any servant of our lord, King Nebuchadnezzar."

Judith said to him, "Listen to my words, permit me to speak, and I shall utter no lie to you this evening. If you follow my advice, God will bring you success in all your aims. I swear by the life of Nebuchadnezzar, king of all the earth, by the power of him who has sent you for the preservation of every living creature—not only do men serve him through you but even the beasts of the field and the cattle and the birds of the air shall live through your might and acknowledge Nebuchadnezzar and all his dynasty. We have learnt of your wisdom and ingenuity and all the world has heard that there is no one else in the whole kingdom who is such a brilliant and successful soldier and general.

"Now, as for what Achior said in your council (we have heard his speech, because the men of Bethuliah saved him, and he told them everything he had said to you): Do not dismiss what he said, my lord and master. Take good note of it; it is true. Our people will not be punished, nor will sword prevail against them unless they sin against their God. But now they are on the threshold of sin, which will provoke their God to anger as soon as they commit the wicked act, so that they shall die, and you, my lord, will not be defeated or frustrated in your aims. Now that their food and water are running out, they have taken a decision to lay hands on the cattle, to eat those things which God in his laws has forbidden them to eat, and to use the first fruits of the corn and the tithes of the wine and oil which they had sanctified and set aside for the priests who serve God in Jerusalem, things which none of the people are permitted so much as to touch. They have sent a deputation to Jerusalem, where this has already been done by some people, to obtain the permission of the Sanhedrin. As soon as word is brought back and they do it, then they will be immediately given over to you and destroyed. That is why I, knowing all this, deserted them. God has sent me to you to do things which will amaze whoever hears of them all over the world. I am a God-fearing woman, my lord, and worship the God of heaven day and night. I shall stay with you, and each night I shall go out into the valley and pray to God, and he will tell me when they have committed their sins, and I shall come and let you know, and then you will set out with all your army, and none of them will stand in your way. I will lead you through the middle of Judea until you come to Jerusalem, and establish you in the heart of the city, and you will drive them before you like sheep without a shepherd, and not a dog will so much as growl at you. All this has been disclosed to me in a revelation and I have been sent to tell you of it.''

What she said pleased Holofernes and all his servants, and they were impressed by her wisdom and said, ''There is no woman to match her for beauty or wisdom from one end of the world to the other.''

Holofernes said to her, ''God did well to send you before the people to bring strength to us and destruction to those who showed contempt to my lord, the king. You a good-looking woman, and you speak wisely. If what you say comes about, then your God will be my God and you will live in the palace of King Nebuchadnezzar, and your fame will spread throughout the world.''

Then he ordered her to be led into the place where his silver vessels were set and told them to prepare some of his own food for her and give her some of his own wine to drink. But Judith said, ''I will not eat it, in case I happen to sin. Let them serve me some of the provisions I have brought with me.''

Holofernes said, ''But if the food you have brought with you runs out, where will we find more like it to feed you? We have none of your people with us.''

''By your soul I swear,'' said Judith, ''I shall not use up the provisions I have brought before God brings about by means of me the things he has decided to do.''

Then Holofernes' servants took her into the tent and she slept till midnight. Towards the morning watch she got up and sent word to Holofernes saying, ''My lord, tell them to let me go out to pray.'' So Holofernes instructed his guard not to impede her. She stayed in the camp for three days and every night she went out into the valley of Bethuliah and bathed in the spring. And each time she rose out of the water she begged the Lord God of Israel to guide her to rescue his people. Then she came back purified and stayed in the tent till the next evening, when she ate.

On the fourth day Holofernes held a banquet, to which he invited none of the officers but only his own servants. He said to the eunuch Bagoas, who was in charge of all his arrangements, ''Go and persuade the Hebrew woman you have in your care to come and eat and drink with us. It would be a disgrace to let a woman like that go without having enjoyed her company; if we do not make an effort to attract her she will laugh us to scorn."

So Bagoas left Holofernes and went to Judith and said, "Let my fair lady not fear to come to my lord and be his honored guest, to drink wine and enjoy herself with us, and become today like one of the daughters of Asshur who wait in the palace of Nebuchadnezzar."

"Who am I," Judith said to him, "to refuse my lord? Whatever pleases him I shall do at once and take pleasure in it till the day I die."

So she dressed herself up in her finest clothes, and her maid went and spread fleeces which Bagoas had given her for her everyday use on the ground opposite Holofernes so that she could recline on them and eat. When Judith came in and sat down, Holofernes was ravished by her beauty, heart and soul. In fact he had been waiting for an opportunity to seduce her ever since the first day he had seen her.

"Have a drink," he said. "Enjoy yourself with us."

"I will," Judith said, "because I feel happier this evening than ever before in my life."

So she took what her maid had prepared and ate and drank with him, while Holofernes, who was intoxicated with her beauty, drank a great deal of wine—more than he had ever drunk in his whole life.

When night fell and his servants hastily took their leave, Bagoas closed the outer door of the tent and dismissed all those who were in attendance on his lord. So Judith was left alone in the tent with Holofernes, who was sprawled on his bed drenched with wine. She had told her maid to wait for her outside the tent till she came out as they did every night. She told her that she would go out to pray as usual, and she had told Bagoas the same. When everyone, great and small, had left and they were all alone in the tent, Judith stood by Holofernes' bed and said in her heart, "O Lord God of all power, be mindful at this moment of what I do for the exaltation of Jerusalem. The time has come to do the thing I have planned to rescue your inheritance and destroy the enemies who have risen up against us."

Then she went up to the bedrail by Holofernes' head and took down his scimitar which was hanging there. She stood close to the bed, took his hair in her hand, and said, "Strengthen me now, O Lord God of Israel."

Then she struck him twice on the neck with all her strength, cut off his head, rolled his body off the bed and took the canopy down from the bedposts. After a short while she went out and gave Holofernes' head to her maid, who put it in her bag of provisions, and the two of them went out as if to pray, as was their custom. They left the camp, walked along the valley and up the mountain till they reached the gates of Bethuliah.

Then Judith called from a distance to the watchman at the gates, "Open, open up the gate. God is with us. Our God has shown his power in Israel again and his might against the enemy."

When the men in the city heard her voice, they hurried down to the city gates and summoned the city elders. Then everyone, great and small, came running (since they had not been expecting her) and opened the gate, let them in, lit torches and thronged round the pair of them.

"Halleluyah," Judith shouted aloud. "Praise God, who has not removed his mercy from the house of Israel. He has destroyed our enemy through me tonight."

Then, taking the head out of the bag and holding it up for them to see, she said, "Look, this is the head of Holofernes, commander-in-chief of the Assyrian army, and this is the canopy beneath which he lay in a drunken stupor. The Lord has struck him down by a woman's hand. I swear by God, who protected me in whatever I did, that my face alone seduced him to his destruction; he did not commit any sin with me, he has not defiled and shamed me."

The people were all amazed. They bowed down and worshipped God, and they recited in unison this prayer: "Blessed are you, our God, who have frustrated the enemies of your people this day."

And Uzziah said to Judith, "Blessed are you, my daughter, in the sight of the Most High God, above all other women in the world; and blessed is the Lord God who created heaven and earth, who guided you to strike down our foremost enemy. Whenever men recount the mighty works of God they will always remember your faith. May God reward you for what you have done; may you be held up as an example forever because you did not hesitate to risk your life on account of the affliction of our people. You averted our calamity while at the same time walking the straight path before our God."

And all the people responded, "Amen, amen."

Then they fetched Achior from Uzziah's house. When he came and saw Holofernes' head in the hand of a man in the crowd he collapsed in a faint. As soon as he had recovered he fell at Judith's feet in deep respect and said, "Blessed are you in every tent of Judah and in every nation which is stirred by the hearing of your name. Tell me the story of what you have been doing these last days."

So Judith told him publicly everything that she had done, from the day she had left until the time she was speaking to them. When she had finished, the people shouted and cheered all over the city. When Achior heard everything that God had done for Israel, he believed in God with all his heart, accepted circumcision, and joined the house of Israel forever.

Then Judith said to them, "Listen, my brothers, to what I have to say: Take this head and hang it on your battlements. As soon as the sun rises and it is day, let all the warriors arm themselves and go out of the city under the leadership of a commander, and make as if to charge down the valley toward the Assyrian guards—but let them not in fact go down. The Assyrians, meanwhile, will pick up their weapons and run back to the camp, to spread the alarm to the commanders of the Assyrian army. They will all go running together to Holofernes' tent but they will not find him there. Then panic will seize them, and they will run away from you. You will pursue them, and all the inhabitants of Israel with you, and leave them lying fallen by the wayside."

So as soon as dawn had broke they hung Holofernes' head on the walls, armed themselves, and marched out in companies onto the mountainside. When the Assyrian guard saw them they sent word to their superior officers, who reported to their own superiors and to all the commanders. These in turn went to Holofernes' tent and said to Bagoas, who was in charge, "Wake our lord at once. The slaves have dared to come down to fight us and to be utterly defeated."

So Bagoas went into the antechamber and clapped his hands, thinking that Holofernes was sleeping with Judith. When he got no answer he drew aside the flap and went into the bedchamber and found him lying dead by the bedside without his head. Then he cried aloud and wept and groaned and screamed and tore his clothes. He went to Judith's tent and found her gone and dashed outside to the people, shouting, "The slaves have cheated us! A Hebrew woman has shamed the house of King Nebuchadnezzar. Holofernes is lying there on the ground without his head!"

When the commanders of the Assyrian army heard this they tore their cloaks in a panic and the whole camp filled with loud shouts and screams.

When the men in the tents heard, they were horrified by what had happened. Panic and terror took hold of them, and they could not keep together but scattered all over the plain and the hill country. The Edomites and Ammonites, too, who had encamped in the hills around Bethuliah, ran away. Then every one of the Israelites who could wield arms sallied forth against them. And Uzziah sent to Bethomesthaim and Bebai and Kobai and Kola, and to all the Israelite settlements to tell them what had happened and to urge them to sally out and destroy the fleeing enemy. When they heard what had happened, the Israelites fell on them with one accord and routed them as far as Kobai. And similarly when the people in Jerusalem and the hill country of Judah heard what had happened in the enemy camp, they too came, and the inhabitants of Gilead and Galilee attacked their flank and butchered them until eventually they escaped beyond the border to Damascus. Meanwhile, those who were left behind at Bethuliah raided the Assyrian camp and carried off a very rich plunder. And when they arrived, the other Israelites took off what remained, and there was rich booty for the towns and villages of the hill country and the plain, for it had been a very rich store.

And then Joakim, the high priest, and the council of the children of Israel in Jerusalem came to see the favors which the Lord had granted Israel and to meet Judith and greet her. When they came to her, they all blessed her in unison in these words:

"You are the exaltation of Jerusalem,
You are the great glory of Israel,
You are the pride of our people.
You have done all this yourself,
You have done Israel a great service, and God is pleased with it.
Blessed may you be with the Lord Almighty forever."

The people plundered the Assyrian camp for a month. They gave Judith Holofernes' tent, all his silver goblets, his beds, his plate, and all his furniture, and she took it all and loaded some of it on her mule and heaped the rest on her wagons. All the Israelite women came running to see her and blessed her and danced in her honor. Then Judith took some branches and gave them to the women who were with her, and they all put olive wreaths on their heads, and Judith led the women in a dance in the presence of all the people while the men of Israel followed behind in their armor, with wreaths on their heads and songs in their mouths. And Judith sang this hymn of thanksgiving, with all the people singing the responses:

"Sing to my God with timbrels,
  chant to my Lord with cymbals.
Hymn him with psalms and praises,
  exalt him and call on his name.
For the Lord is the God who breaks battles:
  he encamped in the midst of the people,
  and delivered me from those who persecuted me.
Asshur came out of the mountains from the north,
  came with an army of ten thousand men,
whose multitudes blocked the rivers,
  and whose horsemen hid the hills.
He threatened to set fire to my lands,
  and to kill my young men with the sword,
to dash my suckling children to the ground,
  to slaughter my tender infants,
  and to ravish my young girls.
The Lord Almighty frustrated their schemes,
  he brought them shame by the hand of a woman.
Their champion was not felled by young men,
  nor did the great giants smite him,
but Judith, the daughter of Merari
  Made him weak with the beauty of her face.
She laid aside her widow's garb
  for the exaltation of Israel in distress.
She anointed her face with oils,
  she bound her hair with a tiara,

and dressed in linen to seduce him.
Her beauty ravished his eye
and her looks imprisoned his soul.
The scimitar cut through his neck;
the Persians shuddered at her daring
and the Medes trembled at her boldness.
Then my lowly ones cried out in triumph
and my weak ones shouted aloud.
The enemy cowered in fright,
they screamed and fled in panic.
The sons of slave girls pierced them
and stabbed them like runaway slaves.
They were slain by the army of the Lord.
I will sing to my God a new song:
O God, you are great and glorious,
marvelous in strength, invincible.
Let all creation serve you:
you spoke and they were made.
You sent your spirit and it formed them,
and none can resist your voice.
Mountains are shaken to their roots like water,
rocks melt like wax at your presence,
But you are merciful still to those who fear you.
All sacrifice is a paltry sweet savor,
all fat is merely a burnt offering,
but he who fears the Lord is great forever.
Woe to the nations who invade my people,
the Lord Almighty will punish them on the Day of Judgment.
He will put fire and worms in their flesh,
and they will weep in pain forever."

They went to Jerusalem and worshipped God, and when the people were purified they offered their whole burnt offerings, free-will offerings and gifts. Judith dedicated all the plate of Holofernes which the people had given her, and she also gave the canopy which she herself had taken from his bedchamber as a gift for the Lord. The people stayed in Jerusalem feasting before the sanctuary for three months, and Judith stayed with them; finally they all went home and Judith went to

Bethuliah, where she lived on her own estate and enjoyed a great reputation. Many men desired her, but she never took another man after the death of her husband, Manasseh. She grew more and more famous and lived to a ripe old age in her husband's house. When she was one hundred and five she freed her maid and died in Bethuliah. She was buried in the same vault as her husband, Manasseh, and all Israel mourned her for seven days. Before she died she distributed her possessions to her own next of kin and her husband's. And Israel was not threatened again in Judith's lifetime or for a long time after her death.

THE STORY OF SUSANNA

The Story of Susanna (in Hebrew, *Shoshannah*) was composed in the latter part of the reign of Alexander Yannai in Judea, at a time of fierce struggles between Pharisees and Sadducees. The point of the story is that witnesses must be closely examined, whatever their social status, and that false witnesses must be punished. This message fits well the recorded statement of Simeon ben Shetaḥ, the leader of the Pharisees at that time: "Examine witnesses closely, and be careful what you say or you may help them to tell lies!" (*Aboth* 1:9). According to a tradition preserved in the Palestinian Talmud (Sanhedrin 6:3, 23[b]), Simeon's son was condemned to death on perjured evidence. The false witnesses confessed to their crime before the sentence was carried out, but the young man insisted that it should be executed so that the perjurers too could be punished with death as they deserved. This accords with the Sadducean interpretation of the law; the Pharisees, on the other hand, held that a false witness in a capital case should be put to death even if the accused person was saved (Mishnah [Makkoth 1:6]), as happens in the Story of Susanna. The separate questioning of witnesses, apparently introduced for the first time here, became a standard feature of judicial procedure (Mishnah [Sanhedrin 3:6]). Simeon ben Shetah is also credited by tradition with the introduction of compulsory education for children (Palestinian Talmud [Ketuboth 8:11, 32[c]]; Babylonian Talmud [Baba Bathra 21[a]]), an interest which may be reflected in the closing words of the story.

The story, told well and simply, soon became popular. It was connected with the names of two biblical figures, Habakkuk and Daniel.

The association with Habakkuk was known to Christian writers as late as the fourth century. The name of Daniel had been inserted in the text before the oldest surviving Greek translation was made, within a century of its composition, and further additions were made which set the story in Babylon in the early period of Daniel's life. Theodotion, in the second century, incorporated these additions in his Greek translation, and it was Theodotion's version which was copied in texts of the Greek Bible, at the end of the Book of Daniel. The Babylonian setting makes many of the details in the text (the elders and assembly, for example) seem incongruous; the present translation tries to follow the earlier version of the story, before the references to Daniel were inserted.

The Story of Susanna was originally written in Hebrew, or possibly in Aramaic, but the original was apparently lost soon after Theodotion's translation was made, no doubt because it had been excluded from the Palestinian canon of scripture. Julius Africanus, in the second quarter of the third century, wrote to the great Christian scholar Origen inquiring about the status of the story; the text of his letter survives together with Origen's reply. Africanus considers, on the basis of the puns on the names of the trees, that the Story of Susanna must have been composed originally in Greek, and this opinion has been followed by scholars up to recent times, although on other grounds it is hardly plausible. Neither Africanus nor Origen knew of a Hebrew text, but Origen offers some very interesting information about the currency of the story in Palestinian Jewish circles. He was acquainted, he said, with a learned Jew who seemed to accept the Story of Susanna as scriptural. He even supplied the names of the two elders: Ahab and Zedekiah, who seduced other men's wives and were roasted to death by the king of Babylon (Jeremiah 29:22–23). Another Jewish informant told Origen an additional story about the two elders: they were in the habit of approaching respectable women privately and telling them that God had given them the power of fathering the Messiah, and by this means they induced the women to fall in with their plans.

Thus, although the original Hebrew was lost and the work was not included in the canon, it was not forgotten by Jews. The Bodleian Library in Oxford contains two medieval Hebrew manuscript translations of the story, one of which again connects the two elders with Ahab and Zedekiah.

This charming story was also extremely popular among Christians, who saw in it an allegory of the Christian church. Apart from numerous references in ecclesiastical writers, its popularity is attested by various paintings, including celebrated ones by Tintoretto, Rembrandt, and Rubens, and by the widespread use of the names Susan and Susanna to this day.

* * *

That year two elders of the people were appointed judges, and cases were brought before them even from other towns. These two both conceived a violent passion for the wife of one of their brother-Israelites, a certain Joakim. The woman's name was Susanna, the daughter of Helkiah. She was a beautiful woman, and she was in the habit of taking a walk in her husband's gardens toward evening. The elders' passion got the better of their good sense and made them forget all thought of Heaven or of justice.

Now although they were both infatuated with Susanna, they concealed their desire from one another, and she had no inkling of it either. They used to part from each other and hurry along stealthily in the hope of a chance to meet her and talk to her. One day, when she was taking her walk as usual, and one of the elders had just arrived, the second appeared on the scene and began questioning him.

"So this is why you rushed off so quickly and left me behind?" he said.

At that they confessed to each other the agonizing condition they were in.

"We must have her," one of them said. So they agreed on a plan and made advances to her and tried to force her to do what they wanted. But Susanna was a model Jewess, and she said to them, "I know that if I give in to you I shall be killed, and I also know that if I refuse I won't escape unharmed. Still, it's better that I should reject you and face the consequences than sin before the Lord."

So the two lechers left her, bent on revenge and determined to bring about her death. They went to the assembly of the town, where all the Jews were gathered in session, and there they stood up and said, "Send for Susanna, the daughter of Helkiah, the wife of Joakim."

Susanna was summoned and soon appeared with her mother and father, five hundred servants, and her four small children.

Susanna was a very attractive woman, and the two scoundrels ordered her to be unveiled so that they could feast their eyes on her beauty. At this her family and friends burst into tears. The two elder-judges came forward and put their hands on her head. Susanna, trusting in the Lord, looked up to heaven and said through her tears, "Lord, eternal God, who knows all things before they happen, you know that I have not done what these vicious men accuse me of."

The two elders said, "We were walking in her husband's garden, and as we were going past the stadium we saw this woman with a man. We stood and watched them making love, and they did not realize we were there. We decided we must find out who they were and moved closer. We recognized her, but the young man, who was masked, escaped. We seized the woman and asked her who the man was but she refused to tell us. This is our solemn testimony."

The whole assembly believed them because they were elders and judges of the people.

As Susanna was being led off to be executed, an angel of the Lord inspired a young man, who parted the crowd and stood in their way.

"Are you such fools, you Israelites," he said, "as to condemn a Jewish woman to death without investigating the charge and discovering the truth? Separate these men and let me cross-examine them."

When they were separated, the young man addressed the assembly. "Don't think," he said, "that these men can't be liars just because they are elders. I am going to confront them both now with a question that has been put in my mind."

He summoned one of the elders, and when he was brought forward, the young man said, "Listen to me, you hardened sinner. The sins you have committed in the past have finally found you out. You were empowered to try capital cases and you convicted the innocent and acquitted the guilty, even though the Lord says, 'You shall not put the innocent and the guiltless to death.'[1]

"Where were you in the garden, what kind of tree were you standing under, when you saw them together?"

[1] Exodus 23:7.

"It was an ash tree," said the wretched man.

"Your perjury rebounds on your own head," replied the young man. "This very day the angel of the Lord will burn you to a fine ash!"

He told them to take him away and fetch the other one. "You are more like a lewd Sidonian than a Jew. You were infatuated by beauty and dragged down by your lust. You had your way, no doubt, with Israelite women; they submitted to you out of fear. But this daughter of Judah was too proud to give in to your disgusting demands. Tell me, now, where exactly were you in the park, what tree were you standing under, when you saw them carrying on together?"

"It was a pear tree," said the elder.

"Sinner!" replied the young man. "At this very moment the angel of the Lord is standing with his sword drawn, waiting for the people to finish with you so that he can pare you to the quick!"

The whole assembly began to shout and cheer the young man because he had convicted them of perjury out of their own mouths. They punished them, in accordance with the law,[2] with the same penalty they had planned to inflict on their sister-Israelite. They gagged them and led them off and hurled them into a chasm, and there the angel of the Lord burned them with flames. And so an innocent life was saved that day.

That is why Jacob favored the young,[3] because they are upright. We, too, should look after our young people so that they will grow to be upstanding citizens and always be God-fearing and intelligent.

[2] Deuteronomy 19:16–21.

[3] Genesis 48:14.

Apocalypse

THE VISIONS OF SHEALTIEL

The Visions of Shealtiel (Salathiel) belong to an important group of documents reflecting the troubled state of mind of Jews after the upheavals and disasters of the tragic revolt against Roman rule which culminated in the capture of Jerusalem and the sack of the Temple. These events provoked a variety of reactions. Some saw the calamity as the beginning of the end and prophesied the destruction of Rome and the coming of the kingdom of God. Others, including many of the rabbis, welcomed Roman rule and blamed the defeat on the sins of the Jews and the fanaticism and mutual hostility of the zealots. For these the remedy lay in loyalty to God and Caesar, study of the Torah and the elimination of sin. The author of *The Visions of Shealtiel* is a deeply religious Jew who was neither a zealot nor a quietist scholar. He struggles to reconcile the disaster with his concept of God's justice and scrutinizes the times for signs of God's future plans. He presents his ideas, not in the form of slogans or interpretations of scripture, but as a revelation from God through a series of dream-visions in which he discusses his problems with an angel. There are four visions, each with similar subject-matter. Shealtiel understands the theory of sin and punishment but he cannot understand why God should punish his own people, even if they have sinned, by means of the even more sinful people of Rome (which he calls Babylon or Esau). The angel answers some of his questions but points out that a full understanding of divine things is beyond the power of mere men. He explains that the present age will soon come to an end; evil will be destroyed and good will flourish. Shealtiel is eager to know more about the end: when will it come? Will he live to see it? The angel refuses to answer the last question but assures him that the end is near and that he himself will be saved although many will perish.

The two themes which run through the work are sin and punishment on the one hand and national redemption on the other. The author's preoccupation with the "evil tendency" (*yeṣer hara*) as a curse which entered the world at the time of Adam's rebellion places him at a point in between the classical Jewish and Christian doctrines of sin.

The visions end, in traditional manner, with a message of hope: a revelation of the splendor of the rebuilt Jerusalem.

The Visions of Shealtiel were written in Hebrew, "thirty years after the destruction of the City," i.e., in 100 C.E. Unfortunately the Hebrew original is lost and the work nowhere survives in the form in which it was written. It is only preserved, heavily edited, in the various translations (Latin, Syriac, Ethiopic, Arabic, and Armenian) of the Christian work known as the Fourth Book of Ezra or 2 Esdras. The editor has pieced together a number of Jewish writings of the period (see also pp. 46–47), and it is not easy to disentangle them. The attempt made here to isolate the Visions of Shealtiel and present them in a continuous form follows the work of several modern editors and commentators, but it must be pointed out that some scholars would challenge the feasibility or desirability of such reconstructions.

The Apocalypse of Ezra 3–10, *abridged*

It was the thirtieth year after the fall of our city. I, Shealtiel, was in Babylon. I lay in bed feeling disturbed, my mind whirling. I kept seeing a picture of Zion in ruins and the Babylonians living in prosperity. My soul was all stirred up, and I voiced my fears to the Almighty:

"Lord God," I said, "surely in the beginning it was you, you alone, who made the world. You spoke to the dust, and it gave you Adam, a dead body. It was you who shaped him, you who breathed the breath of life into him. You led him into the garden that you had planted with your own hands before the world began. You gave him an order, he disobeyed it, and right away you put him under a death sentence, him and his descendants. From him were born countless tribes and peoples. Each one did what it wanted, they were irreligious and unjust, and you did nothing to stop them. But when the right time came you flooded the world and its inhabitants, and destroyed them. So they were all destroyed: Adam had died, and they died in the flood. But you spared one of them with his family, and all the just are descended from him. But when the survivors began to breed and the people became many again, they turned out more ungodly than the earlier ones. When they were behaving so unjustly, you chose one of them, Abraham, to be your own. Because you loved him, you took him aside secretly one night and showed him everything to the end of time, you made an everlasting pact with him and promised you would never abandon his children. You gave him Isaac, and you gave Isaac Jacob and Esau. You made Jacob your heir, but you hated Esau; so Jacob became a great people. You led them out of Egypt and took them to Mount Sinai. You split the sky and shook the earth, you made the world stand still and the depths shudder, you threw the universe into a whirl, and your glory passed through the four gates of fire, earthquake, storm, and ice to give the Torah to Jacob and teachings to the children of Israel. But you did not take away their evil tendency so that your Torah could fruit in them. Because the first man, Adam, wrapped himself in the evil tendency. He rebelled and was crushed, and so were all his descendants after him. So they remained weak; the Torah and the source of evil struggled together in the people's hearts; good gave way, and evil took its place.

"Time passed, and in due course you chose a servant, David, and told him to build a city in your name, where gifts would be offered to you, though really they were yours already. This was done for many years but the inhabitants of the city deserted you, and were no better than Adam and all his other descendants: they also wrapped themselves in the evil tendency. So you gave your own city to your enemies.

"Then I said to myself, 'Perhaps the people of Babylon lead good lives and that is why you have deserted Zion?' But when I came here, I saw more irreligious acts than I could count. For thirty years I have witnessed these misdeeds with my own eyes. My mind is in a whirl because I have seen how you give success to sinners and spare the godless; how you have destroyed your own people and protected your enemies; you give no hint to anyone how to understand your ways. Has Babylon behaved so much better than Zion?''

Then an angel was sent to me, and he replied, ''Your mind is so confused about this world: do you want to understand the way of the Almighty?''

''My Lord, I do,'' I answered.

''I have been sent,'' he said, ''to ask you three things. If you can explain any one of them to me, I shall teach you what you want to know and show you why evil exists.''

''Speak, Lord,'' I said.

''Well, then,'' he said, ''weigh me some fire, measure me some wind, or call me back a day that has passed.''

''What man ever born can do those things?'' I answered. ''How can you ask me to do them?''

He said, ''If I had asked you how many storehouses there are in the heart of the sea, or how many springs feed the deep, or how many paths there are above the sky, or which are the ways out of the underworld and the ways into paradise—then you would have answered, 'I've never been down into the deep or into the underworld, I've never been up to heaven.' As it is, I have not asked you about these, but about fire, wind, and time, things you have known, things you cannot be without, and even so you have not answered me.

''Since,'' he continued, ''you know nothing about things you have grown up with, how can your limited mind comprehend the way of the Almighty? It has been created incomprehensible: the way of the Eternal cannot be grasped by a mortal man living in a transient world.''

When I heard this, I fell prostrate and cried out, ''We would have been better off never to have been born than to be born for a life of suffering and not to understand why we suffer!''

This was his answer: ''The trees of the forest said to one another, 'Let us make war on the sea and drive it off, and make another forest.' Meanwhile the waves of the sea said, 'Let us make war on the forest and have more room for ourselves.' The trees' plan came to nothing because the fire came and burnt them down. So did the plan of the waves because the sand came and blocked their way. Now, if you had to judge between them, which would you acquit and which would you condemn?"

"Both their plans were foolish," I replied. "Forests belong on dry land and the proper place for waves is in the sea."

"That is a very judicious answer," he said. "If only you would judge your own case so acutely. Forests belong on dry land and the proper place for waves is the sea; similarly, those who live on earth can only understand earthly things, and only he who lives in heaven can understand heavenly things."

"Please tell me this, then, my Lord," I said. "Why have I been given the power to think? I wasn't asking about higher things but about our everyday experience. Israel has been handed over to the nations; the people you love is at the mercy of godless tribes; our fathers' holy Torah has been destroyed; the written promises no longer hold; we pass from the world like locusts, our life is like a breath, we are granted no mercy. What will he do for his great name which we bear? That is my question."

He replied, "If you survive you will see; if you live long enough you will be amazed. The present age will quickly come to an end; it is too full of groaning and weakness to contain the reward promised to the just. Evil, which you were asking about, has been sown; its threshing floor is still to come. The land where good is sown cannot come into being until what has already been sown has been reaped and the ground where evil is sown has disappeared. A single seed of evil was sown in Adam's heart in the beginning; what a rich crop of wickedness it has already yielded and will continue to yield before the threshing! Now work it out for yourself: if a single seed of evil can produce so much wickedness, how much richer a harvest will be produced by the grains of good, which are unnumerable!"

"But how long?" I asked. "When will it come? Our lives are so short."

"Do not be in more of a hurry than the Almighty," he replied. "You are in a hurry for yourself, but the Almighty has to consider many. The souls of the just in their present home asked the same question: 'How long are we here for? When will the threshing bring our reward?' And the angel Jerahmiel answered: 'Not until the number of those like you is complete. The Holy One has measured the time; he has counted the years and numbered the hours. He will make no move until the total is reached.' "

"Lord God," I said, "we are so wicked. Is it perhaps because of us that the reward of the just is delayed, because of the sins of those who live on earth?"

He answered, "Go and ask a pregnant woman if she can keep the child in her womb after her nine months are up."

"No, my Lord," I said, "she can't."

"Well," he went on, "the home of the souls in the underworld is like a womb. Just as a woman in labor is impatient to be free of her pains, so it too is impatient to release what has been placed there from the beginning. When the time comes you will be shown what you are so anxious to see."

"Will you grant me a favor," I said, "if I am worthy and if it is possible? Just tell me this, whether there is more time to come than has already passed. I know the past but I know nothing about the future."

"Come and stand next to me," he replied. "I shall show you an image and explain it to you."

I stood beside him and watched. First there came a blazing furnace; the flames disappeared and only smoke was left. Then there came a heavy rain cloud, pouring down rain; when the rain had finished falling, there were only a few drops left.

"Think about it," he said. "Just as there was more rain than drops, more fire than smoke, so what has passed is the greater period: all that are left are drops and smoke."

Then I asked him, "Do you think I shall live to see those days? In whose lifetime will it be?"

"I have not been sent here to tell you about your own life," he answered. "I know nothing about that. But if you pray again and fast for seven days, you will hear more."

Then I woke up. I was trembling all over; I could hardly breathe and I felt close to fainting. But I did as the angel had said. I fasted for seven days, weeping and groaning all the time. At the end of seven days my mind was deeply troubled again. But again I began reasoning things out and I prayed to the Almighty for enlightenment: "Lord

God, out of all the trees of all the forests in the world you have chosen one vine; out of all the countries on earth you have chosen one piece of ground; out of all the depths of the sea you have raised up one stream to be your own; out of all the flowers in the world you have chosen one lily; out of all the cities ever built you have chosen Zion to be holy to you; out of all the birds of creation you have put your name on one dove; out of all the animals ever created you have selected one lamb; out of all the many peoples you have brought one specially near to you; and to this people which you love you have given your own special teaching. Why then, Lord, have you handed over the one to the many? Why have you rejected this one root rather than the many, why have you scattered and dispersed your only one among the many? Why have those who disobey your laws trampled underfoot those who keep faith with you? Surely if you have come to hate your own people you should punish them yourself?"

When I had finished speaking, the same angel was sent to me again. "Listen to me," he said, "and I shall teach you; pay attention, and I shall tell you more."

"Speak, my Lord," I replied.

He said, "You are very worried about Israel. Do you love Israel more than Israel's creator?"

"No, Lord," I answered. "I only spoke because I was so miserable. I felt a pain in my guts as I tried to understand the reasons for the Almighty's judgment."

"You cannot do it," he said.

"Why not, Lord? Why was I born? Why didn't my mother's womb become my grave so that I wouldn't see the agony of Jacob, the despair of the descendants of Israel?"

He answered, "Count me the days that have not yet come, gather in the scattered raindrops, make withered flowers bloom again; release the winds from their sealed storehouses; paint me a picture of a voice or of a face you have never seen; then I shall show you the answer to your question."

I said, "Lord God, only one whose home is not among men can understand these things. How can a poor fool like me answer your questions?"

"Well," he said, "just as you cannot do one of the things I have mentioned, so you can never understand my judgment or the goal of the love I have sworn to my people.''

''But surely, Lord,'' I said, ''that goal is only promised to those who are still living when it comes. What will become of us and of those who went before us and those who follow us?''

''My judgment is like a ring,'' he said. ''Just as those who come last will not be too late, so those who went first will not be too early.''

''Couldn't you have made all men—past, present, and future—at once?'' I asked. ''Then you could pronounce your verdict sooner.''

''Creation cannot go faster than its creator. And the world could not hold all those who are to live in it at once.''

''But you told me that you are going to bring them all back to life at once. If the world will hold them all then, surely it would hold them all now!''

''Ask a woman about her womb. Say to her, 'If you have ten children, why do you have them one by one? Why not have them all at once?' ''

''She cannot, Lord. She has to have them one by one.''

''Well, I have made the earth like a womb, for people to be born one at a time. And just as a woman cannot have children when she is too young or too old, so too my world is governed by time.''

''Since you have raised the subject,'' I said, ''I should like to ask you another question. Is this mother you speak of still young, or is she getting old?''

''Any mother can answer that question. Ask her why the children she bears now are not as strong as her earlier ones. She will tell you that those born in the prime of her youth are very different from those born later in life, when her womb is growing weak. Now consider: Your generation is smaller than men of earlier generations, and later generations will be smaller still. That is because creation is already growing old and has lost the strength of its youth.''

Then I said, ''Grant me a favor, Lord, and tell me whom you will use to punish your creation.''

''At the beginning of the world, before the eternal gateways were set up, before the great winds blew, before thunder sounded or lightning flashed, before the garden was planted and laid out with flowers, before the natural forces were established or the vast armies of angels mustered, before the sky was raised and the divisions of heaven named, before Zion, my footstool, was founded, before the years were set in motion, before the sins of your stupid men had been invented, and before the seal had been set on those who treasure honesty—at that time I thought the thought that brought all this into being, I myself, using no one else. So too the end will come through me and no one else.

"That is all I can tell you tonight," the angel continued. "But if you pray again and fast for another seven days, I shall tell you more. The Almighty has heard your voice. He has seen the purity and holiness you have shown since your youth; that is why he has sent me to show you all this. He also says this: Trust in me, and do not be afraid. And do not give yourself over too easily to fruitless thoughts about the present age, or you may not have an easy time in the age to come."

So I wept and fasted for another seven days. On the eighth night my mind was troubled once more and my soul was on fire, and I started to speak to God again: "Lord God, in the beginning of your creation you spoke. On the first day you said, 'Let heaven and earth exist!' and your word brought them into being. The spirit was hovering; darkness and silence were all around, and there was still no human voice. Then you commanded a ray of light to be produced from your hidden chamber so that your works could be seen.

"On the second day you created the angel of the firmament and ordered him to divide the water, one part rising above and the other part remaining beneath.

"On the third day you commanded the water to collect in a seventh of the earth's surface; the other six-sevenths you dried out and brought part of it into service as sown and cultivated land. As soon as your word went out, the work was done. Immediately countless kinds of sweet-tasting fruits appeared and flowers and trees of different kinds and tantalizing fragrances. All this was done on the third day.

"On the fourth day you gave the order, and the lights were made, the sun, the moon, and the constellations. You commanded them to serve the man you were going to create.

"On the fifth day you commanded the seventh part, where the water was, to produce animals, birds, and fishes, and they appeared. Dumb, lifeless water produced living beings, a wonder for every generation to tell. You set apart two of the animals you had created; you called one

Behemoth and the other Leviathan. You separated them from each other because the wet area was too small to contain them. You gave Behemoth one of the parts which were dried out on the third day to live in, where the thousand mountains are. To Leviathan you gave the wet area. You kept them to serve as food for whom you wish, when you wish.

"On the sixth day you commanded the earth to produce cattle, wild beasts, and creeping things. And finally you made Adam, as ruler of everything you had created. From him we, your chosen people, are descended.

"I have recited all this to you, Lord God, because you have said that you created this world for us. You have also said that the other nations born of Adam are nothing; you have compared their vast numbers to specks of dust and drops from a bucket. Yet now, Lord, those nations which count for nothing are ruling over us and oppressing us while we, your people, whom you honored by the names of firstborn, only son, beloved, are subject to their power. If the world was created for us, why can we not take possession of it? How much longer must we wait?"

When I had finished speaking, the same angel was sent to me as on the previous nights. He said to me, "Stand up and listen to the message I have come to bring you."

"Speak, my Lord," I said.

"Imagine a vast, wide sea approached by a narrow passage like a river. If anyone wants to see the sea and sail on it, how can he reach the open sea without passing through the narrow passage? Again, imagine a rich city built in a plain, which can only be approached by a narrow mountain path, with fire on one side and deep water on the other, just wide enough for one man to pass. Now suppose a man inherits this city, how can he take possession of it without risking the danger?"

"You are right, Lord," I said.

"Israel is like that. It was for them I made the world. But when Adam disobeyed my orders, what I had made was cursed. This world became like a narrow passage, full of pain and sorrow, toil and danger. But the world to come is wide and safe, and its fruits are immortal. The benefits in store, however, can only be reached by passing through this hard and narrow life. Why are you so troubled by the thought of your mortality? Why do you ponder the present instead of what is to come?''

''Lord God,'' I said, ''you have laid it down in your Torah that the just will inherit but the ungodly will perish. The just have a good reason to put up with this narrow life because they hope to reach the wider life to come; but the godless have to suffer the narrows without ever seeing the wide expanse.''

''Don't try to be cleverer than God Almighty! Many men must perish because they have ignored my law. God has given clear instructions for all men what they must do if they wish to live and not be punished. But they reacted disobediently; they conjured up useless ideas, they rebelled, they even said that God did not exist; they laughed at his laws and put no faith in his promises. The result: emptiness for the empty, fullness for the full.''

''Lord God,'' I said, ''I've said it before and I'll say it again: happy are those who keep your commandments. My question is about the others. What living man has never sinned? It seems to me that the age to come will bring joy to few and torment to many. There is an evil tendency in us which leads us to destruction. Not just a few of us, but almost everyone who has ever lived!''

''Listen to what I have to say. That is why the Almighty has made not one age but two. As for the fact that the just are few and the ungodly are many: if you had a few precious stones, would you mix with them beads of lead and clay?''

''It's out of the question,'' I replied.

''If you want further confirmation, look at the earth. It produces gold, silver, copper, iron, lead, and clay, each in greater quantity than the last. Judge for yourself: which is more precious, the common or the rare?''

''Lord God,'' I said, ''the rarer things are the more precious they are.''

''Work it out for yourself, then. A man is happier with a little of something rare than with a lot of something common. My judgment is similar: I am glad about the few who are saved, who add luster to my name, but I am not sorry about the many who perish like the breath and smoke they resemble.''

''Earth, what have you done?'' I cried. ''Better if you had never been created than that you should have produced us with minds which torment us with the knowledge that we must die. Cattle are happier than men: they may not look forward to a life after death but neither do they expect to be tried and punished. What good is our life to us if it leads only to torments? For all men are sinners. We would be much better off without the judgment after death!''

''The judgment was prepared by the Almighty before he created the world and Adam and his descendants. But you have answered your own question. As you say yourself, you are born with a mind. The reason why men have to face torments is that even though they have minds they still do wrong; they do not obey the commands they have been given and they turn their backs on the law which was made for them. So they will have no excuse when the judgment comes. God has put up with them long enough—not for their own sakes but for the sake of the times to come.''

''Lord God,'' I said, ''grant me this favor. Tell me whether, when we give up our souls after death, we shall rest in peace until the time comes for you to renew your creation, or whether our torments will begin right away.''

''Before I answer your question, I have this to say to you: do not count yourself among the wicked who will be tormented. You have stored up a stock of good works with the Almighty which will only be revealed to you when the end of time comes. As for death, this is what happens: When the death sentence is pronounced on a man, his soul leaves the body to be restored to him who gave it. If he was one of those who reject the ways of the Almighty and hate the God-fearers, his soul does not go to a resting place but its punishment begins at once. If, however, he has followed the way of the Almighty during his lifetime, enduring pain and danger and keeping faithfully to his law, then his soul rejoices in the sight of the glory of the Almighty and then rests in peace.''

''And will his soul have an opportunity,'' I asked, ''to see what you have been telling me about after it leaves the body?''

''It has seven days to see all this and then it goes to its resting place.''

''Will you grant me another favor?'' I continued. ''Tell me whether on the day of judgment the just will be able to put in a good word for the ungodly and appeal to the Almighty on their behalf? I am talking about fathers and sons, or brothers, or family and friends.''

"I will grant your favor and tell you. The judgment is final and bears the seal of truth. Just as a father cannot use his son, or a son his father, or a master his slave, or a lover his beloved, to be ill or sleep or eat or be cured on his behalf, so on that day no one will be able to appeal on behalf of anyone else or indeed drag him down with him. Everyone will be judged according to his own good or bad record."

"But we have read how in the old days many men prayed on behalf of others—Abraham, Moses, Joshua, Samuel, and so on. Surely in these days, when wrongdoing is so rampant, the same thing can happen?"

"God's glory is not always present in this world, which is transitory, and that is why the strong can pray for the weak. But the day of judgment marks the end of this world and the beginning of the immortal world to come, in which wrongdoing and doubt will be banished and justice and truth will flourish. When that time comes it will be impossible for anyone to feel pity for those who are condemned or to harm those who are judged worthy."

"All I can say," I replied, "is that it would have been better if Adam had never been created or at least if he had been prevented from sinning. What is the good of this life? We live in misery and face torments when we die. Adam, what have you done! You sinned but we have to suffer for it. What good to us is the promise of eternal life when by our actions we have condemned ourselves to death? We did not think, when we did wrong, that we would have to suffer for it after our death.

"That is the meaning of man's struggle on earth. If he loses he will be punished, but if he wins he will be rewarded. That is what Moses meant when he said to the people, 'Choose life, and then you will live."[1] But they ignored him and the prophets after him, and even me when I spoke to them. That is why there will be no sadness over their destruction, only rejoicing over the survival of those who obeyed."

"But, Lord," I exclaimed, "I know the attributes of the Almighty: He is called

COMPASSIONATE—because he has compassion for those yet unborn;
MERCIFUL—because he shows mercy to those who return to his law;

[1] Deuteronomy 30:19.

PATIENT—because he shows patience to his creatures when they sin;
GENEROUS—because he prefers giving to taking;
FREQUENTLY PARDONING—because over and over again he pardons men, present, past, and future, and so enables the world and its inhabitants to live;
THE GIVER—because without his kind gifts of pardon to wrongdoers not one man in a thousand could hope to live;
FORGIVING—because if he did not forgive and forget the many misdeeds of those created by his word only a tiny fraction of them would be left.''[2]

He replied, ''The Almighty has made this world for many but the world to come for only a few. Think of the earth: it produces plenty of potter's clay but very little gold dust. So it is with this world: many have been created but only a few will be saved.''

''Oh for a gift of understanding,'' I cried. ''We do not choose to come into the world and we do not choose when to leave it. Our life span is so short. Lord God, permit me to offer you a prayer, for myself and for all mankind. We have failed and judgment is certain. O Lord my God, hear my voice and accept my prayer:

''O Lord, you live forever,
heaven is your home,
your throne is beyond imagination,
your glory beyond understanding;
armies attend you with terror,
they turn to fire and wind at your command;
your word is true and lasting,
powerful and awesome is your command;
your glance dries up oceans,
your anger melts mountains,
your truth stands forever.
Hear my voice, my Lord and Creator,
and listen to my words;
while I live I will speak out,

[2] This is a midrashic exposition of the attributes of God listed in Exodus 34:6–7: ''The Lord, compassionate and merciful God, patient, frequently pardoning and just; the giver of pardon to thousands, forgiving misdeeds . . .''

while I am conscious I will address you:
Look not at your people's crimes,
but at those who have served you loyally;
consider not those who have foolishly fomented injustice,
but those who have suffered for keeping faith with you;
ignore those who have acted unjustly before you,
but remember those who have revered you wholeheartedly;
do not destroy those who act like animals,
but take pity on those who have obeyed your glorious law;
do not be angry with those who have behaved worse than beasts,
but love those who have firmly put their trust in your glory.
We and our fathers before us have acted foolishly and wickedly,
but it is only because of our sins that you are called merciful;
the just have a store of good deeds, they have earned their reward,
have mercy on us who have none, and you will rightly be called generous.
What is man, that you should be angry with him,
or the human race, that you should flare up against it?
Truly, no man born has done no wrong,
no one who has ever lived has not sinned;
it is by the mercy shown to those who have no store of good deeds,
Lord God, that your goodness will be made known."

"You are partly right," he answered. "It is true that I give no thought to wrongdoers, to their deeds, their death, and their destruction, but I take pleasure in the just, in their works, their survival, and their reward. So it is as you say. A farmer sows many seeds and plants many plants, but not all the seeds come up and not all the plants take root; so it is with men, not all those who come into the world will survive."

"Grant me a favor," I said, "and let me speak out. The farmer's seed will not come up if it does not receive your rain at the right time, and if it has too much rain it will rot. How can you compare it with man, who was shaped by your hands and created in your image? You have made everything else because of him. I beg of you, Lord God, spare your people and have pity on your heirs because you yourself created them."

"The present is the present, and the future is the future. You cannot love my creation more than I do myself. But why do you keep counting yourself among the godless? You are wrong, but your modesty and humility will win you greater glory before the Almighty while other men will be made to suffer for their arrogance. Still, you should think about yourself and the glory in store for the others who are like you. For you, paradise lies open, the tree of life is planted, the age to come is prepared and delights are in store; for you the city is built, and there you will have rest with perfect goodness and wisdom. From you evil will be eradicated, sickness suppressed, death destroyed; from you hell will flee and decay will depart for ever. All pain will leave you, and the stores of life will be open to you. So ask no more questions about the many who will perish. They were given freedom and they chose to despise the Almighty, to pour scorn on his law and to desert his ways; they trampled his holy ones underfoot and they said to themselves, 'There is no God,' although they knew that they were bringing death upon themselves. The Almighty did not want men to perish but they themselves dishonored their Creator and rejected his good gifts. So stop wondering about the torments of the godless but think instead about the reward of the just: the world to come is theirs and it is for them that it was created."

"I have said it before and will say it again," I replied. "Those who perish vastly outnumber those who are saved; they are like a small drop compared with the ocean."

He answered, "The seed depends on the soil, the color depends on the flower, the work depends on the workman, the harvest depends on the farmer. Once upon a time, before the world began, when I was preparing it as a home for those who now live in it, no man contradicted me because as yet no man existed. But, once created in the world I had prepared for them as a never-failing banquet, an inexhaustible pasture, they followed a path of vice. I looked at my world: it was ruined. My earth was threatened by the wickedness of its inhabitants. I could hardly bring myself to spare it; but I saved one grape from the bunch, one tree from the forest. The majority must perish because they have shown themselves worthless, but my grape, my tree, on which I have lavished so much effort, shall be saved.

"Now wait one more week. Do not fast this time but go to a flowery field where no house has ever been built; eat only the plants of the field, taste no meat and drink no wine, and pray devoutly to the Almighty. Then I will come and talk to you again."

So I went out, as he had said, to the field known as Arpad and sat down among the flowers. I lived on herbs but I felt no hunger.

At the end of a week, as I was lying there on the grass, my mind became troubled again as before. I spoke again and addressed the Almighty: "Lord God, you revealed yourself to our ancestors in the Sinai desert after the Exodus from Egypt when they were crossing the barren, pathless wilderness. You said to them: 'Hear me, Israel, listen to my words, sons of Jacob: I am sowing the seed of my Torah among you, to bear fruit in righteousness and to bring you everlasting glory.' So our ancestors received the Torah but they did not keep it; they received commandments but they did not carry them out. The fruit of your Torah did not perish—it was imperishable because it was yours—but those who had received it perished because they did not take proper care of the seed that had been sown among them. This was contrary to the general rule. Normally, when seed is put in the ground or a ship on the sea or food in a jar, the receptacle survives even if what is put in it perishes. But we, who received the Torah and sinned, perish with our minds which received it whereas your Torah does not perish but survives in all its glory."

While I was framing these thoughts in my mind, I looked round and caught sight of a woman who was weeping and wailing aloud. She was sobbing her heart out; her clothes were torn and there were ashes on her head. I put aside my thoughts and, turning toward her, I said, "Why are you crying? What has made you so miserable?"

"Leave me to my tears and my sobbing, sir," she replied. "My grief is bitter, and I am in deep distress."

"Tell me your troubles."

"For thirty years of my marriage I was barren and childless. I prayed to the Almighty every hour of the day and night throughout those thirty years, and at last he heard my voice and saw my distress. He gave me a son. I was overjoyed, so was my husband and all our neighbors, and we poured out our thanks to the Lord. I worked hard to bring him up properly and when he was grown up I chose a wife for him. I made a lovely party, and we were very happy.

"But when my son went into the bridal chamber he fell down dead. I put out the lights and all my neighbors came to comfort me. I stayed silent for the whole of the next day but that night, when they were all asleep and thought I was also sleeping, I got up and left and came to this field where you see me now. I have made up my mind not to go back to the town but to stay here. I shall not eat or drink but I shall fast and mourn for him uninterruptedly till I die."

At this I abandoned my train of thought and answered her angrily. "You stupid woman! Haven't you noticed that we are all mourning? Don't you know what has happened to us? Zion, the mother of us all, is afflicted with sadness and misery. It is certainly a time for tears: we are all mourners now. You are sad about your son but we are all mourning for our mother. Ask the earth, she will tell you that it is she who ought to be weeping for all her many children. All those who have lived on earth since the beginning and those still to come, they all die, and most of them are doomed to destruction. Who should weep more, you who mourn the loss of one or she who has lost a multitude?

"You may say, 'My sorrow is nothing like the earth's. I have lost the fruit of my womb whom I bore in pain and reared with difficulty. As for the earth, it is only natural that all these multitudes should depart from her just as they came.' But I say to you that just as you gave birth in pain, so the earth too has born her offspring from the beginning: man.

"Contain your grief, then, and bear your disaster bravely. If you accept the justice of the Almighty's decree, in due course you will be reunited with your son and will be praised among women. So go back to the town and to your husband."

"No," she replied, "I am not going back to the town or to my husband. I am staying here to die."

I continued to reason with her. "Don't do it, woman; abandon your plan. Desist because of Zion's misfortunes; be comforted because of Jerusalem's sorrow. Look: our sanctuary is in ruins, our altars are demolished, our Temple destroyed; our worship has been suppressed, our singing silenced, our praises hushed; the light has been extinguished in our sacred lamp, the ark of the covenant has been carried away, our holy vessels have been besmirched; our leading men have been maltreated, our priests burnt alive, our Levites taken captive; our virgins have been defiled and our wives raped, our pious men imprisoned and our saints scattered, our young people enslaved and our fighting men enfeebled. Worst of all, Zion's glorious seal has been broken and she has been handed over to our enemies. So dispel your great grief, cast off your burden of sorrow; may the Lord grant you comfort and may the Almighty soothe your anguish.''

As I spoke to her, suddenly her face began to shine and to flash like lightening. I stood rooted to the spot, too terrified and stunned to go near her. While I was wondering what it meant, she suddenly gave a loud and terrible cry and the whole earth shook. When I looked up, the woman had vanished and instead there was a city built on a massive scale. I exclaimed in terror, ''Where is the angel who came to me before? He is responsible for my terror, and my disillusionment.''

As I spoke the angel appeared. Seeing me lying flat on the ground, almost out of my mind with fear, he took me by the hand, helped me to my feet, and spoke to me reassuringly. ''What's the matter with you? What's the trouble? You look as if you had gone out of your mind.''

''It's because you let me down,'' I said. ''I did exactly as you told me. I came to this field and now I'm seeing things I can't begin to describe.''

''Stand up, and I'll explain everything.''

''I'm listening, Lord,'' I said. ''Only don't leave me. I'm too young to die. I've seen and heard—I don't know what. Or perhaps it's all an illusion or a dream. Please, Lord, tell me about this terrifying vision.''

''Listen to me and I'll tell you all about these things that have frightened you. The Almighty has revealed many secrets to you because he has seen that you are a good man and that you are sincerely sorry for your people and for Zion. This is the explanation of what you saw, the woman who was weeping and whom you tried to comfort, and the tragic story of her son, and then the city that appeared where she had been. The woman you saw is Zion; you see her now as a rebuilt city. She told you that she was barren for thirty years: that is because for three thousand years no sacrifices were offered to her. But at the end of three thousand years Solomon built the Temple and offered sacrifices in it, and that was when the barren woman bore a son.

She said that she worked hard to bring him up: that refers to the time when Jerusalem was the Abode. When she said that her son entered the bridal chamber and died, she was referring to the destruction of Jerusalem. You saw her mourning for her son and you tried to comfort her for her misfortune, and the Almighty, seeing your sincere and heartfelt sympathy for her, showed you her splendor and beauty. That is why I told you to wait for me here. I knew that the Almighty would show you all this. I told you to come to a place where no foundations had been laid for any building because no man-made building could stand in the place where the city of the Almighty was to be revealed.

"Now do not be afraid or disturbed. Go into the city and see its splendor and the magnificence of its buildings so far as your limited powers of seeing and hearing are capable of taking it in. You are more blessed than most men: few have been singled out by the Almighty as you have."

Then he left me and for some time I walked about in the field, and I praised and glorified the Almighty, the Lord of history, for the wonders which he performs at their duly-appointed times.

Philosophy and "Wisdom"

THE MEANING OF THE DIETARY LAWS

The Hellenistic Age was a period of constant interpretation and reinterpretation of the biblical writings. The interpretation of the Mosaic laws had two different aims: to bring the laws up-to-date and make them workable in changed circumstances, and to justify and explain them in Greek terms as a model of inspired and perfect legislation. The first aim is best exemplified in the rabbinic literature, especially the Mishnah; the second, although it is also clearly present in the rabbinic writings, reaches its highest expression in the Alexandrian Jewish writings, and especially in the works of Philo, our fullest witness to the thought and outlook of Hellenistic Jewry.

Philo's prime tool in his labors to harmonize the best of Jewish and Hellenic thought is the allegorical method of interpretation. This technique, borrowed from the work of the Alexandrian literary critics, begins from the assumption of a high degree of subtlety and sophistication in the writer under investigation (in the present case Moses, "the legislator"). "Allegory" means literally "saying something else," and the allegorical method aims to extract hidden meanings from a text. It does not necessarily attempt to invalidate the obvious or traditional meaning, and for all his copious allegorical interpretations of the Mosaic laws, Philo severely criticizes those who go to the extreme of accepting only the allegorical meaning and neglecting the literal observance of the law.

In the Christian church it is this latter tendency which prevailed, and the Christian rejection of the literal observance of the Mosaic law contributed significantly to the eventual rupture of relations between Judaism and Christianity. An important early Christian document on this subject is the so-called *Letter of Barnabas*, which contains a discussion of the dietary laws displaying many common features with the passage before us. Its conclusion is: "In the dietary laws Moses is speaking in spiritual terms, but they [the Jews], being devoted to material things, understood them to refer to food."

The following text is embodied in *The Letter of Aristeas*, where the allegorical interpretation of the laws is put into the mouth of Eleazar, the Jewish high priest. Apart from its intrinsic interest, it serves as a reminder that Philo represents only the culmination of a long process of interpretation and justification of the laws which had been taking place in Alexandria over a very long period of time.

The Letter of Aristeas 130–169

Question: Why, if there was only one creation, are some things considered unclean for food, and some even to the touch?

You have observed the effects of contact and association: by associating with bad men people become corrupted and miserable for the rest of their lives, while if they mix with the wise and sensible they rise from a state of ignorance to a sound life.

Our law-giver defined goodness and justice, and taught us all about them by means of positive precepts as well as prohibitions, and showed us the dangers and divine punishments incurred by the guilty.

First of all, however, he taught that God is one, that his power is displayed in everything and every place is full of his royal might, and that nothing men do secretly on earth escapes his notice, but he sees everything men do clearly, including what is still to happen.

Having explained all this fully he showed that not only what men do but even the evil they merely intend to do is known; throughout his legislation he displays God's power.

Next he showed that all other men except ourselves believe there are many gods, although they themselves are more powerful than the gods they uselessly worship. They make idols of stone and wood and claim that they are images of the inventors of useful discoveries, and they bow down to them in their foolishness. It is absolutely absurd that anyone should be made a god for inventing something; they merely put together things that had already been created and showed that they had some other use, but they did not create the things themselves. To deify men like themselves is useless and foolish. Even today there are men who are more inventive and more learned than the ancients, yet they would never dream of bowing down to them. Yet those who devise these fables consider themselves the wisest of the Greeks. Need I even mention other useless people, like the Egyptians, for example, who put their trust in wild beasts and reptiles and vermin, and bow down to them and sacrifice to them, whether they are alive or dead?

When the law-giver in his wisdom, being endowed with insight by God, had concluded this survey, he fenced us in with impenetrable barriers and iron walls so that we should not mix with any of the other nations but remain pure in body and soul, free from such foolish ideas, worshipping the one powerful God above the whole of creation. That is why the leading priests of the Egyptians, who are very learned and experienced, call us "men of God," a title borne only by those who worship the true God and not by the rest, who are men of food and drink and shelter since they care for nothing else. Our people, however, think nothing of these things but spend their whole lives in contemplation of the might of God.

That is why he hedged us all around with laws of purity in food and drink, in touch, hearing, and sight so that we should not be polluted or corrupted by contact with bad men. It is true that logically everything is the same since the whole world is governed by a single power. Nevertheless in each case there is a deeper reason why we partake of some things and refrain from others. I shall give you one or two examples.

Do not think that it was out of concern for mice and weasels and such that Moses drew up these laws. That is a perverse and unworthy argument. The laws were solemnly drawn up to promote justice, to encourage pure meditation and self-discipline. For instance, the birds which we use are all notably gentle and clean and feed on grain and beans: I mean pigeons, chickens, partridges, geese, and such. But you will find that the forbidden birds are fierce and carnivorous; they use their strength to oppress the others, and unjustly prey on the gentler birds I have mentioned. They even seize lambs and kids and attack men dead and living. By calling these "unclean," he gave us a sign that those for whom the laws were drawn up must practice justice and not oppress others or rob them but guide their lives by justice, just as the tame fowl feed on the grain of the earth and do not oppress and destroy their fellows. If we must not even touch these unclean birds, surely we must take every precaution to prevent ourselves from lapsing into this kind of behavior.

All the dietary laws contain an allegorical teaching. The "parted foot" and "cloven hoof"[1] symbolize the discrimination we must exercise in guiding our actions aright because the strength and activity of the whole body depend on the arms and legs. The symbolic meaning, then, is that we should practice discrimination and pursue justice. And also that we are distinguished from all other men. Most other men defile themselves in their sexual lives, which is a great injustice, and there are whole countries and cities which pride themselves on it; they seduce males and even defile their mothers and daughters. From such men we have been cut off.

Moses also characterizes those who possess this discrimination as endowed with memory. It is clear to those who understand these things that "everything which cleaves the hoof and chews the cud"[2] refers to memory. "Rumination" means recalling both sustenance and life because life is sustained by food. That is why he also exhorts us in scripture when he says, "You shall surely remember the Lord your God who did great and wonderful things in you."[3] When they are properly understood they do seem great and splendid: first of all, the structure of the body; the alimentary system, the division of functions among the organs; and even more important, the organization of the senses, the working and invisible movement of the mind, its practical acuteness and infinite inventiveness. He urges us to remember that all this is in the care of God's creative power. He has appointed each time and place for calling to mind God's power and loving care. For instance, before we eat and drink he tells us to offer the first-fruits to

[1] Leviticus 11:3.
[2] Deuteronomy 14:6.
[3] Cf. Deuteronomy 10:21.

God. He set a sign on our clothing, too, as a reminder. He also commanded us[4] to fix the holy words on our doorposts and gates as a reminder of God, and he explicitly says that we should "bind them as a sign on our hands," clearly indicating that we should perform each action with justice, recalling our creation, and above all, the fear of God. He also says that we should meditate (in word and thought) on God's creation when we lie down and when we rise up; we should ponder the departure and return that take place when we fall asleep and wake up, and consider what a wonderful and incomprehensible transformation this is.

You have now been shown the excellence of the teaching about discrimination and memory, which we have explained as being the meaning of "cleaving the hoof" and "chewing the cud." You see that there is nothing random or haphazard about the laws, but they are aimed at truth and rational behavior. The rules about food, drink, and physical contact are Moses' way of telling us not to do or accept things at random, or to misuse the great power of reason in the pursuit of injustice.

The same could be said about each of the forbidden animals. Each of the creatures on the list—weasels, mice, and so on—has a harmful character. Mice attack and damage everything—not simply to feed themselves, but they also render everything they attack totally unfit for human consumption. Weasels have a further peculiar characteristic: they conceive through the ears and give birth through the mouth. There is a corresponding characteristic in men which is likewise unclean: people who give concrete form in speech to what they have heard through their ears and so get other people into trouble have done something utterly unclean and are themselves thoroughly defiled by their wickedness. It is an unholy thing to brood over other people's destruction. Our law forbids us to harm anybody, by word or deed.

I have given you this brief account to show you that all the regulations are aimed at justice, and that there is nothing haphazard or folkloric about the scriptural rules. Their purpose is that throughout our lives, in all our actions, we should exercise justice toward all men and be mindful of the sovereignty of God. The whole object of the dietary laws and the rules about unclean animals is that they should

[4] Deuteronomy 6:7–9.

point the way toward justice and toward just dealings with our fellow men.

THE WISDOM OF BEN SIRA

The rest of this section takes us out of the world of Greek philosophy and biblical exposition and into the realm of the Jewish "Wisdom Literature." This literature begins in the Bible, especially in the books of Proverbs and Koheleth (Ecclesiastes); although the proverb form is traditional, the personification of the divine Wisdom is a characteristic development of Jewish thought in the Hellenistic Age.

Wisdom, in this literature, is more than an attribute of the human mind. It is an attribute of God himself and one of the manifestations of his will and power on earth. Eventually it comes to be identified with God's Word, the instrument by which he created the world and keeps it in being, and hence also with Torah, which is the embodiment of the Word. There is a beautiful meditation on the role of the Word in the creation at the beginning of the Gospel of John. The Jewish teachings about Wisdom had a powerful appeal among Gnostics and Christians, and in Christian theology Christ is seen as the embodiment of Wisdom and thus takes on something of the role of Torah in Jewish theology. The greatest Byzantine church of Constantinople, Hagia Sophia, is dedicated to Christ as the embodiment of the Holy Wisdom.

The Book of Ben Sira was written in Hebrew in the early second century B.C.E. and translated into Greek later in the same century (for the translator's preface see p. 51). It is a collection of proverbs, maxims, and meditations on a variety of moral themes, of which a selection is given here. The work ends with the celebrated Praise of the Fathers of Old, of which only the opening and closing sections are included here. The last passage, which marks the peroration, is a praise of the contemporary high priest, Simon, son of Onias II.

Like most of the Wisdom Literature, Ben Sira is written in Hebrew poetry. After the work was excluded from the canon of scripture (see the Introduction, p. 9), the Hebrew text fell gradually into disuse although it had once been very popular. It was known to Saadya, in tenth-century Iraq, who says it was equipped with vowel-points and accents like a biblical text; there is no trace of it, however, in medieval Europe. The Hebrew text of a large part of the work was recovered from the Cairo Genizah and more recently from Qumrān and Masada.

The Hebrew text, where it survives, forms the basis of this translation, although the Greek and Syriac translations have also been consulted. The headings from the biblical Wisdom Literature have been added by the present translator.

Ben Sira, selections

The Lord by Wisdom founded the earth. (Proverbs 3:19)

All Wisdom issues from the Lord:
  she is and always has been his.
The seaside sand, the drops of rain,
  and time eternal—who can count?
The height of heaven, the breadth of earth,
  the mighty waters—who can chart?
Before them all was Wisdom made,
  and Understanding long ago.

To whom have Wisdom's roots been shown,
  Or who has known her subtle thoughts?
The Lord alone is wise, and he
  is awesome, seated on his throne.
He made, he saw, he measured her,
  and poured her out upon his works,
In moderation on the rest,
  but in abundance on his own.

The fear of the Lord is the beginning of Wisdom. (Psalm 111:10, Proverbs 9:10)

To fear the Lord brings exultation
  and gladness and a crowning joy.
To fear the Lord delights the heart;
  it gives great joy, and length of days.
Who fears the Lord will die contented,
  and at his death he shall be blessed.

To fear the Lord—yes, that is Wisdom,
  implanted deep in faithful men;
established in the faithful always,
  in faithful men she shall endure.

To fear the Lord is perfect Wisdom,
  who satisfies men with her fruits.
Her house is filled with pleasant things,
  her granaries with rich rewards.

To fear the Lord is Wisdom's crown,
  her gifts are peace, and life, and health,
Great strength and everlasting glory
  she brings to those who cherish her.

To fear the Lord is Wisdom's root,
  and length of days her branches.

The righteous is delivered out of trouble. (Proverbs 11:8)

A wise heart understands a proverb;
  an ear that hears wise words is glad.
As water quells a blazing fire
  so charity atones for sin.
Do good, and it will always help you;
  you may slip, but you shall not fall.

Relieve the oppressed, judge the fatherless, plead for the widow. (Isaiah 1:17)

My son, do not defraud a pauper,
  or mortify a bitter soul.
Do not despise a needy man
  or aggravate his misery.

Do not add insult to misfortune,
  do not reject a poor man's plea;
Do not dismiss him empty handed,
  or turn a haughty back on him.

Look not away from him who asks,
  nor give him cause to curse you.

When broken-hearted men cry out
in anguish, their Creator hears.

Be sure to win the people's love,
and to the rulers bow your head.
Incline your ear to the oppressed,
and humbly answer his "good day."

From his oppressor rescue him
and never judge from cowardice.
Be father to the fatherless,
and like a husband to the widow.
Then God will call you "his own son,"
and love you, and save you from harm.

There is a friend who sticks closer than a brother. (Proverbs 18:24)

Soft conversation brings you friends,
and gentle words acquaintances.
However many friends you have,
make only one your confidant.
Before you make a friend, test him,
and do not lightly trust him.
For some friends only suit themselves,
and when misfortune comes, they go.
And some friends turn to enemies,
and shout your quarrels to the world.
Some friends are only table friends,
who vanish when hard times appear:
so long as you do well they fawn,
they treat your household like their own;
but if you fall on harder times
they turn against you and withdraw.

Keep distance from your enemies,
but also guard against your friends.
A faithful friend is a strong defense,
a treasure, if he can be found.
A faithful friend is beyond price;
there is no measure of his worth.

A faithful friend is a staff of life
which he who fears God shall obtain.
He who fears God respects his friend,
and loves him as he loves himself.

A fool utters all his mind; but a wise man holds it in till afterwards. (Proverbs 29:11)

Never take a judge to court,
for he will always win his case.
Do not go with a cruel man
in case misfortune catches you:
for he will press on heedlessly,
and wreck you through his foolishness.

Do not contradict an angry man,
or travel with him all alone;
a life is nothing in his eyes,
and he will kill you far from help.

Do not consult a fool's advice,
for he will never hold his tongue.
Do nothing secret with a stranger,
or he may use it against you.

Do not reveal your thoughts to all,
or you may suffer later on.

The way of the Lord is strength to the upright. (Proverbs 10:29)

Which is an honored race of men?
A race which fears the Lord their God.
Which is a shameful race of men?
A race which breaks the laws of God.

A prince is honored among men,
but even more he who fears God.
Strangers and paupers, lowly men,
their glory is the fear of God.

The pious poor shall not be scorned,
nor godless rich men honored.

Prince, king, and lord are honored,
 but greater still is he who fears God.
Great men respect a pious slave,
 as men of Wisdom understand.

All good and evil, life and death,
 poverty and riches come from God.
The righteous reaps the gift of God
 and comes to know the Lord's goodwill.

A miser saves and grows in wealth,
 yet this is his assured reward:
when he says, "I can now retire,
 now I'll enjoy my worldly goods"—
he does not realize he will die
 and leave his wealth to other men.

My son, be steadfast in good works,
 and may you live long, fearing God.
Be not impressed by evil-doers;
 trust in the Lord, the savior sure:
for it is easy in God's sight
 suddenly to make a poor man rich.
God's blessing is the righteous' lot;
 in time his hopes will be fulfilled.

Say not: "What more can I desire?"
 or: "What is left for me to want?"
Say not: "I have achieved enough,
 henceforth no harm can trouble me."
As present pleasures drive out sorrows,
 so sorrows cancel pleasures past.
It is an easy thing for God
 to punish or reward men's deeds.

Misfortune cancels out delights;
 men pay their reckoning in the end.
Envy no man before his death,
 for by his end a man is known.

Whither shall I flee from your presence? (Psalm 139:7)

Say not: "I am concealed from God;
up there he'll not remember me.
Among great men I'll pass unseen,
unnoticed in the teeming crowds.
He will not notice me down here,
or pay attention to my deeds.
If I do wrong, what eye can see?
I sin in secret—who shall tell?
And if I do good, who will know?
The day of judgment is far off."

Whoever thinks this lacks good sense;
only a fool would think such things.

Behold the heaven of heavens above,
the earth, the great depth underneath:
they tremble at the Lord's approach
and when he treads on them they quake;
the mountains, and the world's foundations
shudder when he looks at them.

You have made him a little lower than the angels. (Psalm 8:5)

From dust did God create mankind,
and unto dust he turns them back.
He set a limit to their days,
and placed all creatures under them.

With strength he clothed them like his own,
in his own image molded them.
He put their fear upon all flesh
and gave them power over beasts and birds.

He filled their hearts with understanding
and he taught them right and wrong.
He gave them tongues and eyes and ears,
he gave them understanding hearts
to see the splendor of his works
and glory in his wondrous acts.

Declare the glory of his deeds,
sing praises to his holy name.

He offered them the covenant,
bestowed on them the Law of Life;
He made a lasting covenant
and made his judgment known to them.

Their eyes beheld his majesty
and their ears heard his glorious voice.
He said to them: ''Beware of sin,''
and gave them laws to rule their lives.

A time to keep silence and a time to speak. (Koheleth 3:7)

Sometimes reproof is out of place—
then he is wisest who keeps quiet.
To chide a sinner wins no thanks:
if he confesses, spare your wrath.
Doing right with violence is as vain
As a eunuch trying to have a girl.

One man keeps quiet, and counts as wise;
another talks and is despised.
One man keeps quiet for want of words,
another quietly bides his time.

The wise man quietly bides his time,
the boaster takes no note of time.
A man who holds forth is abhorred,
a man who talks too much is hated.

The Lord makes poor and makes rich. (I Samuel 2:7)

Sometimes it pays to suffer ills,
and sometimes riches end in grief.
Sometimes a gift brings no reward,
sometimes a double recompense.
Honor leads sometimes to disgrace,
disgrace can sometimes lead to honor.
Some men buy much for little gold
and end up paying sevenfold.

Wise men are loved for saying little,
While fools' effusiveness is wasted.

The foolishness of man perverts his way. (Koheleth 19:3)

A fool's gift brings you no advantage:
he looks to sevenfold returns.
Little he gives and much complains,
and shouts his grievance to the world;
what he lends one day he asks back the next,
he is despised by God and men.
The fool declares, "I have no friends,
my kindnesses receive no thanks;
those whom I helped are evil-tongued,"
So he becomes a laughing-stock.

A good wife is a crown to her husband. (Proverbs 12:4)

A good wife's husband is a happy man,
the days of his life are doubled.
A worthy wife cares for her husband,
and he ends his days contented.

A good wife is a precious gift,
the lot of the God-fearer.
Be he rich or poor his heart is glad
and his face is always cheerful.

Her grace will give him happiness,
her wisdom makes him healthy.
A quiet woman is a precious gift,
a prudent wife is priceless.

A good housewife is as beautiful
as sunrise on the mountains.
Like the lamp on the holy candlestick
is her lovely face on her fine body.
Like columns of gold on a silver base
are her shapely legs on well-turned ankles.

He who makes haste to be rich shall not go unpunished.
(Proverbs 28:20)

It is better to be poor and healthy
than rich and tortured with disease.
Good health is worth more than fine gold,
a cheerful heart than precious stones.
No wealth is worth more than good health,
no good worth more than a good heart.
Better is death than a wretched life,
eternal rest than constant pain.

Great riches for an invalid
are like the sacrifices which
the pagan idols cannot enjoy,
since they can neither eat nor smell;
like them the wealthy invalid
cannot enjoy his worldly goods;
he contemplates them and he sighs
just like a eunuch with a girl.

He who loves gold shall not go free;
he who hunts gain is led astray.
Many have sold themselves for gold,
and put their trust in precious stones.
It is a trap for foolish men
and simple men are snared by it.

Happy the rich man who is pure,
who has not followed mammon's lure!
Who is he? Let us honor him:
he has achieved a worthy aim.
Who has been rich and not been spoilt?
He has good reason to be proud.
Who had the chance, and did no wrong?
Who could have done harm, but refrained?
His fortunes will be ever sound,
And all men shall declare his praise.

Happy is the man who finds Wisdom and acquires Understanding. (Proverbs 3:13)

A life of liquor and wine is sweet,
but sweeter than either is moral wealth.

Children and works give us permanence,
  but better than either is to be wise.

Cattle and crops may bring increase,
  but richer than both is a woman loved.
Both wine and song gladden the heart,
  but better than either is falling in love.

Flute and harp sweeten a song,
  but sweeter than these is an honest tongue.
Grace and beauty charm the eye,
  but fairer than both are the crops of the field.

A friend or companion will lend support,
  but firmer than these is a prudent wife.
A brother or comrade will save your life,
  but safer than either is righteousness.

Silver and gold give security,
  but sounder than either is common sense.
Wealth and strength lift up the heart,
  but better than both is the fear of God.

He who fears God shall know no lack,
  nor need to look elsewhere for help.
The fear of God is paradise,
  And all that is glorious stands in its shade.

The earth is the Lord's and its fulness. (Psalm 24:1)

I shall recount the works of God,
  and call to mind what I have seen.

By God's own word his works were formed,
  and his will shaped what he decreed.
The rising sun shines over all,
  and the glory of God over all his works.

God's holy ones have not the power
  to tell his wondrous works of might;
he gives his armies special strength
  to stand before his glorious face.

He pierces the deep and the heart of man,
and all their secrets he surveys;
for knowledge of all things is with God,
and he sees what will be forevermore.

The past and future he declares,
the deepest secrets he reveals.
No knowledge is denied to him,
nothing escapes his eagle eye.

His powerful Wisdom stands secure,
and ever has been so, unchanged;
nothing is added or removed,
he need consult no one's advice.

His works are truly beautiful,
as fair as blossoms to behold.
All things exist forever, and
contribute to each other's needs.

All things are different and distinct,
but nothing is superfluous.
They harmonize and interact,
their beauty never fails or palls.

PRAISE OF THE FATHERS OF OLD

I sing the praise of famous men,
of our fathers who begot us.
Greatness and glory from the Lord
are theirs from days of old.

World rulers in their royalty,
men famous for their power;
men gifted with discernment and
all-seeing prophecy;
accomplished rulers of the state
and understanding leaders;
enlightened teachers of the Law,
guardians of the traditions;

able composers of the Psalms,
compilers of the Proverbs;
men of great worth and girt with strength,
secure in their habitations:
all these were honored in their time,
and in their day had glory.

Some of them left behind a name
that men might sing their praises;
others left no memorial—
they faded with their passing:
these were as though they had not lived,
both they and their descendants.

But there were men of piety
whose hope shall not prove empty;
they left a precious covenant
unto their children's children.

Their memory stands for all time,
nor are their deeds forgotten;
their bodies in peace were laid to rest,
their fame survives forever.
The congregation sings their praise,
the people laud their wisdom.

ENOCH: an example of knowledge for all time;
he walked with the Lord and was taken.[1]

NOAH, the righteous and perfect man:[2]
he alone survived destruction.
Thanks to him mankind survived,
his covenant signaled the end of the flood,
an eternal sign from God
that he would never destroy mankind.[3]

[1] Genesis 5:24.
[2] Genesis 6:9.
[3] Genesis 9:11ff.

ABRAHAM, "father of many nations,"[4]
a man of unblemished record:
he kept the Almighty's commands
and made a covenant with him;
he sealed it in his flesh,
he was tested and found faithful;
therefore God swore him an oath
to bless nations through his descendants,
to multiply them like the sand,
to exalt them like the stars,[5]
to make their home from sea to sea,
from the river to the ends of the earth.[6]

ISAAC was promised the same
for his father Abraham's sake.[7]

ISRAEL inherited the blessings
bestowed upon his ancestors.
He received the title of firstborn
and came into his inheritance.
He was divided into twelve
and these became the tribes.

From him descended a man
who charmed all living beings,
beloved of God and men:
MOSES of blessed memory.
He was called "the man of God,"[8]
he was bold and fearless;
he worked wonders by his word
and he bravely faced a king.
God gave him command of his people
and revealed to him his glory.[9]

[4] Genesis 17:5.
[5] Genesis 22:17ff.
[6] Psalm 72:8.
[7] Genesis 26:3f.
[8] Psalm 90:1.
[9] Exodus 30:18ff.

He chose him out of all mankind
for his humility and faith.
He let him hear his voice
and summoned him into the cloud.
He handed him the law,
Wisdom, life, Torah,
to teach his rules to Jacob,
his law and judgment to Israel.[10]

[*Ben Sira continues with the praise of Aaron, Phinehas, Joshua and Caleb, the Judges, Samuel, David, Solomon, Elijah, Elisha, Hezekiah and Isaiah, Josiah, Jeremiah, Ezekiel, Job, the Twelve Prophets, Zerubbabel, Jeshua, son of Jozadak, and Nehemiah. He concludes with a description of the glory of the high priest of his own day*:]

Greater than his brothers, the glory of his people,
is Simeon, son of Johanan the priest.
Under him the Temple was repaired
and fortified like a royal palace;
the city was strengthened against its enemies
and a vast reservoir was dug.

How glorious he is when he comes out of the shrine,
when he emerges from the sanctuary:
like a bright star among the clouds,
like the full moon on a feast day,
like the sun blazing on the shrine,
like a rainbow in the clouds,
like a summer flower against the foliage,
like a lily growing by a stream,
like the cedars of Lebanon,
like incense in the censer,
like a finely-worked gold cup
adorned with precious stones,
like a flourishing olive tree
rich in branches and berries;
clothed in splendid robes,
wrapped in magnificent splendor,

[10] Cf. Psalm 147:19.

lighting the courtyard with his brilliance
  as he climbs the steps to the altar,
standing by the woodpile,
  receiving the offerings from his brothers,
surrounded by his sons
  like young cedars of Lebanon,
the sons of Aaron in their glory
  surrounding him like willows,
holding the Lord's burnt offerings
  before the whole congregation of Israel.

THE WISDOM OF SOLOMON

The Wisdom of Solomon, a typical representative of the Wisdom Literature, contains some of the most attractive and fascinating passages of this kind. Although it seems probable that it was written in Greek, much of it is composed in the style of Hebrew poetry, with the pairs of parallel lines characteristic of ancient Hebrew verse.

The work falls broadly into three main parts. The first, from which the first of our extracts is taken, is concerned with sin and death. God intended man to be immortal but man by his own sin brought death into the world. The author insists that death is not to be taken at its face value. The righteous, even if they die young or childless, are destined for a life of immortality while the wicked, even if they seem to prosper, will eventually be punished.

The second part consists of a panegyric in praise of Wisdom which is thoroughly typical of this literature. From this is taken Solomon's prayer, which, like other prayers in this anthology, is a Hellenistic prayer put into the mouth of a biblical character. It takes its inspiration from the prayer of Solomon in 1 Kings 3:6–9, in which Solomon prays not for long life or wealth but for understanding to rule the people wisely. Its opening words identify Wisdom with the Word by which the world was created, and in the closing words Wisdom is seen as the only means of salvation.

The third part (not quoted here) is an exposition of the events surrounding the Exodus from Egypt, based once again on the theme of rewards and punishments. It was because of their sins that the Egyptians were punished and thus, indirectly, that the Israelites were rescued. This section is interrupted by an extended and interesting excursus on the origins and evils of idolatry.

Like several of the other Wisdom writings, the book is attributed to King Solomon. The real author is unknown, but it was suggested in antiquity that it was written by Philo. Though this suggestion is not to be taken seriously, there are similarities between the outlook of the author (or authors) of the Wisdom of Solomon and that of Philo.

Wisdom of Solomon 1–3, *adridged;* 9

WICKEDNESS LEADS TO DEATH

Earthly judges, cherish justice
  and seek the Lord with sincerity.
Those who trust him find him,
  but crooked thoughts are a barrier.
Wisdom cannot abide deceit or evil,
  education flees from foolishness and insincerity.
Wisdom loves man,
  but does not tolerate arrogant remarks.
God's spirit fills the world
  and sees into every heart,
so no impious remark passes unnoticed:
  it will be sought out and punished.

Do not court death by misguided actions
  or tempt destruction by your deeds.
God did not create death,
  he is not glad when the living perish;
he formed everything for life,
  and death had no dominion;
but the ungodly fell in love with him
  and wooed him like a friend,
they made a compact with death
  and they reap their proper fate.

This is their false logic,
listen to what they say:
Our life is short and miserable,
and death is a one-way trip,
Chance put us here on earth,
and there's nothing afterwards.
Breath is just so much air
and the brain depends on the heartbeat,
when that stops we'll be finished,
and in no time at all we're forgotten.
So let's make the most of it while we're here,
drink our fill and wallow in perfume,
gather our rosebuds while we may,
and cover the countryside with our litter.
It's our right, after all,
and you're only young once.
Might is right, weakness is useless,
so to hell with the poor and the old.
Gang up against godly folk:
they're always getting at us,
Trying to run our lives for us,
telling us we're doing wrong.
They live pretty weird lives themselves,
they avoid us like the plague.
They claim that God looks after them:
well, we'll soon see who's right:
We'll torture them and kill them
and see if their God saves them.

This is how they reason because they are blinded by evil,
and do not understand God's secret plan.
He created man to be immortal,
he formed him in his own image,
It was the Devil's spite that brought death into the world,
and those who choose to follow him will experience it.
But God holds the souls of the just in his hand:
no harm can touch them.

They may appear to perish,
but really they are at peace.
God has tested them, and found them worthy,
they will live with him in truth and love.
But the wicked will reap their just rewards,
they will perish miserably and be forgotten.

SOLOMON'S PRAYER FOR WISDOM

God of our fathers, merciful Lord, who created all things by your Word and by your Wisdom made man to rule over your other works and to govern the world with holiness and justice, give me Wisdom, who is enthroned beside you, and do not judge me unworthy to serve you. I am your slave, the son of your maidservant, a weak, short-lived man with little power to understand law and justice. Even the most perfect man is nothing without your Wisdom. You have chosen me to be king of your people and judge of your sons and daughters; you have told me to build a temple on your holy mountain and an altar in the city you have made your home, a copy of the sacred tabernacle you prepared from the beginning. Wisdom is with you, she knows everything you do, she was present when you created the world, she knows what you approve of and what is in accord with your commands. Send her down from the holy heavens, from your glorious throne, to labor by my side and show me what is pleasing to you. She knows and understands everything; she will guide my actions with sense and protect me with her splendor. Then whatever I do will be acceptable: I shall judge your people with justice and be worthy of my father's throne. How can any man know God's plan? How can he perceive God's will? We poor mortals have inadequate brains; our best-laid plans fail. A corruptible body weighs down our soul, our inventive minds are trammeled by our earthly form. We have difficulty figuring out what is close at hand here on earth; how can we track down what is in heaven? How can we know your will unless you give us Wisdom and send your Holy Spirit down to us? Only thus can men be set on the right path and discover what is pleasing to you. Only by Wisdom can they be saved.

TWO WISDOM POEMS

As has already been mentioned, most of the Wisdom Literature is poetic in form. The two Hebrew poems which follow are specimens of the short poems in praise of Wisdom which were probably numerous in antiquity.

The first is addressed to the people of Israel and dates from the period of gloom following the destruction of the Temple. It blames the disaster on the neglect of Wisdom, who is here clearly identified with Torah. It has been suggested that it was produced in the circle of Johanan ben Zakkai, the founder of Rabbinic Judaism, although this is by no means certain. It is preserved in Greek translation in the Book of Baruch, a miscellaneous collection of literary fragments of the period.

The second poem is partly an autobiographical description of the poet's discovery of Wisdom, to which there are parallels in the middle section of the Wisdom of Solomon. The poet appears to be a teacher addressing his public. He describes his relationship with Wisdom in openly erotic terms, for which he later apologizes. This idea of a mystical sexual union with the divine Wisdom is found in other texts as well and recurs in the medieval and later Jewish mystical literature.

The poem has come down to us in a collection of short poems which form a kind of appendix to Ben Sira. The ancient versions have considerably toned down the sexual imagery but the original Hebrew has been recovered in a manuscript from Qumrān, which also shows (as had been suspected) that the poem is an acrostic, each line beginning with a successive letter of the Hebrew alphabet.

I Baruch 3:9–4:4

EXHORTATION TO WISDOM

Hear, O Israel, the commandments of life,
  be attentive to Wisdom and understanding.

Israel, why these long years in hostile lands
  and the taint of foreign exile?
Why do they speak of you as dead?

You have forgotten the Fountain of Wisdom.
If you had followed God's road
  you would enjoy peace forever.
Learn where to find Wisdom and strength,
  long life, understanding, and peace.

Who knows the place where the treasure is hidden?

What has become of the kings of the earth?
  They lorded it over the birds and the beasts,
  they stored up gold and silver—
  a human weakness but a vain pursuit—
  and they built untold monuments.
Death took them, they disappeared,
  and younger men came in their place,
but did they have understanding or Wisdom?
  No, not even their children were wise.

Do not seek her in Canaan or Teman—
children of Hagar, merchants of Midian,
spinners of stories and seekers of truth,
not one of them knows Wisdom's way.
Israel, God's world is vast,
  boundlessly wide, endlessly high.
Once, long ago, there were giants,
  huge men, who won all their wars;
God did not choose them, he did not give them Wisdom,
  and they perished through their own lack of sense.

Who can go up to heaven to fetch her,
  or buy her far over the seas?
No man can know Wisdom's ways.
But he who knows all things knows them:
  he made the world and all its creatures,
  he sent the light and it obeyed him,
  the stars keep bright watch in response to his Word.
He is our God and he has no equal.
  Wisdom was his possession,
  but he gave her to his servant Jacob.

This is the book of God's eternal law,
to follow it is life, to abandon it, death.
Turn, Jacob, and follow its bright light;
do not abandon its glory to strangers.

Happy are we, Israel,
who know what is pleasing to God!

Ben Sira 51:13–30

THE QUEST FOR WISDOM

A s an innocent youth I wooed her.
B eautifully she came to me: I plumbed her depths.
C allow youth yielded to ripeness,
D evotedly I dogged her footsteps.
E ars strained to catch each whisper,
F lexing my manhood to her service,
G reedily I sucked her milk,
H ungrily I clung to my teacher.
I felt no hesitation, no remorse.
J oy seized me as I unveiled her secret parts,
K eenly I parted her gates and entered,
L ove for her set my loins on fire—
M y mistress, my treasure!

N ow therefore I praise God who put words on my lips.

O ignorant men, let me be your teacher:
P repare to shoulder the burden of knowledge,
Q uench your thirst at Wisdom's fountain,
R efresh yourselves at no expense.
S ee for yourselves how easily I have found relief.
T rust me, be glad, and do not be shocked by my song.
U phold the truth, and lead the virtuous life:
V irtue brings rich rewards.

History

THE CONTEST OF THE THREE YOUNG MEN AND THE DECREE OF DARIUS

The Greek Ezra presents a free Greek translation of the story of the sack of the Temple in Jerusalem by Nebuchadnezzar (586 B.C.E.) and of its eventual rebuilding, which is told in the biblical books of 2 Chronicles, Ezra, and Nehemiah. In some respects it agrees with the biblical story but in certain details it represents a different tradition. The most important divergence is the decree of King Darius (521–486 B.C.E.) permitting a group of Jewish exiles under Zerubbabel to rebuild the city and the Temple, which clashes with the account of the return under Cyrus (d. 529 B.C.E.). This passage is introduced by another story, which is likewise not found in the biblical books, in which three young men of the king's bodyguard hold a competition to name the strongest thing in the world. The young man who wins the contest with his celebrated Praise of Truth is identified with Zerubbabel.

It is generally accepted now that the Greek Ezra is not based on Ezra and Nehemiah but represents an independent tradition. The two versions of the story circulated side by side, and its popularity is demonstrated by the fact that it was extensively exploited by the historian Josephus in the first century C.E. What reasons made the Jewish authorities accept Ezra and Nehemiah and reject the Greek Ezra from the canon of sripture we can only surmise.

The Greek Ezra (1 *Esdras*) 3–4

One night King Darius held a great feast for all the officials who served him, for all the members of his household, for all the princes of Media and Persia, and for all the satraps, commanders, and governors who served him in the hundred and twenty-seven provinces from India to Ethiopia. When they had eaten and drunk their fill and gone home, King Darius went to his bedchamber and slept.

Meanwhile, the three young men who made up the king's personal bodyguard said to one another, "Let us each name one thing which he considers to be the strongest. Whichever of us puts forward the wisest argument shall be rewarded with great gifts and honors by King Darius. He shall be dressed in purple, drink from a gold cup, sleep on a bed of gold, drive in a chariot with gold-trimmed bridles, wear a headdress of fine linen and a chain around his neck. He shall sit next to Darius in recognition of his wisdom and be called Darius' kinsman."

So each of them wrote out his saying, sealed it with his seal, and put it under the king's pillow. "When the king gets up," they said, "he will be given the notes, and whoever is judged by the king and the three princes of Persia to have written the wisest saying will be the victor."

The first wrote: *Wine is strongest.*

The second wrote: *The king is strongest.*

The third wrote: *Women are strongest, but Truth is victorious over all.*

When the king rose he was given the notes and he read them. He summoned all the princes of Persia and Media, the satraps, the commanders, the governors, and the senior officers. He sat on the royal throne of judgment and had the sayings read out to them. Then he said, "Call the young men, and let them explain their sayings." So they were called and came, and he said to them, "State your reasons for writing what you have written."

The first, who had said that wine was strongest, spoke first. "My lords," he said, "consider how strong is wine. It befuddles the wits of everyone who drinks it. King and orphan, slave and free man, poor and rich, it makes them all alike. It turns all thoughts to merriment and joy and drives out all memory of sorrow or debt. It enriches every heart, so that men care nothing for king or satrap. It makes men talk in millions. When men drink, they forget their love for friends and family and readily draw their swords: but when they wake from their drunkenness they do not remember what they have done. Is not wine, then, the strongest thing, my lords, since it forces men to behave like this?''

When he had said this much, he stopped speaking.

Then the second, who had said that the king was strongest, said, ''My lords, consider how strong are men who rule over land and sea and everything in them. Yet the king is even stronger. He is their overlord and rules over them, and they obey his every command. If he orders them to make war on one another they do so, and if he sends them out to fight against the enemy, they conquer mountains, walls, and towers. They kill and are killed, yet they do not disobey the king. If they win the war, they bring all their spoils to the king. It is the same with those who have nothing to do with soldiering and wars, who farm the land; when they harvest their crops they bring them to the king, and they compel each other to pay him tribute. He is only one man but if he orders them to kill, they kill; if he orders them to spare, they spare; if he orders them to attack, they attack; if he orders them to ravage, they ravage; if he orders them to build, they build; if he orders them to cut down, they cut down; if he orders them to plant, they plant. So all his people and his armies obey him. Even when he sleeps or eats or drinks or rests they keep watch over him; no one may go off and attend to his own business or disobey him in anything. Surely then, my lords, the king must be the strongest since he is obeyed in this way.''

When he had finished speaking, the third, who had spoken of women and truth, began his speech. ''My lords, the king is indeed great, and men are great, and wine is strong. But who is it who rules over them and controls them? Women! The king was born of a woman and all those who rule by land and sea were born of women. They also raised those who planted the vineyards from which the wine comes. They make men's clothes and bring them honor. Without women men cannot exist. Men who have amassed gold and silver and other valuables, if they catch sight of a beautiful woman, forget their possessions and gaze at her open-mouthed; they desire her more than gold or silver or all other valuables. A man leaves his own father who reared him, and his own country, and lives with his wife. He gives himself up wholly to his wife and does not remember his father or his mother or his country. Here is another proof that women dominate us: do we not toil and labor and give everything we earn to our wives? A man takes his sword and travels abroad, robbing and stealing, sailing seas and rivers and braving lions and darkness; and when he has stolen, robbed, and plundered, he brings his booty home to his love.

"So a man loves his wife more than he loves his father and mother. Many men have gone out of their minds for women or become slaves for their sake. Others have died or committed crimes or sins for women. If you do not believe me, consider this: The king is mighty and powerful, and no nation dares touch him. Yet I myself saw Apame, the king's concubine, daughter of the illustrious Bartakos, sitting at the king's right hand and taking the crown off the king's head and putting it on her own. She slapped him with her left hand and the king simply stared at her, gazing open-mouthed. If she smiles at him, he smiles, but if she frowns at him, he fawns and flatters her to win her favor. Can you deny, my lords, that women are strong since they behave like this?"

At this the king and the nobles looked at one another. Then he began to speak about Truth. "My lords, women are strong, are they not? Great is the earth, high is the sky, and swift is the sun in its course, for it runs the circuit of heaven and returns to its place in a single day. And is he not great who rules all these? But Truth is great and stronger than all things. All the earth praises Truth and heaven blesses her. All created things shake and tremble but with her there is no injustice. There is injustice in wine, in the king, and in women; all mankind are unjust and everything they do is unjust. If there is no truth in them, they perish for their injustice. Truth endures and is strong forever; she lives and rules for all time. She does not respect persons or take bribes; she does what is right and abhors injustice and wrong, and all men approve of her doings. There is nothing unjust in her judgment; hers is the strength, the kingdom, the power, and the majesty of all ages. Blessed be the God of Truth."

With this he finished speaking and all the people shouted aloud,

"Great is Truth, and strongest of all."

Then the king said to him, "If there is anything you desire besides what was decided, ask for it and I shall give it to you since you have proved to be the wisest: you will sit next to me and be called my kinsman."

"Your Majesty," he replied, "remember the vow you made on the day you became king: to rebuild Jerusalem and to send there all the objects which were taken from Jerusalem which Cyrus put aside to send back when he swore that he would destroy Babylon. You vowed to rebuild the Temple, which the Edomites burned when Judea was ravaged by the Chaldeans. This is the favor I ask you, Your Majesty, to perform with kingly generosity: I beg you to make good the vow which with your own mouth you vowed to the King of heaven."

Then King Darius stood up and kissed him and wrote letters for him to all the treasurers and governors and commanders and satraps, instructing them to afford a safe passage to him and to all those who went with him to rebuild Jerusalem. He also wrote letters to all the governors in Coele-Syria and Phoenicia and in Lebanon, telling them to transport timber from Lebanon to Jerusalem and to help him rebuild the city. He wrote guarantees of freedom for all those Jews who were to go up and settle in Judea, forbidding any officer, governor, or satrap to interfere with them and granting immunity from taxation to all the land they should acquire. He ordered the Edomites to hand over the Jewish villages they had occupied. He decreed that twenty talents should be given annually for the building of the Temple until it was completed, and another ten talents annually for burnt offerings to be sacrificed daily on the altar according to the commandments, and that all those who went from Babylonia to rebuild the city and their descendants after them should have their freedom. As for the priests who went, he issued orders for their maintenance to be given to them as well as the priestly vestments in which they would serve; and for the Levites he ordered their dues to be paid to them until the Temple was completed and Jerusalem rebuilt. He ordered lands and money to be given to those who defended the city. He also decreed that all the objects which Cyrus had set aside and had stipulated in his decrees should be sent back to Jerusalem from Babylonia.

As soon as the young man went outside, he turned toward Jerusalem, raised his eyes, and praised the King of heaven in these words:

"From you comes victory, from you comes wisdom, yours is the glory, and I am your servant. Blessed are you, who have given me wisdom, and to you I give thanks, O Lord of our fathers."

Then he went to Babylon, taking the letters with him, and told his fellow Jews everything. They too praised the God of their fathers because he had given them freedom and liberty to go up and rebuild Jerusalem and the Temple which is called by his name. And they feasted with music and merrymaking for seven days.

THE HISTORY OF THE HASMONEANS

The First Book of Maccabees is the most imposing of the surviving examples of Hellenistic Jewish historical writing, with the exception of the works of Josephus, who paraphrases 1 Maccabees extensively in Books XII and XIII of his *Jewish Antiquities*. It displays a striking blend of Jewish and Greek influences: as a work of history it is firmly in the Greek tradition; events are described with care and accuracy, they are placed in a chronological framework and supplied with copies of official documents. On the other hand, the historical narrative is interspersed with Hebrew poems and there is a constant emphasis on Jewish religious values. The word "God" is never used, being always replaced by "Heaven."

The period covered runs (after a short preface about the death of Alexander) from the accession of Antiochus Epiphanes in 175 B.C.E. to the death of Simeon in 135—that is, the period of the establishment and consolidation of Hasmonean rule.

Even though the original Hebrew text was lost, the story of the war against the Jewish Hellenizers and Syrian Greeks remained popular among Jews throughout the Middle Ages and was remembered especially at the festival of Hanukkah, the establishment of which is recorded in this book.

The present translation is based on the text found in Greek Bibles but the Hebrew names have been restored wherever possible. The passages omitted in this translation describe successively the campaigns of Judah after the rededication of the Temple, the history of his successor, Jonathan, and the reign of Simeon to his murder at Jericho in 135 B.C.E. The book ends with the succession of his son John.

1 Maccabees 1–4; 8–9; 14

ALEXANDER OF MACEDON

Alexander, the son of Philip of Macedon, came from Greece, defeated Darius, king of the Medes and Persians, and succeeded him as king. He fought many battles, capturing fortresses and killing rulers; he pressed on to the ends of the earth and pillaged many peoples. When he had subdued the world he became proud and overbearing. He had gathered a powerful army and become the ruler of lands and peoples and provinces that now served him.

When he realized he was about to die, he took to his bed and summoned his principal officers, who had all been his comrades since their youth, and divided his kingdom among them. Alexander had reigned for twelve years when he died. His officers ruled their respective provinces, and after his death they all assumed the royal diadem, as their sons did after them. This situation continued for many years, and the rulers caused a greal deal of hardship.

ANTIOCHUS EPIPHANES

Out of them came an evil shoot, Antiochus Epiphanes, son of King Antiochus, who had been taken to Rome as a hostage and come back as king in the year 137 of the Greek era.[1] At that time there were some evil-doers in Israel who tried to win popularity for a policy of integration with the surrounding nations. It was because the Jews had kept themselves aloof for so long, they claimed, that so many hardships had befallen them. They acquired a following and applied to Antiochus, who authorized them to introduce the Greek way of life. They built a Greek gymnasium in Jerusalem and even had themselves uncircumcised, in repudiation of the holy covenant. Thus they affected Greek ways and committed themselves to a policy of wrongdoing.

When, in his opinion, Antiochus' rule was thoroughly established in Syria, he decided to gain control of Egypt as well so as to rule over two kingdoms. He advanced into Egypt with a heavy force of chariots, elephants, and horsemen and with a large fleet, and made war on

[1] 175 B.C.E.

Ptolemy, king of Egypt. Ptolemy turned and fled and there were heavy casualties. The Syrians captured the fortified cities and pillaged the land of Egypt.

In the year 143,[2] after conquering Egypt, Antiochus turned and led his large army against Israel and Jerusalem. He had the arrogance to enter the sanctuary and carry off the golden altar, the lamp-stand, all the accessories, the table of the shewbread; the cups, bowls, and golden censers; the veil, the crowns, and the golden ornaments on the Temple facade. He took the silver, the gold, and the precious plate, and all the hidden treasure he could discover and returned to his own land.

Israel was filled with lamentation;
the rulers and elders mourned.
Youths and maidens languished,
and the women's beauty faded.
Bridegrooms broke into weeping,
and brides went into mourning.
Even the land sighed for her people,
and the house of Jacob was clothed with shame.

Two years later Antiochus sent one of his principal tax-collectors into Judea, and he arrived at Jerusalem with a strong force. Being a cunning man, he addressed them peacefully so that they trusted him. Then he suddenly attacked the city, conquered it, and killed many of the inhabitants. He plundered the city and burnt it, demolished the houses and destroyed the walls. They took the women and children captive and appropriated the cattle. They fortified the city of David with a great wall and strong towers and made it their citadel; inside they installed a crowd of evil, lawless men. They laid in a store of arms and provisions and they also collected there the spoils of Jerusalem. The place now became a dangerous threat; it menaced the sanctuary and harassed the people.

They shed innocent blood round about the shrine,
and defiled the sanctuary.
The people of Jerusalem fled from them,

[2] 169 B.C.E.

and she was settled by strangers;
she was estranged from her offspring,
and her children forsook her.
Her sanctuary became desolate as a wilderness,
her festivals turned into mourning,
her sabbaths into shame,
her honor into contempt.
Her dishonor was low as her glory had been high,
and her former magnificence turned to degradation.

Antiochus then issued an edict saying that all his subjects were to form a single people and that they should give up their individual customs. The Gentiles all acceded to the king's command, and even among the Jews many people accepted this form of worship, sacrificing to idols and profaning the Sabbath. The king also sent written instructions to Jerusalem and the other cities of Judea ordering the adoption of foreign customs. They were to stop the whole burnt offerings, sacrifices and drink offerings in the sanctuary, profane the sabbaths and festivals, and desecrate the sanctuary and the holy things. In addition, they were to erect altars and sacred groves and shrines to idols and to sacrifice pigs and other unclean animals. They were to abandon circumcision and practice everything that was unclean and profane so that they should forget the Torah and subvert all the commandments. Whoever refused to obey the king's command was to be put to death. He wrote in these terms to his entire kingdom, appointed supervisors, and commanded all the citizens of Judea to sacrifice. Large numbers of the people who had abandoned the Torah went over, and they instituted a reign of terror, driving the faithful Jews into hiding.

On the fifteenth of Kislev in the year 145[3] they set up an "abomination of desolation" on the altar and put up altars throughout the cities of Judea, and made the people sacrifice at the doors of their houses and in the streets. They tore up and burnt the scrolls of the Torah which they found, and whoever was found in possession of a book of the covenant, if he was an observer of the Torah, was sentenced to death in accordance with the king's decree. This was how, month after month, they terrorized the Jews in the cities. On the twenty-fifth day

[3] 168 B.C.E.

of the month they sacrificed on the altar which had been placed on top of the altar of burnt offering. In accordance with the king's decree, whenever they found a child which had been circumcised they hung the baby round its mother's neck and put her to death together with her whole family and the person who had performed the circumcision. Nevertheless, many Jews stood firm and resolved not to eat unclean meat and to die rather than be defiled and profane the holy covenant. And die they did. It was a time of great suffering for the Jews.

MATTATHIAH'S REVOLT

There was a man in those days called Mattathiah, son of John, son of Simeon, a priest of the line of Joarib, from Jerusalem. He lived in Modiin, and he had five sons: John, surnamed Gaddis; Simeon, who was called Thassis; Judah, who was called Maccabee; Eleazar, who was called Auaran; and Jonathan, who was called Apphos.

When Mattathiah saw the sacrilege which was being performed in Judea and Jerusalem, he said, "Alas, why was I born to behold the ruin of my people and of the Holy City, to sit still and watch it fall into the hands of enemies, the sanctuary into the hands of strangers?

Her house is like that of a man in disgrace;
her precious plate is taken in spoil.
Her infants are slain in the streets,
her youths by the enemy's sword.
What nation has the kingdom not occupied,
of what nation not taken the spoils?
Her ornaments have all been taken away,
instead of a free woman she is now a slave.
Our Temple, our pride and our glory, is laid waste
and profaned by the heathen. Why should we live?"

Then Mattathiah and his sons tore their clothes, dressed in sackcloth, and went into deep mourning.

When the king's officers came to Modiin to make the people sacrifice, many of them obeyed, but Mattathiah and his sons kept themselves apart. The king's officers turned to Mattathiah and said, "You are an important man in this city, you belong to the ruling class, and you have sons and brothers to support you; come up now and be the first to carry out the king's decree, as all the nations have done, and all the people of Judea and all those who remained in Jerusalem. If you do so, you and your sons will be enrolled among the king's friends; you will all receive high honors, rich rewards of silver and gold, and many other benefits besides."

To this Mattathiah replied resoundingly, "Even if all the nations in the kingdom forsake their ancestral religion and submit to the king's demands, my sons, my brothers and I will, nevertheless, follow the covenant of our fathers. Heaven forbid that we should ever abandon the Torah and the commandments. We will not obey the king if it means deviating by a hair's breadth from our own forms of worship."

No sooner had he finished speaking than a Jew stepped forward in full view of all to sacrifice on the pagan altar in obedience to the royal command. Mattathiah was outraged at this sight. He trembled with fury. In a fit of righteous indignation he rushed forward and cut the traitor down on the very altar. Then he killed the officer sent by the king to enforce sacrifice and demolished the altar. Thus he showed his fervent zeal for the law, just as Phinehas did when he killed Zimri, son of Salu.[4] "Follow me," he shouted through the town, "everyone who is zealous for the Torah and aims to uphold the covenant." Then he and his sons took to the hills, leaving their belongings behind in the town.

Meanwhile, large numbers of people who wanted to maintain their religion and the Torah had gone down to live in the desert. They took their children, their wives, and their cattle with them, since they could bear their hardships no longer. Word soon reached the king's officers and the garrison in David's citadel in Jerusalem that men who had defied the king's edict had gone into hiding in the desert. A large body of men immediately went out to follow them and took up positions opposite them. They prepared to attack them on the Sabbath. "There is still time," they shouted; "come out, obey the king's command and your lives will be spared." "We will not come out," the Jews replied; "we will not obey the king's command or profane the Sabbath." At that the attack was launched, but the Jews did nothing to defend themselves. They did not even hurl stones or barricade their caves. "Let us all meet death with a clear conscience," they said; "we call heaven

[4] Numbers 25:6–15.

and earth to witness that this slaughter is unjust." So they were attacked and massacred on the Sabbath; about one thousand men, women, and children along with their cattle.

When Mattathiah and his comrades heard the news they were overcome with grief. They said to one another, "If we all do as our brothers have done and refuse to fight the Gentiles, not only for our laws and customs, but for our very lives, then they will soon wipe us off the face of the earth." So they decided that day that if they were attacked on the Sabbath they would fight back rather than be wiped out like their brothers in the caves.

Then they were joined by a company of Hasidim, pillars of Israel, who had volunteered to fight for the Torah. Their strength was also added to by large numbers of refugees from the troubles. Now that they had an organized force they turned on the wrongdoers and renegades, and those who escaped their onslaughts took refuge with the Gentiles.

Mattathiah and his comrades then swept through the countryside, pulling down the pagan altars and forcibly circumcising all the uncircumcised Jewish boys they could find. They hunted down their oppressive enemies, and their cause flourished. So they saved the Torah from the Gentiles and their kings and broke the power of the tyrant.

THE DEATH OF MATTATHIAH

When the time came for Mattathiah to die, he said to his sons, "Tyranny still stands firm against us, and it is a time of disaster and havoc. It is up to you, my sons, to fight bravely for the Torah and to give your lives for the covenant of your fathers. Remember the deeds they did in their generations, and great glory and eternal fame shall be yours. Abraham stood firm under trial and he was credited with righteousness. Joseph, in times of hardship, kept the commandments and became lord of Egypt. Our father, Phinehas, fought unstintingly and received a covenant of everlasting priesthood. Joshua kept the Torah and he became a Judge in Israel. Caleb bore witness against the majority and was rewarded with a share in the land. David remained loyal and was rewarded with an everlasting kingdom. Elijah fought steadfastly for the Torah and he was taken up bodily to heaven. Hananiah, Azariah, and Mishael had faith and they were rescued from the fiery furnace. Daniel kept his integrity and was saved from the lions. Follow their example, generation by generation; no one who trusts in Heaven shall ever lack strength. Do not fear a wicked man's words; all his success will end in filth and worms. He may be held in awe today but tomorrow he will be gone without trace; he will have returned to the dust and all his schemes will have come to nothing. You, my sons, must draw your courage and strength from the Torah for by it you will win great glory.

"Your brother, Simeon, here, I know to be blessed with great insight; always listen to him and treat him as your father. Judah Maccabee has been strong and brave from his childhood; he shall be your commander in the field and fight his people's battles. Gather to your side all those who revere the Torah and avenge your people's wrongs. Repay the Gentiles in their own coin and always keep to the commandments."

Mattathiah blessed them and passed away. He died in the year 146,[5] and his sons buried him in the family tomb in Modiin. He was deeply mourned by all Israel.

JUDAH MACCABEE

Judah Maccabee came forward to take his father's place. He had the support of all his brothers and his father's followers, and they carried on the fight for Israel with spirit.

He enhanced his people's glory.
Like a giant he donned his breastplate,
  and girt himself with weapons of war.
Battle upon battle he fought,
  protecting his army with his sword.
He was like a lion in his exploits,
  like a young lion roaring for prey.
He hunted and tracked down the lawless,
  he shattered his people's oppressors.
The lawless cowered in fear of him,
  all evil-doers were stricken with panic.

[5] 166 B.C.E.

He furthered the cause of freedom,
and stirred many kings to anger.
He made Jacob glad by his deeds,
and is remembered forever for a blessing.
He passed through the towns of Judea
and destroyed the godless there.
He turned away wrath from Israel,
his fame spread to the ends of the earth,
and he rallied a desperate people.

Apollonios now collected a Gentile force and a large contingent from Samaria to fight against the Jews. Judah, when he heard of it, marched out to meet him and defeated and killed him. Many of the Gentiles fell and the rest took to flight. When they despoiled the fallen, Judah took Apollonios' sword and he fought with it for the rest of his life.

Seron, who was the commander of the army in Syria, heard that Judah had raised a large force from those of his followers who were of military age. He determined to attack them as a means of enhancing his own reputation. He was reinforced by a strong contingent of renegade Jews who had marched up to help him retaliate against Israel. When he reached the pass of Beth Horon, Judah advanced to meet him with a handful of men. His followers, seeing the great army which was advancing toward them, said to him, "How can so few of us fight against such a huge force? Besides, we have eaten nothing all day, and we are exhausted."

Judah replied, "A small force can easily overpower a large one. It makes no difference to Heaven whether the agents of deliverance are few or many. Victory does not depend on numbers; strength comes from Heaven alone. Our enemies come with arrogance and lawlessness to kill and plunder us and our wives and our children. But we are fighting for our lives and our religion. Heaven will crush them before our eyes. You need not fear them."

When he had finished speaking he launched a sudden attack and Seron and his army broke before him. They pursued them down the pass of Beth Horon as far as the plain. Some eight hundred of the enemy fell and the rest fled to Philistia.

After that Judah and his brothers came to be regarded as a force to be reckoned with, and consternation spread to the Gentiles round about. His fame reached the ears of the king and the story of his battles was told in every nation. When King Antiochus heard the news he flew into a rage and gave orders for all the forces of his empire to be assembled, an immensely powerful army. He gave his troops a year's pay and ordered them to be prepared for any duty. He now found, however, that his resources were running low; his tribute, too, had dwindled as a result of the violent rebellion he had brought about by abolishing traditional laws and customs. He saw now with alarm, and not for the first time, that he might be short of money both for his normal expenses and for the gifts which he had been in the habit of distributing even more lavishly than his predecessors on the throne.

For a time he was perplexed. Then he decided to go to Persia to collect the tribute due from the provinces and to raise a large sum of ready money. He left a distinguished member of the royal family, named Lysias, as viceroy of the territories between the Euphrates and the Egyptian border, and he also appointed him guardian of his son Antiochus until his return. He transferred half the armed forces to Lysias, together with the elephants, and told him everything he wanted done, particularly to the population of Judea and Jerusalem. Lysias was to send a force against these to shatter the strength of Israel and those who were left in Jerusalem and to wipe them out entirely. He was to settle all their territory with foreigners. The other half of his forces the king took with him. He set out from his capital, Antioch, in the year 147,[6] crossed the Euphrates, and marched through the upper provinces.

Lysias chose three prominent members of the order of King's Friends: Ptolemy, son of Dorymenes, Nikanor, and Gorgias; sent them with forty thousand infantry and seven thousand cavalry to invade Judea and devastate the country as the king had commanded. They set out in force and camped in the lowlands, near Emmaus. The local merchants, impressed by what they had heard of the army, arrived in the camp with quantities of silver and gold and a supply of fetters, to buy the Jews for slaves. The army was also reinforced by troops from Syria and Philistia.

Judah and his brothers had heard of the orders the king had given

[6] 165 B.C.E.

for the complete destruction of the nation. When they saw the seriousness of their plight, with the enemy encamped inside their frontiers, they made up their minds to fight for the nation, for the holy place, and for the restitution of national power. They gathered in full assembly to prepare for battle, to pray, and to seek divine mercy and compassion.

Jerusalem lay abandoned like a desert;
none of her children went in or out.
Her holy place was trampled down;
aliens and pagans had occupied her citadel.
Joy had been banished from Jacob,
and the flute and the lyre were dumb.

They rallied at Mizpah, opposite Jerusalem, which had once been a religious center. They fasted all day, dressed in sackcloth, sprinkled ashes on their heads, and tore their clothes. Opening the scroll of the Torah, they sought the kind of guidance which Gentiles seek from the images of their gods. They brought the priestly vestments, the first fruits and the tithes, and they presented the Nazirites who had completed their vows. "What shall we do with these Nazirites?" they cried; "Where shall we take them? Your holy place is trampled and defiled, and your priests are grief-stricken and downcast. See, the Gentiles have gathered to destroy us. You know the fate they plan for us; how can we withstand them unless you help us?" Then the trumpets sounded and a great shout went up.

Judah then appointed officers over units of one thousand, one hundred, fifty, and ten men. In accordance with the law,[7] he also sent home all those who were building houses, who were newly wed, who were planting vineyards, or who felt afraid. Then the army moved and camped to the south of Emmaus. Judah here addressed them as follows: "Prepare for action and show your mettle. Tomorrow you must be ready to fight these Gentiles who have gathered together to destroy us and our holy place. It is better for us to die fighting than see disaster strike our people and the holy place. But it will be as heaven wills."

Gorgias took a detachment of five thousand men and one thousand

[7] Deuteronomy 20:5–8.

picked cavalry and advanced by night, using men from the citadel as guides, so as to take the Jewish army unawares. But Judah heard of this and set out to attack the king's army, which was at Emmaus, while it was still scattered. Gorgias entered Judah's camp by night and found it empty, and he went up into the hills to look for them, thinking that they had run away from him. Meanwhile, at daybreak, Judah appeared in the plain with a force of three thousand men, though they did not have all the armor and swords they might have wished. They found the Gentiles' camp strongly fortified and patrolled by mounted guards. The enemy, furthermore, were experienced soldiers.

Judah addressed his men: "Do not be afraid of their great numbers, and do not panic when they charge. Remember how our fathers were saved at the Red Sea, when Pharaoh pursued them with a vast army. Let us call on heaven to have mercy on us, to remember the covenant made with our fathers and to destroy this army before us today. Then all the Gentiles will know that there is One who rescues Israel."

The Greeks saw them coming and advanced out of their camp to meet them. Then Judah's men sounded their trumpets and joined battle and the Gentiles were routed and fled into the plain. Picking off those in the rear, they pursued them as far as Gezer and Ashdod and Yavneh, and about three thousand of the enemy were killed.

When Judah and his army had returned from the pursuit, he addressed them as follows: "Do not be hungry for plunder. There is more fighting ahead of us. Gorgias and his army are not far away, in the hills. Take up your positions now to fight the enemy and after that you will be free to plunder."

Before Judah had finished speaking, a detachment of the enemy appeared, reconnoitering in the hills. The smoke which they could see was enough to tell them that their army had been routed and that the Jews were burning the camp. This in itself set them in a panic. Then, when they saw Judah's army drawn up ready for battle in the plain, they all fled into Philistia. Judah's men went back to plunder the camp and took a rich booty of gold and silver, blue- and purple-dyed cloth and precious objects. As they marched home they sang a hymn of thanksgiving, praising heaven "for it is good, for his mercy endures forever."[8]

[8] See Psalm 136.

So that day Israel was saved.

Those of the Gentiles who had survived, however, went and reported back to Lysias. When he heard the news he was desperately upset, both because Israel had not suffered the defeat he had hoped for and because he had failed to carry out the king's command.

The following year he mustered an army of sixty thousand picked infantry and five thousand cavalry to make war on the Jews. They advanced into Judea and camped at Beth Sur, where Judah met them with ten thousand men. When he saw the strength of the army he offered up this prayer:

"Blessed are you, Savior of Israel, who by your servant David foiled the giant's attack, delivered the army of the Philistines into the hand of Jonathan, son of Saul, and his armor-bearer. Deliver this army too into the hand of your people, Israel, and put them to shame, with all their great number and their cavalry. Spread panic among them, dissolve their confidence, and let them shudder at their defeat. Overthrow them by the sword of those who love you so that all who know your name may praise you with hymns of thanksgiving."

Then they joined battle and about five thousand of Lysias' men fell in the melee. When Lysias saw that his great army had been routed and when he saw the spirit of Judah's men, who were ready to live or to die valiantly, he withdrew to Antioch, where he collected an army of mercenaries to invade Judea again with an even larger force.

Judah and his brothers, meanwhile, said, "Now that our enemies are defeated, let us go up to Jerusalem to cleanse and rededicate the holy place." So they gathered the whole army and went up to Mount Zion. They found the Temple laid waste, the altar desecrated, the gates burned down, the courts overgrown like a forest or a mountainside, and the priests' quarters in ruins. They tore their clothes, wailed with grief, put ashes on their heads, and fell on their faces on the ground; they blew solemn blasts on the horns and cried aloud to Heaven.

Judah detailed troops to fight the men in the citadel until he had finished cleansing the holy place. He selected priests without blemish, who were devoted to the Torah, and they cleansed the holy place and carried away to an unclean place the stones which defiled it. They discussed what to do with the altar of burnt offering, which had been profaned, and rightly decided to demolish it in case it became a source of reproach to them, seeing that it had been defiled by the Gentiles. So they pulled down the altar and stored the stones in a convenient place on the Temple Mount until such time as a prophet should come who would decide what to do with them. They took unhewn stones, according to the Torah, and built a new altar modeled on the previous one, and they rebuilt the holy place and restored the interior of the Temple and reconsecrated the courts. They made new sacred vessels and set up the lamp-stand, the incense altar and the table in the Temple. They burned incense on the altar and lit the lamps on the lamp-stand to light the Temple. They laid loaves on the table, hung the veil, and put the finishing touches to their work. On the twenty-fifth day of the ninth month, the month of Kislev, in the year 148,[9] they rose early and sacrificed, in accordance with the Torah, on the new altar of burnt offering they had made. The altar was rededicated on the exact anniversary of the day on which the Gentiles had profaned it, to the sound of hymns, harps, lutes, and cymbals. The people all fell on their faces and worshipped, praising Heaven for the success they had been granted. For eight days they celebrated the dedication of the altar, joyfully offering up burnt offerings and sacrificing peace offerings and thanks offerings. They decorated the façade of the Temple with gold wreaths and miniature shields, and restored the gates and the priests' quarters, which they fitted with doors. There was great rejoicing among the people and the disgrace caused by the Gentiles was removed.

Then Judah and his brothers and the whole congregation of Israel decreed that the rededication of the altar should be celebrated every year for eight days, beginning on the twenty-fifth of Kislev, with joy and gladness.

THE ALLIANCE WITH ROME

Judah had heard about the Romans: they were a great military power who were glad to enter into friendly relations with any nation which approached them. He had heard of their achievements in the wars against the Gauls, whom they had conquered and made into a satellite state. He had heard about what they had done in Spain, how

[9] 164 B.C.E.

they had obtained the gold and silver mines, and how by determination and diplomacy they had conquered the whole of that far-off land; he had also heard how they had been attacked by kings from the farthest parts of the earth and how they had routed some of them and inflicted very severe losses on them so that the others had agreed to pay them an annual tribute. He was told how they had defeated the Greek kings Philip[10] and Perseus[11] in battle together with all those who sided with them and how they had even routed Antiochus the Great,[12] the king of Asia, who had marched against them with one hundred and twenty elephants, cavalry, chariots, and an enormous army; they had captured Antiochus alive and exacted from him and his successors a considerable tribute and hostages and some of their finest lands in India, Media, and Lydia, which they took and gave to King Eumenes.[13] He was told how the Greeks had planned to attack and conquer them, how they had found out about it and sent an army against them and inflicted heavy losses; they had taken their wives and children captive, plundered and ravaged their land, dismantled their fortifications, and made them their subjects, as they are to this day. He had heard how they had destroyed and enslaved all other kingdoms and islands which had resisted them but how they remained on good terms with those who were friendly to them or relied on their protection. They had conquered kings both near and far and inspired fear in all those who had heard of their fame. Yet, though they made and unmade kings, none of them ever aspired to wear the crown or the imperial purple. They had a senate house, where three hundred and twenty men sat in council daily deliberating for the welfare of the people, and they entrusted the government each year to one man, whom they all obeyed without envy or rivalry.

So Judah chose Eupolemos, son of John, son of Akkos; and Jason, son of Eleazar, and sent them to Rome to make an alliance with them to liberate Israel from the yoke of the Syrians, who they could see

[10] Philip V of Macedon (220–179 B.C.E.). Defeated by the Romans at Cynoscephalae in 197 B.C.E.

[11] The last king of Macedon, Philip's illegitimate son and successor, defeated at Pydna in 168 B.C.E.

[12] Antiochus III, the Great, king of Syria 223–187 B.C.E, defeated at the battle of Magnesia, 190 B.C.E.

[13] Eumenes II of Pergamum, 197–158 B.C.E.

were enslaving Israel. They made the long journey to Rome, went into the Senate House, and said, "Judah Maccabee and his brothers and the whole Jewish people have sent us to you to make peace and an alliance with you and to be counted among your allies and friends."

The Senate agreed to their proposals. The following is the text of the message they sent to Jerusalem written on tablets of bronze, to be kept as a record of the peace and the alliance:

> Success to the Romans and the Jewish nation, by land and sea, forever. May sword and enemy be far from them. But if Rome, or any of her allies anywhere, shall be in a state of war, the Jewish nation as allies shall render them wholehearted assistance as the occasion demands and shall not give or supply provisions, arms, money or ships to the enemy, as Rome sees fit; they shall observe their obligations, without compensation.
>
> Likewise, if the Jewish nation is in a state of war, the Romans shall help them wholeheartedly as allies as the occasion may demand; their enemies shall not be given provisions, arms, money, or ships, as Rome sees fit. These obligations shall be observed, without deceit.
>
> These are the terms of the treaty made between the Romans and the Jewish nation. If at any future date either party shall decide to insert or delete anything, they shall be free to do so and any such insertion or deletion shall be valid.
>
> As regards the wrongs done to you by King Demetrios, we have written to him as follows: Why have you oppressed our friends and allies the Jews? If they make any further complaint against you, we will see that justice is done them and make war on you by land and sea.

THE DEATH OF JUDAH

When Demetrios heard that Nikanor and his army had fallen, he sent Bacchides and Alkimos back into Judea once more with the right wing of his army. They took the road to Gilgal and camped opposite Mesadoth in the Arbel, which they captured with great bloodshed. Then, in the first month of the year 152,[14] they encamped outside Jerusalem. However, they soon moved on to Berea with twenty thousand infantry and two thousand cavalry.

Judah was encamped at Elasa with three thousand picked men. When they saw the overwhelming numbers of the enemy forces, they

[14] 160 B.C.E.

panicked and many of them absconded, leaving not more than eight hundred men. Judah saw that his men were deserting but he also saw that battle was imminent, and that he had no time to round them up. So, in great distress, he said to those who were left, "Let us make a move and attack the enemy, and fight them as best we can."

But they turned away from him and replied, "There is nothing we can do. Better to save our lives for the time being, and come back later with the others to fight them. There are too few of us."

Judah said, "Heaven forbid that we should run away. If our time has come, let us die like men for the sake of our people and not disgrace our name."

So when the Syrian army left their camp the Jews stood ready to meet them. The cavalry was divided in two, and the slingers and archers led the way together with the front-line troops. The phalanx advanced from both sides, with Bacchides on the right wing. The trumpets sounded, the trumpeters on Judah's side responded, and the earth shook with the shouting of the troops. So battle was joined and they fought from morning to evening.

Judah, seeing that Bacchides and the main strength of his army were on the right wing concentrated the whole of his forces on them. They routed the right wing, and drove them as far as Mount Azotos. But when the left wing saw that the right had been routed, they turned and pressed in pursuit of Judah and his men. There was heavy fighting and many fatal casualties on both sides. Judah fell and the rest took to flight. Jonathan and Simeon took charge of their brother's body and buried him in the family tomb at Modiin. They wept over him and all Israel went into deep mourning for several days.

They said, "A hero has fallen, the savior of Israel!"

The rest of Judah's acts, his wars, his great and courageous deeds, are too numerous to have been recorded.

THE REIGN OF SIMEON

Judea prospered throughout Simeon's reign. He worked for the welfare of his people and they were satisfied with his glorious rule all his life. Among other achievements, he took the port of Joppe and opened it up to shipping.

He broadened his nation's borders
and mastered all the land.
He recovered many captives;
he took Gezer, Beth Sur, and the citadel,
He purged them of pollution,
and no one stood in his way.
They tilled their land in peace;
the land yielded her produce
and the trees of the plains their fruit.
Old men sat on street corners
discussing their good fortune;
young men dressed in glory and military pomp.
He provided the cities with food
and with the means of defense;
his fame was proclaimed far and wide.
He made peace in the land
and there was great rejoicing in Israel.
Each man sat under his vine and fig tree,
and no one could make them afraid.
No enemy was left in the land,
the kings were all defeated.
He strengthened the poor of his people,
he studied the Torah,
he eradicated wrongdoers.
He beautified the Temple
and added to its sacred vessels.

When the news of Jonathan's death reached Rome and Sparta, there was great sadness. As soon as they heard that his brother Simeon had been made high priest in succession to him and that he was ruling the country and its cities, they sent him messages inscribed on tablets of bronze, renewing the ties of friendship and alliance they had established with his brothers Judah and Jonathan. These were read out publicly in Jerusalem. The following is a copy of the letter from the Spartans:

> The rulers and city of the Spartans send greetings to our brothers Simeon, the high priest, the elders and priests, and the rest of the Jewish people. The envoys who were sent to us gave us an account of your glory and honor.

> We were glad to welcome them. We have registered their message in the public records as follows:
>
> > Numenios, son of Antiochus, and Antipater, son of Jason, envoys from the Jews, came to renew their alliance with us. The people resolved that they should be received with honor and that a copy of their speeches should be placed in the public archives as a record for the Spartan people. A copy of this has been made for Simeon, the high priest.

Simeon also sent Numenios to Rome with a great golden shield of one thousand pounds' weight to confirm the alliance with them.

When the people heard of all this they said, "How can we demonstrate our gratitude to Simeon and his sons? He and his brothers and his father's family have shown great courage; they have defeated and driven out the enemies of Israel and liberated Israel."

So they had the following proclamation inscribed on tablets of bronze and set up on a pillar on Mount Zion:

> On the eighteenth day of Elul in the year 172,[15] which is the third year of the rule and high priesthood of Simeon, the following decree was promulgated in a great assembly of the priests and the people, the princes of the nation, and the elders of the land. At a time when the land had been much troubled by wars, Simeon, son of Mattathiah, of the family of Joarib, and his brothers risked their lives in opposing the enemies of their nation and defending their Temple and the Torah, and they brought great glory on their nation.
>
> Jonathan led the people and became their high priest. After his decease, the enemies resolved to invade the land, to devastate it and to lay hands on the sanctuary. Then Simeon took up his nation's fight. He spent his own resources liberally on arming the fighting men and paying their wages. He fortified the cities of Judea and also Beth Sur on the borders of Judea, which had been the enemy arsenal, and garrisoned it with Jews. He also fortified Joppe on the coast and Gezer on the border of Ashdod, which had previously been held by the enemy; these he settled with Jews and provided them with everything they needed. When the people saw Simeon's patriotism and his dedication to the cause of the national honor, they made him their ruler and high priest, in recognition of all he had done, his justice, his devotion to the national cause, and his efforts on its behalf. The Gentiles were successfully driven out of the land, including those who had fortified themselves in the citadel of David in Jerusalem, from which base they raided the precincts of the Temple and defiled its purity. Simeon settled

[15] 141 B.C.E.

Jews in it and fortified it for the protection of the city and the countryside, and he built up the walls of Jerusalem. King Demetrios, when he heard that the Romans had received Simeon's envoys with honor and declared the Jews to be their friends and allies and brothers, confirmed him in the high priesthood, made him one of his friends, and accorded him great honor.

The Jews and the priests decreed that Simeon and his descendants should be their leaders and high priests forever until a true prophet should appear. He was to be their general and appoint officers and governors and overseers of arms and fortifications. He was to be in charge of the sanctuary. He was to be obeyed by all and all orders should be issued in his name. He should dress in purple and gold.

No one among the priests or people might lawfully override any of his orders or issue instructions contrary to his, or convene any assembly in the land without his consent, or wear purple or a gold buckle. Anyone who disobeyed or disregarded these provisions should be liable to punishment.

The people unanimously decided to appoint Simeon to these honors and Simeon accepted them and agreed to serve as high priest and to be the leader and ruler of the Jews and the priests and to have supreme power.

They ordered this to be inscribed on tablets of bronze and set up in a prominent place in the Temple precincts, and copies to be placed in the treasury, in the keeping of Simeon and his sons.

THE MARTYRDOM OF ELEAZAR AND THE SEVEN BROTHERS

The Second Book of Maccabees covers part of the same history as 1 Maccabees: it starts with political troubles in Jerusalem and the accession of Antiochus (175 B.C.E.) and ends with the celebration of Judah's victory over the Greek commander Nikanor (161 B.C.E.). 2 Maccabees is prefaced by two letters from the Jews in Jerusalem to their fellow Jews in Egypt, urging them to join them in celebrating the festival of Hanukkah, and a foreword explaining that the present work is a popular abridgment of a five-book work by Jason of Cyrene describing the history of Judah Maccabee and his brothers.

It would seem, therefore, that the purpose of the abridgment was to encourage the Greek-speaking Jews of Egypt to identify themselves with the victory of the Hasmoneans, which was in part a victory over Hellenized Jews, and to cement their common feeling by the celebration of Hanukkah.

Since, although it is an independent history, 2 Maccabees repeats so much of the ground already covered by 1 Maccabees, we have selected here a passage not found in 1 Maccabees and which has come to be widely celebrated. It is the story of the "Maccabean Martyrs," put to death by the Greeks for their refusal to abandon the Jewish observances. This story retained great popularity not merely among Zealots but in every branch of Judaism; it is retold in rabbinic aggadah and in the philosophical work known as *4 Maccabees* and is frequently referred to in the early Christian literature. In fact, in the Church the martyrs became canonized as saints.

The story is set during the persecution of Judaism by Antiochus, shortly after the beginning of the Maccabean revolt.

2 Maccabees 6–7

Shortly after this Antiochus sent an Athenian elder to induce the Jews to abandon their traditional observances and to give up living by the laws of God. He gave orders, moreover, for the sanctuary in Jerusalem to be desecrated and rededicated to Olympian Zeus, and for the sanctuary on Mount Gerizim to be named after Zeus Xenios, "the hospitable," in token of the hospitable character of the local people.[1]

This hit all the Jews as a cruel and crushing blow. The Gentiles filled the Temple with their rowdy merrymaking. They took their pleasure with harlots and slept with women inside the sacred precincts, and also brought in forbidden things, while the altar was heaped with impure sacrifices forbidden by the Torah. A man could not keep the Sabbath or the traditional festivals or even so much as admit that he was a Jew. On the king's birthday every month they were compelled against their will to eat the sacrificial meat, and when the festival of Dionysia[2] came round they were forced to wear ivy wreaths and join the procession in honor of Dionysos. On the suggestion of Ptolemy[3] an edict was published in the neighboring Greek cities ordering them to treat the Jews there in the same way, forcing them to eat the sacrificial meat and killing all those who refused to adapt to the Greek way of life.

[1] The Samaritans.

[2] The festival of Dionysos, god of wine, was a highlight of Greek religious life.

[3] Some texts read: "of the people of Ptolemais" (Acre).

Their misery was made public for all to see. Two women, for example, who were brought to trial for circumcising their sons were paraded round the city with their babies hanging at their breasts and then flung from the battlements. Some other Jews who had hidden in some nearby caves so as to be able to observe the Sabbath in secret were betrayed to Philip[4] and burned alive since they refused to defend themselves out of respect for the holy day.

I must implore the readers of this book not to be disheartened by such calamities but to reflect that our people were only being punished, not destroyed. It is a mark of great kindness when the wicked are punished immediately and not left alone for a long time. In dealing with the other nations, the Lord refrains from punishing them until they have reached the utmost limits of sinfulness, but in our case he has decided otherwise and will not wreak his vengeance on us in days to come when our sins have reached their height. Thus he has never withdrawn his mercy from us, and though he punishes his own people with disasters yet he does not forsake them. Having reminded ourselves of this fact, let us return to the story.

One of the leading teachers of the Torah, Eleazar by name, a man of advanced years and distinguished bearing, who was being forced to eat pork, chose to die gloriously rather than live a polluted life. He advanced of his own accord to the torture, setting an example of how men ought to act if they have the courage to refuse what the Torah forbids to be tasted even to save one's life. The officials who were in charge of the sacrilegious feast, out of consideration for their long acquaintance, took him aside and urged him to provide some permitted meat prepared by his own hand and only to pretend to eat the sacrificial meat as the king had commanded. If he did this, they said, he would escape death and they would treat him kindly out of consideration of their long-standing friendship. Eleazar's reply was well reasoned and worthy of the wisdom and distinction of his old age, of his exemplary behavior from childhood on, and, above all, of the holy God-given Torah: "Dispatch me at once," he said. "It would be a disgrace for a man of my age to mislead our youth into supposing that Eleazar, in his ninetieth year, has adopted pagan ways. Merely for the sake of enjoying this brief and transitory life I should be leading them

[4] Who had been appointed governor of Jerusalem by Antiochus.

astray and bringing disgrace and dishonor on my own old age. I might succeed in escaping for the time being the punishment of men but I should not escape the punishment of the Almighty, in life or in death. By acquitting myself as a man now I shall prove myself worthy of my old age, and I shall leave behind a noble example to our youth of how to die willingly and nobly for the sake of our holy and revered laws."

With these words he stepped forward to be tortured, and those who had befriended him a few moments before now turned against him, considering his words to be those of a madman. As he expired under torture he groaned, "The Lord, who has holy knowledge, knows that, although I had an opportunity to escape death, I die suffering cruel bodily torments, and gladly too, because I fear him."

Thus he died, leaving behind him by his death an example of noble action and a memorial of virtue not only to the young but to the whole body of his people.

Another episode involved seven brothers and their mother, who were arrested and flogged by order of the king in an attempt to force them to disobey the Torah and eat pork. One of them, acting as spokesman, said, "Why question us? What do you want to know? We are ready to die sooner than transgress our ancestral laws."

The king, enraged, gave orders for large pots and pans to be heated, and as soon as they were hot he ordered the spokesman's tongue to be torn out and had him scalped while his brothers and his mother looked on. When he was thoroughly mutilated he had him put on the fire and fried alive. As the smell of frying rose from the pan, mother and sons encouraged each other to die nobly. "The Lord God observes this," they said, "and he truly has mercy on us, as Moses declares[5] in his song in which he bears witness against us: 'He will have mercy on his servants.' "

When the first had been killed in this way, they began to insult the second, tearing the skin of his head off with the hair and saying to him, "Will you eat or shall we torture your body limb by limb?" But he replied in his ancestral language and refused. So he too suffered the full torture, as the first had done. As he breathed his last he cried out, "You tyrant! You may dispatch us from this life but the King of the

[5] Deuteronomy 32:36.

world, for whose laws we die, will raise us up again to everlasting life.''

Next they tortured the third. When he was told to put out his tongue he did so at once and bravely stretched out his hands, saying, ''I got these from Heaven; for his laws' sake I consider them as nothing and from him I hope to get them back again.'' The boy's spirit amazed the king and his attendants; he seemed to think nothing of his sufferings.

When he too was dead they tortured the fourth in the same way. When he was nearing his end, he said, ''Those who are slain by man may rightly hope to be resurrected by God; but you shall have no resurrection to life.''

Then they took the fifth and began to torture him. He looked straight at the king and said, ''You, a mere mortal, have power over men and do what you please. Do not think, though, that God has forsaken our people. Continue in this way and you will discover how his sovereign power will torment you and your descendants.''

Next they took the sixth. When he was at the point of death he said, ''Do not deceive yourself. We are suffering this on our own account, for our sins against our own God. That is why these horrors have befallen us. But do not think that you will go unpunished for daring to fight against God.''

The mother was absolutely amazing. She deserves fame and glory for having the courage, bred of hope in God, to bear the sight of her seven sons dying in a single day. She kept her spirits high and, rousing with manly courage her woman's heart, she encouraged each of them in the language of our forefathers, saying, ''I do not know how you were formed in my womb; I did not breathe the breath of life into you; I did not give order and shape to your bodies. It is the Creator of the world who forms men and brings all things into being, and he it is who in his mercy will restore the breath of life to you, as you now give yourselves unstintingly for his laws' sake.''

Antiochus felt he was being insulted. Disregarding the taunt in her words, he appealed to the youngest brother, who was still alive, and even vowed to him that if he abandoned the ancestral ways he would make him rich and famous, and a friend and a trusted official. When the young man persisted in ignoring him, he summoned the mother and urged her to advise the boy to save himself. He urged her at great length and eventually she agreed to persuade her son. She bent down close to him and whispered to him in the language of his forefathers, fooling the cruel tyrant.

"Have pity on me, my son," she said. "For nine months I carried you in my womb and for three years I suckled you. I have cared for you and supported you and brought you up till now. My child, I beg of you, look up to heaven, look at the earth and everything that is in them, and realize that it was out of nothing that God made them and that humankind was created. Do not be afraid of the executioner but show that you are worthy of your brothers and accept death so that by his mercy I may receive you again with your brothers."

Before she had finished speaking, the boy exclaimed, "What are you waiting for? I will not obey the king's command. I shall obey the command of the law given by Moses to our forefathers. But you, who have plotted every kind of evil against the Hebrews, you shall not escape the hands of God. We are suffering for our own sins, and though our living Lord is angry with us for a little while and rebukes and chastens us, one day he will be reconciled to his servants. As for you, impious wretch, scum of the earth, do not try to encourage yourself with arrogant and uncertain hopes and raise your hand against the children of heaven. You have not yet escaped the judgment of almighty, all-seeing God. My brothers, after a brief moment of pain, have now attained everlasting life in accordance with God's covenant, but you will receive the just penalty for your arrogance in accordance with God's justice. So I too, like my brothers, give up my body and my soul for our ancestral laws, calling on God to show favor to our nation soon and to force you with torments and with plagues to acknowledge that he alone is God. I pray that the Almighty's wrath, which has justly fallen on the whole of our nation, may come to an end with me and my brothers."

Then the king fell into a fury and had him treated even worse than the others, so enraged was he by his insults. So he too died unpolluted, trusting steadfastly in the Lord. Finally, after her sons, the mother also perished.

Now we have spoken at sufficient length of enforced sacrifices and barbaric excesses.

A TOURIST'S DESCRIPTION OF JERUSALEM

The description of a visit to Jerusalem which follows has the air of an eyewitness account by a tourist or pilgrim of the type familiar from Christian visitors to the city from the fourth century on. It is preserved in *The Letter of Aristeas*, at the point where Aristeas goes to Jerusalem to ask the high priest to send a panel of translators to Alexandria (see p. 47), and purports to be Aristeas' own account of his tour of the city. Though it is generally recognized that this section of the letter is an insertion from an independent source, the precise nature of this source is hard to pin down. It is not easy to form a clear impression of the date of the visit: it seems to be a time when the Temple was functioning and when Jerusalem was under independent Jewish rule. It has been argued that this points to a date before the Seleucid occupation at the beginning of the second century B.C.E., although a later date would not necessarily be ruled out. But some scholars believe that this is not a genuine account of a visit to Jerusalem but an idealized description, perhaps even dating from after the destruction of the Temple.

Several descriptions of Jerusalem survive from antiquity. The fullest and most detailed are in the writings of Josephus (*Jewish War* V. 136–237; *Jewish Antiquities* XV.391–420), who also preserves a brief description attributed to Hecataeus of Abdera (*Against Apion* I.197–9). The terse remarks of Tacitus (*Histories* V.11–12) present several parallels with our text:

> The commanding position of the city had been reinforced by engineering works. . . . More inner walls surrounded the palace, and the Antonian Tower was a conspicuous landmark. . . . The Temple was like a citadel with its own walls, more carefully built than the rest. . . . It had an inexhaustible spring of water and underground tanks and cisterns for storing rainwater hollowed out of the mountain. Its founders had foreseen that separateness would lead to frequent wars. . . .

The description of the Temple and the priestly service calls to mind the fuller accounts in the Mishnah tractates Middoth and Tamid, and the splendor of the high priest is reminiscent of Ben Sira's rapturous description of Simeon (see p. 172). The account of the priestly vestments, which leans heavily on the language of the Bible, is complemented by the fuller information of Josephus (*Jewish Antiquities* III.150–174; *Jewish War* V.227–236). The reader interested in pursuing this topic further should consult Alfred Rubens's *A History of Jewish Costume* (London: Weidenfeld, 1973), which contains handsome illustrations of the costumes and full translations of the passages from Josephus.

The Letter of Aristeas 83–106

Arriving in the country, we beheld the city set in the center of the whole of Judea, on top of a mountain which rose to a great height. The Temple stood magnificently on its crest, surrounded by three walls which were more than one hundred feet high and thick to match and ran right round the whole building. The total effect was one of outstanding lavishness and splendor. From the doorway and the fastenings which held it to the doorposts and the solidity of the lintel it was evident that no expense had been spared. The curtain was conceived with the same lavishness, especially since it was kept in constant motion by a current of air from beneath which made it billow upward and outward with an effect which was so charming it was hard to tear oneself away.

The altar was constructed on a scale in keeping with its situation and the sacrifices burnt on it. Out of a proper regard for decency it was approached by a gently sloping staircase and the ministering priests wore fine linen robes reaching down to their ankles.

The Temple itself faces east, with its back to the west. Its whole floor area is paved with stone and slopes in a convenient direction for it to be flushed with water to wash away the blood of the sacrifices because on feast days many thousands of beasts are offered.

There is an inexhaustible supply of water, not only from an abundant natural spring which bubbles up inside the compound but also from an indescribably amazing system of underground reservoirs. I was told that these extended for well over half a mile beyond the foundations of the Temple round about and were connected by countless numbers of pipes. The floors and sides of the reservoirs, I was told, were lined with lead covered with a thick layer of plaster, which was very effective, and there were numerous outlets at the base of the altar which were invisible to everyone except those officiating so that the transported to another world. I would go so far as to affirm that any man who witnessed the scene I have just described would find his mind so stirred by the sanctity of the whole service that he would reach inexpressible heights of wonder and amazement.

To obtain an overall view we climbed the nearby citadel of the city and looked around. The citadel is situated on very high ground and is fortified with several towers built entirely of large-sized blocks of stone from base to top. The purpose of the towers, we were told, is to protect the Temple precincts so that in case of attack, revolution, or enemy invasion no one could reach the outer walls surrounding the shrine. Added protection is afforded by the eminence on which the citadel is built as well as the artillery and various other installations which are mounted on its towers. The towers were guarded by loyal men who had given ample proof of their patriotism. They had no authority to leave the citadel except at the festivals, and even then only in shifts. They allowed no one in; even when they had orders from their commanding officer to admit individual sightseers, they exercised top security. We experienced this ourselves: even though there were only two of us and we were unarmed, they were reluctant to let us in to get a view of the sacrifices. They were bound by a solemn oath that even if there were five hundred of them they would not admit more than five persons at a time because the citadel had been conceived by its founder for the total security of the Temple.

The city itself is of modest proportions, being of some five miles in circumference, so far as it was possible to judge. The arrangement of the towers makes it look like a theater and the layout of the streets contributes to this impression, the main roads running in tiers above one another and joined by the side streets. This is because the city is built on a mountain, and the streets are reached by flights of steps. Some people take the upper routes and some the lower; they keep a good distance from one another so that those who are in a state of purity do not come into contact with anything they should not touch.

huge accumulation of sacrificial blood could be washed away
twinkling of an eye. I had no cause to doubt the accuracy of tl
count, and it was confirmed when I was taken half a mile outsi
city and told to bend down and listen to the rushing sound of the
as it reached a junction. Here was clear proof of the great size
cisterns.

The service of the priests is an unrivaled display of physical stı
and silent and orderly management. Each has his appointed task
they labor at their arduous work without supervision. They are
stantly on duty, some bringing wood, others oil or flour or s
Others again bring the carcasses for the burnt offerings, with a re
able show of strength: gripping the calves, most of which weigh
hundredweight apiece, by the legs with both hands, they hurl th
fair height into the air and never miss their target. It is a wond
performance. They do the same with the sheep and goats, whicl
remarkably heavy and fat, since those responsible for selecting
beasts choose them for plumpness as well as flawlessness. There
special place for them to rest. As soon as one priest sits down to
one of those already resting immediately leaps to his feet. There i
need for anyone to supervise the work. Total silence prevails so
one might suppose that there was not a man in the place, despite
presence of some seven hundred officiants and a fair crowd of pe
bringing sacrifices to be offered. The whole service is performed
reverence and in a manner appropriate to the great holiness of
place.

We were absolutely bowled over by the sight of the high priest
ficiating and by the magnificence of his vestments. He was coverec
precious stones; the gold bells along the hem of his long robe made
unusual and attractive sound, and beside each bell there was a por
granate embroidered with flowers in wonderful colors. On his chest
wore the so-called "oracle," with twelve different stones set in go
inscribed with the names of the ancient heads of the tribes, each fla
ing a different color. On his head he wore the turban covered by
incomparable crown and the consecrated diadem mounted with a go
plate, between the eyebrows, inscribed with the name of God in ho
letters, radiating splendor. Such were the vestments worn when he
ficiated by the man who was chosen to be high priest. The total effe
filled me with such awe and excitement that I felt as if I had be

Prayers and Psalms

This short anthology of historical prayers and devotional poetry is selected from the wide range found in the ancient literature. Many similar examples can be found in the preceding pages. To mention only the most outstanding:

The Prayer of Asenath (pp. 74ff)
The Hymn of Deborah (pp. 91ff)
The Prayer of Judith (pp. 117f)
The Hymn of Judith (pp. 126f)
The Prayer of Shealtiel (pp. 146f)
Solomon's Prayer for Wisdom (p. 176)
Wisdom Poems (pp. 177ff)

THE PRAYER OF MANASSEH

[Included among the Odes of the Greek Bible, this is a prayer of penitence put into the mouth of Manasseh, king of Judah, as a prisoner in Babylon. Its language is reminiscent of the liturgy for the Day of Atonement.]

Lord of Hosts,
God of our fathers Abraham, Isaac, and Jacob, and their righteous descendants,

who made heaven and earth with all their array,
who confined the ocean by your word of command,
who shut up the deep and sealed it with your terrifying, glorious name,
before whose power all things tremble and quake
because the magnificence of your glory is unbearable
and no one can stand up to the threat of your wrath against sinners:
your promise of mercy is infinite and incomprehensible.
You are Lord Almighty,
compassionate, long-suffering and merciful,
and pitying men's sins.
Out of your great goodness, Lord, you have promised repentance and forgiveness to those who sin against you,
you have mercifully established repentance as a way by which sinners can be saved.
Lord God of the righteous, you did not make repentance for Abraham, Isaac, and Jacob, who were righteous and did not sin against you,
you made it for sinners like me.
My sins are more numerous than the grains of sand on the seashore,
my transgressions are many,
and because of my vast record of wrongdoing I am not worthy to behold the heavenly heights.
Hence, Lord, my punishment is just and my sufferings are deserved:
I am a captive, weighted down by iron chains,
you have cast me off and I can find no relief,
because I provoked your wrath, I acted wickedly,
I set up pagan shrines and encouraged abominations.
Now therefore with a prostrate heart I implore your goodness.
I am a sinner, Lord, I am a sinner,
I willingly acknowledge my transgressions.
I beg you, I implore you,
spare me, Lord, spare me,
do not destroy me together with my transgressions.
Do not be angry with me forever, do not prolong my sufferings,
do not condemn me when I am lost in the depths of the earth.
Lord, you are God of the penitent,
in me you will make known your goodness.

Unworthy though I am, you will save me in your great mercy,
and I will praise you forever all the days of my life.
All the army of heaven sings your praise,
and glory is yours forever.

Amen.

THE PRAYER OF MORDECAI

[The Prayer of Mordecai and the Prayer of Esther that follow are obviously composed to fit their context in the Book of Esther. Equally obviously they reflect the language of genuine ancient prayers.]

Lord, Lord and King who rules over all things,
everything is in your power
and if you wish to save Israel no one can prevent you.
You made heaven and earth and all the wonders that are under heaven,
you are Lord of all and no one can stand in your way.
You know everything, Lord.
You know that it was not from pride or arrogance that I refused to bow before Haman.
I would have gladly kissed the soles of his feet if it would have helped Israel.
I did it so as not to honor man above God;
I will bow to no one but you, my Lord. It is not a question of arrogance.
Now, Lord and King, God of Abraham, spare your people.
They are plotting to wipe us out,
they want to destroy your chosen heritage.
Do not despise your own possession, which you rescued from Egypt.
Hear my plea, and have pity on your heritage.
Turn our mourning into celebration.
Let us live and sing praises to your name,
do not silence the voices of those who praise you.

THE PRAYER OF ESTHER

My Lord, you are our only King.
Help me, I am alone, I have no one to help me but you,

I am hemmed in by danger,
Ever since I was born I have heard from my people
how you, Lord, chose Israel out of all the nations to be your eternal heritage,
and everything you promised them you did.
Now we have sinned before you,
and you have placed us at the mercy of our enemies,
because we honored their gods.
This is a mark of your justice, Lord.
But they are not content to embitter our lives by enslaving us;
they have pledged themselves to their idols to annul your decree,
and to destroy your heritage,
to silence the voices of those who praise you,
to extinguish the glory of your house and your altar,
and to raise the voices of the nations in praise of false gods
and pay everlasting honor to a king of flesh and blood.
Do not yield your scepter, Lord, to worthless gods,
do not let them mock us in our misfortune.
Turn their plot against themselves,
and make an example of the architect of our disaster.
Remember us, O Lord.
Make yourself known in our time of distress.
Give me courage, King of gods, Ruler of all power.
Grant me eloquence when I brave the lion.
Divert his mind to hatred of our enemy,
to make an end of him and those who think like him.
But save us by your power,
and help me: I am alone, I have no one to help me but you, Lord.
Everything is known to you;
you know that I hate the honor of the ungodly,
I detest sleeping with an uncircumcised man or any Gentile.
You know what I am compelled to do.
I loathe the symbol of pride which I wear on my head when I make my appearances,
I loathe it like a bloodstained rag, and I never wear it when I am off duty.
I have not eaten at Haman's table,
I have not graced a royal banquet,

I have not drunk pagan wine.
From the day I came here till now my delight has been only in you,
Lord God of Abraham.
God mighty over all, hear our desperate plea,
rescue us from the power of these cruel men,
and rescue me from my fear.

THE PRAYER OF AZARIAH

[The Prayer of Azariah is preserved in the Greek Daniel but is clearly an extraneous insertion. As with the Prayer of Manasseh, its language is strongly suggestive of the Atonement liturgy and would appear to date from shortly after the capture of Jerusalem and the destruction of the Temple. The survival of Judaism after the destruction was greatly helped by the conscious attempt to replace sacrifice as the means of atonement by prayer and penitence.]

Blessed are you, Lord God of our fathers,
praised and glorified is your name forever.
You are just in everything you have done to us:
all your works are true, your paths are straight, and all your judgments are just.
In everything you have brought upon us and upon Jerusalem, your holy city and the city of our fathers, your sentence was just;
justly and truly you did it all, because of our sins.
We sinned and transgressed and rebelled against you in everything we did;
we did not observe or keep the laws of your Torah,
we did not do as you had commanded us for our good.
Everything you have brought upon us, everything you have done to us, is just and true:
you have placed us at the mercy of our bitterest enemies, lawless rebels, and an unjust king, the cruellest in the world.
We have nothing to say for ourselves; shame and abuse have overtaken your servants and worshippers.
For your name's sake, do not abandon us forever, do not annul your covenant with us.
Do not withdraw your mercy from us, for the sake of Abraham,

your beloved; of Isaac, your servant; of Jacob, your holy one.
You told them you would multiply their descendants like the stars in the sky and the sand on the seashore,
but today, Lord, for our sins we have become the least of the nations, the most wretched people on earth.
We have no ruler now, no prophet or leader, no burnt offering, no sacrifice, no incense, no place to make an offering to you and find mercy,
but may our contrite heart and humble spirit be found acceptable,
may this sacrifice of ours today be considered like burnt offerings of rams and bullocks and thousands of fat lambs,
and grant us atonement, for those who trust in you shall not be shamed.
Now we wholeheartedly follow and fear you and seek your presence:
do not shame us, but in your great mercy and kindness have mercy upon us.
As you have worked wonders in the past so save us now and gain glory for your name, O Lord.
Let all who wish to harm your servants be confounded, and put to shame,
may they be stripped of all power and may their strength be shattered;
let them know that you alone are the Lord God, glorious throughout the world.

THE PRAYER OF BARUCH

[The Prayer of Baruch (*2 Baruch* 48:2–24) seems to originate in similar circumstances. Torah, identified with Wisdom, is here seen as the means by which Israel will survive.]

Lord, you summon the times and they stand before you,
you dismiss the ages and they yield to you,
you arrange the seasons and they obey you.
You alone know the duration of history,
few are those who share your secrets.

You can measure fire, you can weigh the wind,[1]
you can span the heights and plumb the dark depths.
You supervise the survival of those who pass away,
you prepare a dwelling place for those who are yet to be.
You remember the creation which you made,
you do not forget the destruction that is to come.
You bring things to life by your word,
you hold back the future by your great power.
You instruct creation in your understanding,
you wisely order the spheres in your service.
Innumerable forces stand before you,
their ranks obey your every nod.

Listen to your servant, Lord,
be attentive to my plea.
We are born for a short time, after a short time we return;
but for you hours are like moments, like days our generations.
Do not be angry with man, he is nothing;
do not judge our actions—what are we?
We come into the world at your bidding,
and we do not leave of our own choice.
We did not tell our parents to give us birth,
nor do we ask Sheol to receive us.
What strength do we have to withstand your wrath?

How can we survive your judgment?
Protect us in your compassion,
and in your mercy help us.
Take pity on your humble subjects
and save all those who turn to you.
Do not destroy your people's hope,
do not put an end to your help.
This is the nation you have chosen,
the people you proclaimed unique.
Let me address you now,
let me speak my mind.
We trust you because we have your Torah,

[1] See p. 136.

we know we shall not perish while we keep your law.
We are the one special people,
who have received the one Torah from the one God.
The Torah which is among us will help us,
the great Wisdom which is in us will aid us.

A PSALM OF DAVID, SON OF JESSE

[Psalm 151 is translated here from the Hebrew text discovered at Qumrān. Previously known in Greek and Syriac translation only, it is based on the biblical story of Samuel's anointing of David (1 Samuel 16:1–13). The interpretation of David's meditation in the middle of the poem is extremely problematical and various different renderings have been proposed.]

I was smaller than my brothers,
the youngest of my father's sons,
so he made me the shepherd of his flock,
the ruler of his kids.
My fingers made a reed pipe,
my hands a lyre,
and I paid tribute to the glory of the Lord.
I said to myself:
"The mountains will not speak up for me,
the hills will not tell of me,
the trees will not report my words
or the flock my deeds.
So who will tell, who will describe,
who will narrate my deeds?"
But the Lord of All Things saw,
the God of All Things listened and heard:
He sent his prophet to anoint me,
Samuel to make me great.
My brothers went to meet him,
handsome and good-looking,
tall of stature
with beautiful hair;
but it was not them the Lord God chose,

he sent and took me, the shepherd boy,
he anointed me with holy oil
and made me the ruler of his nation.

THREE PSALMS (1)

[The three psalms which follow (Psalm 154; Psalm 155; Ben Sira 51:1–12) are typical psalms of the period, mingling praise of God's might and saving power with pleas for personal or national salvation. The first two are preserved in Syriac; the third is in the collection appended to Ben Sira.]

Sing God's praise aloud,
proclaim his splendor in a mighty throng;
praise his name among the upright,
recount his greatness with the steadfast.
Join the good in praising the Almighty
gather together to tell how he saves;
do not fail to tell of his strength
and splendor to all simple men.
Proclaim the glory of the Lord,
for that is why Wisdom was given;
recount his many great deeds,
for that is why he was made known to man:
to proclaim his strength to the simple,
to expound his greatness to the ignorant
who are far from her doorways
and remote from her gates.
For the Almighty is the Lord of Jacob
and his splendor is in all his works,
and men's praise of the Almighty
is as welcome as burnt offerings.
Wisdom's voice is heard in the gatherings of the godly,
it resounds while they eat and drink:
their talk is of the Torah of the Almighty,
in their conversation they proclaim his greatness.
But the wicked are far from speaking with her
and the arrogant from knowing her.

The eyes of the Lord
look kindly on the good;
he loves those who praise him
and saves them from danger.
Bless the Lord who rescues the humble from the arrogant
and saves the innocent from the power of the wicked.
He will give us a prince from Jacob's line,
a judge of the nations from the sons of Israel,
he will pitch his tent on Zion
and dwell forever in Jerusalem.

(2)

Hear me, Lord, I am calling to you,
my hands are stretched toward your holy dwelling.
Listen to me and grant my petition,
do not refuse my request.
Help me, do not reject me,
do not abandon me in the face of the wicked.
O True Judge, preserve me from the fruits of evil.

Enable me, Lord, to understand your Torah,
educate me in your laws.
Far and wide make known your deeds,
so that all nations will honor your glory.
Guard me from problems too great for me,
remember me, do not forget me.
Hurl away my youthful sins,
discount my indiscretions.
I pray you, Lord, destroy the taint within me,
excise it, root and branch.
Judge me not according to my sins,
for no man alive is righteous before you.
King and Lord are you,
therefore you have granted my petition.
Lo, I cried out to you and you heard;
what more can human power do to me?
My trust is yours, O Lord:

I called, you answered, and healed my broken heart.
Nodding, I slept and dreamed,
and then awoke in peace.
O Lord, you supported me:
I have named you my salvation.
Placing my trust in you I was not laid low,
but I saw my enemies' humiliation.
Quickly, Lord, rescue Israel, your faithful servants,
and the house of Jacob, your chosen ones.

(3)

I praise you, God my rescuer,
I thank you, God my father,
I sing your praises, refuge of my life,
You have spared my body from destruction
and stopped me going down to Sheol.
You have freed me from public scandal,
from whiplash tongues and lying lips.
You stood by me when I was attacked,
and lovingly helped me
against those who were trying to trap me
and those who were waiting to kill me.
You rescued me from terrible troubles,
from flames closing in all around,
from unquenchable fire,
from the jaws of the bottomless pit,
from false accusations,
from arrows from lying tongues.
My soul was close to death,
my life to the depths of Sheol,
I looked round—there was no one to help me,
I sought support—there was none.
Then I remembered God's mercy
and his eternal love:
He rescues those who trust him
and saves them from every danger.
I raised my voice from the ground,

I cried out from the gates of Sheol,
I shouted: Lord, you are my father,
you are my rescuing hero;
do not desert me in time of trouble,
in time of destruction and devastation:
I will always praise your name
and remember you with prayers.
Then the Lord heard my voice
and listened to my plea;
he freed me from all my troubles
and saved me in desperate times.
Therefore I offer thanks and praise
and bless the name of the Lord.

HYMN OF OUR FATHERS

[The psalm bearing this title in the Odes of the Greek Bible is also found in the Greek Daniel immediately after the Prayer of Azariah. It is a repetitive, almost incantatory song of praise, whose formulae of blessing conjure echoes of the Hebrew Liturgy.]

Blessed are you, Lord God of our fathers,
praised and highly exalted forever,
and blessed is your holy and glorious name,
highly praised and highly exalted forever and ever.
Blessed are you in your holy glorious Temple,
highly sung and highly glorified forever.
Blessed are you on your glorious royal throne,
sung and highly exalted forever.
Blessed are you who survey the deep, seated on the cherubim,
praised and glorified forever.
Blessed are you in the firmament of heaven,
sung and glorified forever.

Bless the Lord, all the works of the Lord,
sing his praise and highly exalt him forever.
Bless the Lord, angels of the Lord,
sing his praise and highly exalt him forever.
Bless the Lord, O heavens,

sing his praise and highly exalt him forever.
Bless the Lord, all waters above the sky,
sing his praise and highly exalt him forever.
Bless the Lord, all forces of the Lord,
sing his praise and highly exalt him forever.
Bless the Lord, sun and moon,
sing his praise and highly exalt him forever,
Bless the Lord, stars of the sky,
sing his praise and highly exalt him forever,
Bless the Lord, all rain and dew,
sing his praise and highly exalt him forever,
Bless the Lord, all winds,
sing his praise and highly exalt him forever.
Bless the Lord, fire and heat,
sing his praise and highly exalt him forever.
Bless the Lord, frost and cold,
sing his praise and highly exalt him forever.
Bless the Lord, dews and snowstorms,
sing his praise and highly exalt him forever.
Bless the Lord, ice and frost,
sing his praise and highly exalt him forever.
Praise the Lord, nights and days,
sing his praise and highly exalt him forever.
Bless the Lord, light and darkness,
sing his praise and highly exalt him forever.
Bless the Lord, lightnings and thunderclouds,
sing his praise and highly exalt him forever.
Let the earth bless the Lord,
sing his praise and highly exalt him forever.
Bless the Lord, mountains and hills,
sing his praise and highly exalt him forever.
Bless the Lord, all that grows on the earth,
sing his praise and highly exalt him forever.
Bless the Lord, showers and springs,
sing his praise and highly exalt him forever.
Bless the Lord, seas and rivers,
sing his praise and highly exalt him forever.
Bless the Lord, whales and all that move in the waters,

sing his praise and highly exalt him forever.
Bless the Lord, all birds in the sky,
sing his praise and highly exalt him forever.
Bless the Lord, all quadrupeds and beasts of the earth,
sing his praise and highly exalt him forever.
Bless the Lord, all mankind,
sing his praise and highly exalt him forever.
Bless the Lord, O Israel,
sing his praise and highly exalt him forever.
Bless the Lord, you priests and servants of the Lord,
sing his praise and highly exalt him forever.
Bless the Lord, you upright and righteous of soul,
sing his praise and highly exalt him forever.
Bless the Lord, you holy and humble of heart,
sing his praise and highly exalt him forever.

A SONG OF THANKSGIVING

[This psalm (Ben Sira 51:12[a–o]), which bears no title in the Hebrew, is found in the appendix to Ben Sira, although it is not in the Greek and Syriac translations. It has obvious similarities with the biblical Psalm 136, and also with the Jewish liturgy. Several of its phrases recur prominently in the central prayer of the liturgy, the Amidah or Eighteen Blessings, and its closing verse is identical with Psalm 148:14, which is also used in the liturgy.]

Give thanks to the Lord, as is right:
his love is everlasting.
Give thanks to the God of praises:
his love is everlasting.
Give thanks to the guardian of Israel:
his love is everlasting.
Give thanks to the Creator of all things:
his love is everlasting.
Give thanks to the rescuer of Israel:
his love is everlasting.
Give thanks to the gatherer of Israel's exiles:
his love is everlasting.

Give thanks to the builder of his city and temple:
his love is everlasting.
Give thanks to the restorer of the fortunes of the house of David:
his love is everlasting.
Give thanks to him who chose the sons of Zadok as priests:
his love is everlasting.
Give thanks to the shield of Abraham:
his love is everlasting.
Give thanks to the rock of Isaac:
his love is everlasting.
Give thanks to the warrior of Jacob:
his love is everlasting.
Give thanks to the chooser of Zion:
his love is everlasting.
Give thanks to the emperor of emperors:
his love is everlasting.
He restores the fortune of his nation,
praise to all his loving servants,
the sons of Israel, the nation which is close to him.
Halleluyah!

PSALMS OF SOLOMON

[The three psalms that follow are from the *Psalms of Solomon* (6;9;11). The second, headed Punishment, dwells on the contrast between God's mercy and his justice, a central theme of rabbinic theology. (The verses have been slightly rearrranged so as to improve the sense and rhythm.) The third (Expectation), a hopeful paean for Jerusalem, is one of several similar poems expressing the confident hope in the restoration of Zion.]

Trust

Happy is the man whose heart readily calls on the name of the Lord;
when he remembers the name of the Lord he will be saved.
His paths are directed by the Lord.
his deeds are protected by the Lord his God.
He will not be troubled by bad dreams,

he will not be alarmed crossing rivers and stormy seas.
He wakes from his sleep and blesses the name of the Lord,
for his mental well-being he praises the name of God.
He prays to the Lord for the sake of all his household,
and the Lord hears the prayer of all who fear him.
The Lord grants the request of every soul that trusts in him:
Blessed be the Lord who has mercy on those who truly love him.

Punishment

When Israel was led away to captivity in a foreign land,
when they rebelled against the Lord, their rescuer,
they were deprived of the inheritance which the Lord had given them,
at God's bidding they were scattered among all the nations,
to testify, God, to your justice and our crimes,
for you are a just judge of all the peoples of the earth.

No one who acts unjustly can hide from your knowledge,
but the just deeds of your holy ones are before you, Lord.
It is in our own power to choose to act justly,
and in your justice you examine mankind:
He who acts justly stores up treasure with the Lord,
he who acts unjustly forfeits his own life.

Lord, you pronounce just sentence on each man and household,
but you show your goodness to repentant sinners.
To whom do you show your goodness, God, if not to those who appeal to you?
You cleanse a man from sin when he pours out his soul in confession.
Whose sins do you forgive if not those who have sinned?
You bless them like the just, you do not hold their sins against them.

God, we are the people you love,
we are ashamed of everything we have done.
Look at us and pity us, God of Israel; we are yours.
Do not withold your mercy and let our enemies attack us.

You have chosen the seed of Abraham from all the nations,
you have put your name on us, Lord: it will never fail us.
You made a covenant about us with our fathers;
we put our trust in you and turn our hearts toward you.

May the mercy of the Lord be upon the house of Israel
forever and ever.

Expectation

Blow the trumpet in Zion!
Sound the good news in Jerusalem!
God has had mercy on Israel,
he has come to their rescue.
Stand up, Jerusalem, and see your children
gathered by the Lord from the east and the west;
they come from the north rejoicing in their God,
he gathers them in from the furthermost isles.
He has flattened the mountains in their path,
the hills flee at their approach.
Forests shelter them on their way,
sweet-smelling woods spring up around them,
for Israel rescued by the glory of their God.
Dress yourself in glory, Jerusalem,
don the cloak of your holiness,
for God has promised good things for Israel
forever and ever.

May the Lord keep his promise for Israel and Jerusalem,
May the Lord raise up Israel by his glorious name.
May the Lord's mercy be on Israel
forever and ever.

THE GLORY OF JERUSALEM

[This psalm (I Baruch 4:30–5:9) is close in language and sentiment to the preceding poem. It adds, however, a sinister anticipation of the destruction of Rome, of the kind popular in certain circles in the years following the defeat at the hands of Titus.]

Be happy, Jerusalem,
your protector will comfort you.
Terror will strike your tormentors
and those who rejoiced at your fall;
panic will fill the cities which enslaved your sons—
one especially which took your offspring captive.
As she rejoiced at your fall and celebrated your ruin,
so will she mourn for her own desolation.
I shall remove the pride of her greatness
and her boasts will turn to laments;
The Almighty will turn her to a charnel house,
and a perpetual haunt of demons.

Jerusalem, look to the east
and see the joy God is sending you.
The sons you lost are mustering
from east to west, glorying in God.
Jerusalem, take off your widow's weeds,
dress in God's eternal radiance,
don the cloak of his goodness,
the crown of his glory.
God will show the world your splendor,
as the home of justice, piety, and peace.

Stand up, Jerusalem, on your mountain
and look toward the east;
see your lost sons mustering from east to west,
glorying in God, who has remembered them.
They left on foot, led as captives in chains;
they will return carried high, as on royal thrones.
Mountains and hills will be flattened and valleys filled
to make a safe path for Israel's glorious return;
forests and fruit trees will grow again in Israel.
God in his great mercy will bring Israel back,
rejoicing in the splendor of his glory.

HYMN TO ZION

[Previously unknown, this psalm was recovered in its Hebrew original from Qumrān. It is an alphabetical acrostic.]

A blessing on you, Zion,
  I love you with all my might.
Blessed be your memory for all eternity.
Confidently may you hope
  for peace and long-awaited salvation,
Dwelling-place of generations,
  adorned with faithful adorers,
Each longing for your rescue,
Fed on the hope of beholding your glory:
Great will be their rejoicing
  when they tread your splendid streets,
Hallowed by the love of the prophets
  and beautified by the deeds of your adorers.
Injustice will be eradicated,
  violence and deceit will be stamped out.
Jubilantly your children will rejoice,
  and your lovers will return to you.
Keenly they hope for your triumph,
  deeply the pure share your sorrow.
Love of Zion will never fade,
  the hope will never perish.
Men's lives are all examined
  and each receive his fit reward:
Never are the virtuous destroyed
  nor can the sinful escape.
O Zion, your foes will be scattered,
  your enemies will be wiped out.
Pleasant is your praise, O Zion,
  it spreads to the ends of the earth.
Quickly may you attain eternal justice
  and be blessed by all decent men.
Reach out for the vision that is promised you,
  let the dreams of the prophets come true.
So often have I called down blessings upon you;
  I bless you with all my heart.
Truly my soul shall rejoice in your splendor;
Unto the Almighty your savior sing praises:
Victory and peace, O Zion, shall be yours.

Suggestions for Further Reading

The list that follows is intended for the serious but general reader and is therefore restricted to books available in English.

GENERAL INTRODUCTIONS TO APOCRYPHAL LITERATURE

Goodspeed, E. J. *The Story of the Apocrypha*. Chicago: University of Chicago Press, 1939.

Metzger, B. M. *An Introduction to the Apocrypha*. New York: Oxford University Press, 1957.

Moore, G. F. *Judaism in the First Centuries of the Christian Era*. 2 vols. New York: Schocken Books, 1971.

Oesterley, W. O. E. *The Jews and Judaism during the Greek Period: the Background of Christianity*. Repr. of 1941 ed. Port Washington, N.Y.: Kennikat Press, 1970.

Pfeiffer, R. H. *History of the New Testament Times with an Introduction to the Apocrypha*. Repr. of 1949 ed. Westport, Conn.: Greenwood Press, 1972.

Schurer, E. *A History of the Jewish People in the Time of Jesus Christ*. Various translators. New York: Schocken Books, 1961.

Surburg, R. F. *Introduction to the Intertestamental Period*. St. Louis: Concordia Publishing House, 1975.

Torrey, C. C. *The Apocryphal Literature: a Brief Introduction*. New Haven: Yale University Press, 1945. Second ed., Hamden, Conn.: Shoe String Press, 1963.

HISTORY

Bickerman, E. J. *From Ezra to the Last of the Maccabees*. New York: Schocken Books, 1962.

Farmer, W. R. *Maccabees, Zealots and Josephus*. Repr. of 1956 ed. Westport, Conn.: Greenwood Press, 1974.

Grant, M. *The Jews in the Roman World*. New York: Charles Scribner's Sons, 1973.

MacMullen, R. *Enemies of the Roman Order*. Cambridge, Mass: Harvard University Press, 1966.

HELLENISM

Eddy, S. K. *The King is Dead: studies in the Near Eastern Resistance to Hellenism, 334–31 B.C.* Lincoln, Nebr.: University of Nebraska Press, 1961.

Hadas, M. *Hellenistic Culture: Fusion and Diffusion*. New York: Columbia University Press, 1959.

Hengel, M. *Judaism and Hellenism*. 2 vols. Trans. J. Bowden. Philadelphia: Fortress Press, 1975.

Momigliano, A. D. *Alien Wisdom: the Limits of Hellenization*. Cambridge: Cambridge University Press, 1975.

Tarn, W. W. *Hellenistic Civilization*. Rev. ed. New York: New American Library Press, 1961.

Tcherikover, V. *Hellenistic Civilization and the Jews*. Trans. S. Applebaum. New York: Atheneum, 1970.

THEOLOGY AND PHILOSOPHY

Efros, I. I. *Ancient Jewish Philosophy: a Study in Metaphysics and Ethics*. Detroit: Wayne State University Press, 1964.

Goodenough, E. R. *By Light, Light: the Mystic Gospel of Hellenistic Judaism*. New Haven: Yale University Press, 1935.

Herford, R. T. *Talmud and Apocrypha: a Comparative Study of the Ethical Teachings in the Rabbinical and non-Rabbinical Sources*. Repr. of 1929 ed. New York: Ktav Publishing House, Inc., 1971.

Klausner, J. *The Messianic Idea in Israel from its Beginning to the Completion of the Mishnah*. Trans. W. F. Stinespring. New York: Macmillan, 1955.

Scholem, G. *Major Trends in Jewish Mysticism*. 3rd ed. New York: Schocken Books, 1961.

Wicks, H. J. *The Doctrine of God in the Jewish Apocryphal and Apocalyptic*

Literature. Repr. of 1915 ed. New York: Ktav Publishing House, Inc., 1971.

GREEK JEWISH WRITERS

Wacholder, B. Z. *Eupolemus: A Study of Graeco-Judean Literature*. New York: Ktav Publishing House, Inc., 1974.

Goodenough, E. R. *An Introduction to Philo Judaeus*. Naperville, Ill.: Alec R. Allenson, Inc., 1962.

Wolfson, H. A. *Philo: Foundations of Religious Philosophy in Judaism, Christianity and Islam*. 2 vols. Rev. ed. Cambridge: Harvard University Press, 1962.

Thackeray, H. St. J. *Josephus, the Man and the Historian*. Rev. ed. New York: Ktav Publishing House, Inc., 1968.

Williamson, G. A. *The World of Josephus*. Boston: Little, Brown & Co., 1965.

Wasserstein, A. *Flavius Josephus: Selections from his Works*. New York: The Viking Press, 1974.

THE BIBLE IN THE HELLENISTIC AGE

Ackroyd, P. R., and Evans, C. F., eds. *From the Beginning to Jerome*. The Cambridge History of the Bible, Vol. I. Cambridge: Cambridge University Press, 1975.

Bickerman, E. J. *Four Strange Books of the Bible: Jonah, Daniel, Koheleth, Esther*. New York: Schocken Books, 1968.

Jellicoe, S. *The Septuagint and Modern Study*. Oxford: Oxford University Press, 1968.

Leiman, S. J. *The Canonization of Hebrew Scripture: the Talmudic and Midrashic Evidence*. Hamden, Conn.: Shoe String Press, 1976.

Rankin, O. S. *Israel's Wisdom Literature: its Bearing on Theology and the History of Religion*. New York: Schocken Books, 1969.

Sanders, J. A. *Torah and Canon*. Philadelphia: Fortress, 1972.

TRANSLATIONS OF TEXTS

The Apocrypha in the narrow sense can be found in or added to some Bibles. The most important versions are: The King James Version (1611); The American Standard Version (1901, based on the English Revised Version of 1895); The Revised Standard Version (1952) and The New English Bible (1970).

See also:

Goodspeed, E. J. *The Apocrypha, an American Translation.* New York: Random House, 1959.

The fullest collection of translations, however, is still:

Charles, R. H. *The Apocrypha and Pseudepigrapha of the Old Testament.* 2 vols. London: Oxford University Press, 1913.

The following list comprises more recent translations, and translations of works not included by Charles:

APOCALYPSE OF ABRAHAM

Box, G. H., and Landsman, J. I., eds. and trans. *The Apocalypse of Abraham.* New York: Macmillan, Inc., 1919.

BIBLICAL ANTIQUITIES

James, M. R. *The Biblical Antiquities of Philo.* Repr. of 1917 ed. New York: Ktav Publishing House, Inc., 1970.

EZRA

Myers, J. M. *I and II Esdras, a New Translation with Introduction and Commentary.* (Anchor Bible). New York: Doubleday, 1974.

JUDITH

Enslin, M. S., and Zeitlin, S. *The Book of Judith.* New York: Ktav, 1973.

LETTER OF ARISTEAS

Hadas, M., ed. *Aristeas to Philocrates.* New York: Ktav, 1951.

MACCABEES

Fischel, H. A. *The First Book of Maccabees.* New York: Schocken Books, 1948.

Tedesche, S., and Zeitlin, S. *The First Book of Maccabees.* New York: Ktav, 1950.

Zeitlin, S., and Tedesche, S. *The Second Book of Maccabees.* New York: Ktav, 1954.

Hadas, M. *The Third and Fourth Books of Maccabees.* New York: Ktav, 1953.

PSALMS

Sanders, J. A. *The Dead Sea Psalms Scroll.* Oxford: Clarendon Press, 1965.

Charlesworth, J. H. *The Odes of Solomon.* New York: Oxford University Press, 1973.

TOBIT

Zimmerman, F. *The Book of Tobit.* New York: Ktav, 1958.

WISDOM OF SOLOMON

Reider, J. *The Book of Wisdom.* New York: Ktav, 1957.

For collected translations of the Qumrān texts, see:

Gaster, T. H. *Dead Sea Scriptures in English Translation*. Third ed., rev. Garden City, New York: Anchor Books (Doubleday), 1976.

Vermes, G., trans. *The Dead Sea Scrolls in English*. New York: Penguin Books, 1968 (rev. ed.; first pub. 1962).

SPECIALIZED REFERENCE WORKS

Eissfeldt, O. *The Old Testament, an Introduction*. Trans. P. R. Ackroyd. New York: Harper & Row, 1965.

Marcus, R. "A Selected Bibliography of the Jews in the Hellenistic-Roman Period." *Proceedings of the American Academy for Jewish Research,* v. 16 (1946–47), pp. 97–81.

Index

Aaron, 27, 172
Abal, 99
Abdon, 87
Abimelech, 87
Abinoam, 91
Abraham, 21, 27, 28, 78, 91, 105, 116, 135, 145, 171, 192, 215
  Apocalypse of Abraham, The, 18, 32, 54, 58
  death of, 64–67
  discovers the true God, 53–57
  in Egypt, 61–63
  legends about, 53–67
  ordeal of, 58–61
  Testament of Abraham, The, 30
Achior, 114, 120, 124
Adam, 65, 94, 110, 134–35, 137, 142, 144, 145
  Book of, 27
  Life of Adam and Eve, The, 26, 30, 32
  Testament of Adam, The, 30
Africanus, Julius, 129
Aggadah, 25, 26, 31, 206
Ahab, 129
Ahasuerus, 104
Ahikar, 17, 18, 28, 34
Akiba, Rabbi, 9, 10
Alexander of Macedon, 14, 17, 187
Alkimos, 201
Allegory, 153–54, 156
Anna (Hannah), 104, 105, 107, 112, 113
Antiochus, 187, 195
  Scroll of, 37
Antiochus III, the Great, 200
Antiochus Epiphanes, 17, 37, 186, 187–190
Anti-Semitism, origins of, 15
Apocalypse, 31–34, 133–152
Apocrypha
  historical background, 14–19
  as a Jewish heritage, 1–2
  meaning of term, 2–3, 8
  philosophical and religious background, 19–24
  problem of the, 11–14
Apocryphal writings, list of, 24–39
  translations of, 4–6, 11, 12, 27, 29, 50, 51, 104, 134, 159, 181, 212
Apollonios, 194
Aquila, 5
Arabian Nights, 28
Aramaic language, 5, 6, 12
Aristeas, 36, 211
  Letter of Aristeas, *The*, 17, 34, 36–37, 44, 45, 47, 154, 211, 212
Aristobulus I, 17
Aristobulus II, 18
Aristotle, 21

Artaxerxes, 7
Ascension of Isaiah, The, 27
Asenath, 18, 26, 86
  Joseph and Asenath, 68–78
  Prayer of, 26, 74
Asshur, 122
Astyages, King, 98
Azariah, 107, 108, 111, 192
  Prayer of, 39, 219–220

Baal, 99
Babel, tower of, 58
Bacchides, 201–202
Bagoas, 121–22, 124–25
Barak, 87, 89–91
Barnabas, Letter of, The, 154
Baruch, 19, 33
  Book of, 177
  Prayer of, 220–22
Bel and the Serpent, 27, 98–101
Belshazzar, 16
Benjamin, 69
Ben Sira, 3, 4, 9, 34, 211
  Book of, 6, 9, 10, 17, 35, 158, 177, 223, 228
  translator's preface to Book of, 50–51
  Wisdom of, 158–173
Bible
  Christian, 2
  Greek, 5, 6, 20, 24, 27, 33, 35, 36, 38, 104, 129, 186, 215, 226
  Hebrew, 2, 3–10, 20, 24, 25, 38, 43
Biblical stories, 24–28, 53–101
Book of Biblical Antiquities, The, 58, 87, 88, 95
Book of the Hasmonean Dynasty, The, 37

Caesar, Julius, 18
Caleb, 192
Christianity, 2, 17, 19–20
  comparison with Judaism, 19–20, 154
Chronicles, Book of, 7, 26, 36, 181
Codex, 4
Constantine, Emperor, 19
Contest of the Three Young Men, 181–86
Council of Trent, 2
Cyrus the Persian, 98, 181, 185

Daniel, 27, 98–101, 128, 129, 193
  Book of Daniel, 3, 4, 6, 7, 14, 25, 29, 39, 98, 103, 129
Darius, King, 181–86, 187
David, 39, 135, 172, 192
  Psalm of, 222
Dead Sea Scrolls, 2
Death, 23
Deborah, 24, 87–95, 114
  Hymn of, 91
Demetrios, King, 201, 205
Demetrios of Phaleron, 47, 49, 50
Demetrius, 36
Dietary laws, meaning of the, 153–58
Dorotheos, 48, 49

Ecclesiastes. *See* Koheleth
Ecclesiasticus, 35
Edna (Reuel's wife), 109, 110, 111, 113
Eleazar, 35, 47, 49, 154
  martyrdom of, 205–208
Elijah, 172, 192
Elisha, 172
Elon, 87
Enoch, 170
  Book of Enoch, The, 6, 17, 32
  Secrets of Enoch, The, 32
Ephraim, 69, 78
Esau, 92, 135
Esdras, 36, 134
Esther
  Book of, 6, 7, 9, 17, 25, 36, 37, 217
  Greek, 36, 39
  Prayer of, 217–19
Eumenes II, King, 200
Eupolemos, 200
Eupolemus, 36
Eve, 110
  Life of Adam and Eve, The, 26, 30, 32
  Testament of Eve, The, 30
Evil, 23, 135–37
Exhortation to Wisdom, 177–79
Ezekiel, 172
  Book of, 6, 10
Ezra, 8, 33, 41–44
  Apocalypse of, 8, 19, 33, 39, 42, 43, 134
  Book of, 41, 134, 181–82
  Greek, 17, 36, 181–82

Fasting Scroll, The, 38, 46

Gabael, 104, 105, 106, 111, 112
Gabri, 105
Genesis, Book of, 54, 68, 78

Genesis Apocryphon, The, 28
Genizah, Cairo, 1, 2, 31, 35, 159
Gideon, 87
Gilyonim, 9
Ginzberg, Louis, 28
Gorgias, 195, 196, 197
Greek language, 5, 6, 12, 15, 173

Habakkuk, 98, 101, 128, 129
Hadrian, 19
Hagar, 63
Ham, 58, 66
Hananel, 107
Hananiah, 192
Hannah. *See* Anna
Hanukkah, 13, 29, 37, 114, 186, 205
Haran, 53, 56, 58
Harkenosh, 62, 63
Hasmoneans, history of the, 186–205
Heber the Kenite, 87, 90
Hebrew, 5, 11, 12, 42, 51, 57, 114, 129, 134, 158
Hecataeus of Abdera, 211
Helkiah, 130
Herod, 18
Hezekiah, 172
History, 35–38, 181–214
Holofernes, 29, 114–128
Hymn of Our Fathers, 226–28
Hymn to Zion, 232–33
Hymns, 38, 39, 91, 126, 226, 232
Hyrcanus, John, 17
Hyrcanus II, 18

Isaac, 21, 64, 67, 78, 92, 105, 116, 135, 171, 215
  Testament of, 30
Isaiah, 172
  Martyrdom of Isaiah, The, 19, 27, 32
  Targum of, 27
Ishmael, 64, 67
Israel, 171, 172

Jabin, 88
Jacob, 21, 30, 64, 65–67, 71, 78, 85, 92, 95, 105, 116, 132, 135, 172, 194, 196, 215
  sons of, 31, 79–86
  Testament of, 30
Jael, 87–91, 93
James, M. R., 28
Jamnes and Jambres (or Mambres), Book of, The, 27
Japheth, 58
Jason, 37, 200, 204, 205
Jephthah, 87, 95–97
Jephthah's daughter. *See* Sheila
Jerahmiel, 137
Jeremiah, 8, 33, 172
  Book of, 24, 99
  Letter of, 17, 27
Jerome, 29
Jerusalem
  Glory of (Psalm), 231–32
  tourist's description of, 211–14
Jeshua, 172
Jesus, execution of, 18
Joakim, 125, 130
Job, 172
  Book of, 7, 24
  Testament of Job, The, 31
Johanan ben Zakkai, 177
John (son of Simeon), 186, 190
John, Gospel of, 158
Joktan, 58, 59, 60
Jonathan, 186, 198, 202, 203, 204
Joseph, 18, 26, 68–86, 192
  death of, 78, 86
  Joseph and Asenath, 18, 26, 68–78
  last words of, 78–86
  Testament of Joseph, The, 79–86
Josephus, 7, 8, 9, 11, 15, 19, 21, 36, 37, 45, 54, 181, 186, 211, 212
Joshua, 31, 42, 51, 88, 89, 93, 145, 172, 192
Josiah, 172
Jozadak, 172
Jubilees, Book of, 6, 17, 25–26, 30, 32, 54, 58, 64
Judah, 17, 85, 186, 193–202, 205
Judaism, 3, 11, 14, 16, 19–22, 36, 37, 98, 219
  comparison with Christianity, 19–20, 154
  Hellenistic Age of, 14–19
Judges, 8, 26, 87, 172
Judith, 29, 114–128
  Book of, 13, 17, 29
  Hymn of, 126–27
  Prayer of, 117
Justus of Tiberias, 36

Kabri, 115, 118
Karmi, 115, 118
Kenaz, 87, 89
Koheleth (Ecclesiastes), 6, 8, 9, 10, 158, 165, 166

Laban, 116
Lakish, Resh, 42
Lamech Scroll, 28
Lamentations, 6, 8
Legends of the Jews, The (Ginzberg), 28
Lesser Genesis, The, 25
Levi, 85
Logos, 22
Lost Apocrypha of the Old Testament, The (James), 28
Lot, 53, 56, 62, 63
Luke, Gospel of, 7
Lysias, 195, 198

Maccabee, Judah. *See* Judah
Maccabees, Books of the, 13, 17, 18, 34, 35, 37–38, 186, 187, 205–206
Machir, 78
Manasseh, 27, 69, 78, 115, 118, 128
  Prayer of, 38, 39, 215–17, 219
Marduk, 99
Mattathiah, 190–93
Megillath Ta'anith, 38
Messiah, 32, 79, 129
Midrashim, 46, 54, 114
Milcah, 53
Minim, books of the, 9, 10
Mishael, 192
Mishnah, 8, 13, 43, 153, 211
Moral tales, 28–30, 103–132
Mordecai, 39
  Prayer of, 217
Moses, 7, 18, 21, 25, 27, 33, 41, 42, 43, 45–46, 88, 89, 92–93, 108, 110, 145, 153–57, 171, 208, 210
  Testament of Moses, The, 31

Nahor, 53, 56
Nathan, 107
Nebuchadnezzar, 16, 29, 114, 119–122, 125, 181
Nehemiah, 172
  Book of, 7, 36, 181–82
New Testament, 2, 103
Nikanor, 195, 201, 205
Nimrod, 58, 60
Noah, 28, 54, 65, 105, 170

Old Testament, 2
Origen, 10, 29, 129

Paleography, 12
Paralipomena of Jeremiah, The, 33
Paul, St., 18
Penech, 58, 60
Pentateuch, 3, 4, 5, 6, 7
Perseus, King, 200
Philip V of Macedon, 200
Philo, 6–7, 11, 15, 18, 21, 26, 34, 36, 45–46, 50, 153, 154, 174
Philosophy, 34–35, 153–58
Phinehas, 172, 191, 192
Plato, 15, 21
Poetry, 38, 158, 173, 177–79, 186, 215
Pompey, 18, 39
Potiphar, 79, 83
Potiphar's wife, 79–84
Potiphera, 68–78
Praise of the Fathers of Old, 158, 169–173
Prayers, 38–39, 215–222
Prophets, 3, 4, 7, 26, 42, 51, 89, 105, 172
Proverbs, Book of, 10, 34, 35, 158, 159–162, 166, 167, 170
Psalms, 4, 7, 38–39, 103, 159, 164, 168, 170, 222–26, 228, 229–231
Pseudepigraphia, 3
Pseudo-Philo, 26
Ptolemy, son of Dorymenes, 195
Ptolemy II, 45
Ptolemy IV, 37
Ptolemy VII, 37
Purim, 37

Quest for Wisdom, The, 179
Qumrān Scrolls, 1, 28, 29, 32, 35, 38, 39, 61, 103, 159, 177, 222, 232

Rachel, 86
Raphael, 104, 106–111, 113
Rebecca, 64, 67
Rembrandt, 130
Rubens, Alfred, 212
Rubens, Peter Paul, 130

Saadya, 158
Salathiel. *See* Shealtiel

Salome Alexandra, 18
Samson, 87
Samuel, 145, 172, 222
Sarah (Abraham's wife), 53, 56, 62–63, 65, 67
Sarah (Reuel's daughter), 108–114
Saul, 26
Scripture, canonization of, 3–11
Secrets of Enoch, The, 32
Sefer Torah, 4
Septuagint, 5
Seron, 194
Seth, 65
Seven Brothers, martyrdom of the, 208–210
Shalmaneser, 103
Shealtiel, 23, 33, 133–152
  Prayer of, 146
  Visions of Shealtiel, The, 23, 133–152
Sheila (Jephthah's daughter), 95–97
Shelomiah, 107
Sheol, 23
Shoshannah. *See* Susanna
Sibylline Oracles, 34
Simeon ben Azzai, 27
Simeon ben Shetah, 128
Simon, 17, 37
Sirach, Wisdom of (Ben Sira), 35
Sisera, 87–91, 93
Solomon, 34, 151, 172, 174
  Prayer for Wisdom, 176
  Psalms of, 18, 39, 229–231
  Wisdom of Solomon, 18, 23, 35, 173–76, 177
Song of Songs, 6, 8, 10
Susanna, 17, 29, 98, 128–132

Tacitus, 211
Talmud, 9, 10, 13, 27, 38
  Babylonian, 9, 27, 42, 128
  Palestinian, 27, 128
Temech, 91
Terah, 53, 54, 55, 57
Testaments, 30–31
Testaments of the Twelve Patriarchs, The, 31, 79
Theodotion, 5, 27, 129
Therapeutae, 6, 7, 9
Tintoretto, 130
Titus, 16, 19, 231
Tobias (Tobiah), 29
  Adventures of Tobiah, 103–114
Tobit (Tobi), 103–114
  Book of, 6, 13, 17, 28–29, 103
Torah, 3, 22, 23, 25, 34, 36, 41–48, 50–51, 83, 89, 95, 133, 135, 143, 149, 158, 172, 177, 189, 192, 193, 196, 198, 199, 203, 204, 206, 207, 208, 220
  translation into Greek, 44–50
Trajan, 16, 19
Translations, 4–6, 11, 12, 27, 29, 50, 51, 104, 134, 159, 181, 212

Uzziah, 115–17, 118, 123–24, 125

Vespasian, 16, 18
Visions of Shealtiel, The, 23, 133–152

Wisdom, 22, 34–35, 152–179

Xerxes, 7

Yannai, Alexander, 17, 128
Yose, Tanna, 42

Zebul, 87, 89
Zedekiah, 129
Zerubbabel, 172, 181
Zimri, 191
Zion, 23, 134, 135, 136, 150–51, 229
  Hymn to, 232–33